Religious Experience and the End of Metaphysics

Edited by Jeffrey Bloechl

INDIANA UNIVERSITY PRESS
BLOOMINGTON AND INDIANAPOLIS

Bloomington & Indianapolis

Publication of this book is made possible in part with the assistance of a Challenge Grant from the National Endowment for the Humanities, a federal agency that supports research, education, and public programming in the humanities.

This book is a publication of

Indiana University Press
601 North Morton Street
Bloomington, IN 47404-3797 USA

http://iupress.indiana.edu/~iupress

Telephone orders   800-842-6796
Fax orders   812-855-7931
Orders by e-mail   iuporder@indiana.edu

The paper used in this publication meets the minimum requirements of American National Standard for Information Sciences— Permanence of Paper for Printed Library Materials, ANSI Z39.48-1984.

MANUFACTURED IN THE UNITED STATES OF AMERICA

Library of Congress Cataloging-in-Publication Data

Religious experience and the end of metaphysics / edited by Jeffrey Bloechl.
p. cm. — (Indiana series in the philosophy of religion) Includes bibliographical references and index.
ISBN 0-253-34226-0 (alk. paper) — ISBN 0-253-21592-7 (pbk. : alk. paper)
1. Experience (Religion). 2. Religion—Philosophy.
3. Postmodernism. I. Bloechl, Jeffrey, date. II. Series.
BL53.R444 2003
291.4′2—dc21
2002155228

1 2 3 4 5 08 07 06 05 04 03

Religious Experience and the End of Metaphysics

INDIANA SERIES IN THE PHILOSOPHY OF RELIGION
MEROLD WESTPHAL, GENERAL EDITOR

Contents

PREFACE

A number of the contributions to this volume are elaborations of texts presented in a seminar on "Religion Experience in the Wake of Modernity," itself a component of a research project exploring the nature and expression of sacramental presence in a context often identified, with persistent ambiguity, as postmodern. The research project was conducted between 1996 and 2000 in the Theology Department of the Catholic University of Louvain (Flemish campus); the seminar met monthly during the academic year 1999–2000.

As its title indicates, the seminar was conceived to widen focus from Christian sacramentality to include religious experience of any sort (and indeed few of the essays in this volume approach the former theme),[1] while also stepping back from the notion that emergent dissatisfaction with modern culture and rationality concludes necessarily to any of the various definitions of "postmodernity." Thus, whereas the essays included here—and a few have been added to those originating from the seminar—begin with some reservation about our modernity, or at least some of its features, they are recognizably divergent in their conceptions of how one ought to think about and respond to it on the important but troubled matter of religious experience.

The fact that the title of the volume differs from the title of the seminar is an indication of the direction taken by the contributions more or less as a whole, and without prompting. Among these theologians and philosophers schooled in continental European thought, the conjunction of "religious experience" with "modernity," or perhaps modernity as the site of its crisis, brings to mind the philosophy of Martin Heidegger, specifically where he associates theology with a metaphysics coming to its final achievement in our own time, so that thinking must accept for itself the task of now overcoming it. This matter of overcoming (a certain) metaphysics, or of recognizing its "end" and thus escaping its limits, is recorded in the title of this volume, and therefore commands immediate commentary.

It is a central claim of Heidegger that the history of philosophy has in fact been a history of metaphysics whose various forms each display an inclination to what he calls "onto-theology." This metaphysics, he says, has always tended to search for some particular entity that most exemplifies what it is to be. In this regard, occidental thought would be most familiar with the specific form that calls this most exemplary entity "God," and classifies and explains all other entities in its light or by reference to it. In such a manner, we are told, thinking begins by asking what it is for beings to be—under Heidegger's pen virtually the *Leitfrage* of western philosophy—only to immediately turn away from an inquiry that would get beneath beings to being (*Sein*). Against this, and as the avenue back to a thinking not yet encumbered by onto-theological pretensions, his early work proposes to think in constant view of the ontological difference between being and beings.[2] Somewhat later, he attempts a leap beyond the preliminary question of the being of beings directly to asking about "the truth of Seyn itself."[3]

Regardless of which path Heidegger is seen to follow, his argument that the history of metaphysics, as onto-theology, is a history of the forgetfulness of being may be recognized as the counterpart of resistance to what Jacques Derrida in particular has made us understand as the "metaphysics of presence," whereby it is considered that thinking is able to grasp the enduring reality of a thing—its essential meaning—by penetrating its appearance in fluid time and space. Onto-theology would be in solidarity with the metaphysics of presence insofar as the former will have secured the ultimate foundations on which the latter bases its distinction between founded and unfounded meaning. From the onto-theological premise of arrival at a first, exemplary being, the metaphysics of enduring presences would seem to be not only possible but at some level inevitable. Recognizing this, Heidegger seeks to abandon the transcendental subject that would grasp such presences as if from a commanding distance as a prerequisite to deep reflection on being. In *Being and Time*, this is a matter of opposing any attribution of "transcendental knowledge" in Dasein, as if it has some priority over being, dictating its meaning, or even grasping it once and for all, as if from one step back.[4] With this, the philosophy of Heidegger becomes simultaneously a departure from traditional metaphysics such as he conceives it, and the modern philosophy he considers to have peaked in the work of his teacher, Husserl. Within the context of his own work, this means a move to acknowledge not only that understanding is irreducibly concrete and historical (against Husserl), but also—as developed increasingly in later works—that being is itself deeply historical. It is there that his idea of the "end of philosophy," which is to say metaphysics (or onto-theology), receives its proper meaning. And it is this meaning, surrounded by the responses since ventured by Levinas, Derrida, Marion, and others, that is intended by the word *end* appearing in the title of this volume.

Heidegger understands the word *end* in its older sense of *place*, such as we use it in the expression "from this place here to that place over there." The end of philosophy as metaphysics is thus the place of philosophy as metaphysics (or onto-theology)—that place in which "the whole of philosophy's history is gathered in its extreme possibility."[5] The overcoming of metaphysics becomes possible—and for Heidegger necessary—precisely as its place comes into view, and the bare fact that we can catch sight of this place already puts us on the way to overcoming its limits. The historical scope of the claim is breathtaking and well known: according to Heidegger, philosophy embarked on this course only now fulfilling itself already with Heraclitus, whose preoccupation with Logos developed into a search for ultimate grounds recognizable all the way down to the advent of technology, where indeed it is virulent. But again, to witness the place wherein philosophy reveals its inner truth is already to have a foot planted outside it, and to recognize its closure is already to think through it, rather than according to it or within it.

After Heidegger, the thought of the end of philosophy and the overcoming of metaphysics as onto-theology has sometimes received new inflection from thinkers also interested in religion. Of these, Derrida has sometimes seemed closer to Heidegger, at least in the early works that share Heidegger's conviction that the last vestige of transcendentality is also a last vestige of the metaphysics of presence. Before Derrida, and later as a source of inspiration for him, Emmanuel Levinas has attempted to include Heidegger himself as a philosopher to be overcome. For Levinas, the end of philosophy as onto-theology comes into view precisely in *Being and Time*, which is still a philosophy of totality, whereas it has always been the proper definition of metaphysics to hold thought open to an infinity beyond any totalization. According to the great theme of *Totality and Infinity*, being is a concept susceptible to deployment by an imperial subject, enabling it to reduce otherness to "the Same." The imperative to overcome such a philosophy is therefore simultaneously metaphysical-religious and ethical: only the otherness of the Other lies beyond the reach of onto-theological pretension, but because it does, it is possible to pass beyond the philosophy rooted in ultimate grounds to one inspired by absolute desire. Finally, this same distinction between a philosophy of ultimate grounds, or theology, and one already open to transcendent inspiration (theology), defines the attitude of Jean-Luc Marion. For Marion, the end of philosophy recognized by Heidegger is simultaneously the (re)emergence of the correct nature of certain phenomena that have never submitted themselves to onto-theology—above all, the divine word. It is difficult to know whether a basic sympathy with Barth opens the way to considerable willingness to accompany Heidegger, or it is the appeal of Heidegger that leads the way back toward Barth, but in either case, the startling conclusion must be that the end of philosophy would be a new beginning for theology.[6]

None of this is yet to ask about the promises and perils of the history of philosophy supporting these notions of an end and an overcoming. Nor is it to ask whether the most traditional theology and metaphysics do not already possess the means to protect themselves against onto-theology and its pitfalls. Nor, finally, is it to question the capacity of western thought to free itself from these difficulties without help from other traditions. These are the themes of the various essays gathered here, as well as of the essay that introduces them against the background of the modern developments that have made them urgent.

* * *

Much of the work for this collection was conducted within the theology department of the Katholieke Universiteit Leuven. My sincere thanks go first to the director of that project, Professor Lambert Leijssen, whose remarkable generosity made such work possible, and to Professors George De Schrijver, Lieven Boeve, and Stijn Vandenbossche, whose love of dialogue made it both desirable and, I believe, fruitful. This volume may be read as a companion to the collection of more theological essays also assembled by that research project, and published as *Sacramental Presence in a Postmodern Context* (Leuven: Peeters/BETL, 2001).

I have translated the essays by Emilio Brito and Jean-Yves Lacoste from the French, and the essay by Ignace Verhack from the Dutch. I thank each author for having kindly reviewed, and in some cases corrected, my translation. I wish also to thank Dee Mortensen, Richard Kearney, Merold Westphal, and Joyce Rappaport for suggestions that have improved this volume, and Merold Westphal for also welcoming it into the distinguished company of other volumes appearing in his series at Indiana University Press.

JEFFREY BLOECHL

COLLEGE OF THE HOLY CROSS

DECEMBER 8, 2001

NOTES

1. Close and more properly theological study of the theme may be found in L. Boeve and L. Leijssen, eds., *Sacramental Presence in a Postmodern Context* (Leuven: Peeters/BETL, 2001).

2. This "ontological difference" is present by visible assumption already in the early movements of *Being and Time*, where Heidegger distinguishes the ontic transcendence by which we relate to beings and the more originary transcendence by which we comprehend being. M. Heidegger, *Being and Time*, trans. J. Macquarrie and E. Robinson (London: SCM Press, 1962), pp. 118–19.

3. See Heidegger, *Contributions to Philosophy (from Enowning)*, trans. P. Emad and K. Maly (Indianapolis: Indiana University Press, 1999), § 34.

4. Heidegger, *Being and Time*, p. 62.

5. Heidegger, "The End of Philosophy and the Task of Thinking," in *On Time and Being*, ed. and trans. J. Stambaugh (New York: Harper Torchbooks, 1972), p. 57.

6. The question is well captured in John Milbank's characterization: "it is as if (albeit in a mode already inscribed by Levinas) Marion seeks to be both Barth and Heidegger at once." J. Milbank, *The Word Made Strange* (London: Blackwell, 1997), p. 37.

Religious Experience and
the End of Metaphysics

Editor's Introduction

Jeffrey Bloechl

I

The authors contributing to the present collection share a conviction that religious thinking cannot afford to disengage from the challenges of modern European philosophy, and more specifically from the strand running from Kant to Husserl and Heidegger before fraying into the diverse lines visible today. Until the late twentieth century, most philosophy of religion drawing on that tradition tended to rely heavily on either the transcendental methods of Kant or Husserl, or else the more hermeneutical and narrative phenomenologies inspired by early Heidegger. As different as they are, what those two approaches evidently share is a commitment to some conception of subjectivity, selfhood, or if one insists, *Dasein,* as the irreducible locus of everything capable of becoming a theme for investigation. The common heritage is of course Cartesian, at least if the philosophy of Descartes can be made to stand simply for a style of thinking that insists on correlating every concrete datum given to experience with a formal basis in individual consciousness. The status of the subjective pole of this intentional relation has, for better or worse, preoccupied much of continental European philosophy ever since then. And its persistence, seeming to command the conclusion that individual conscious-

1

ness is the horizon for all meaning, provides modern philosophy of religion with much of its present ferment. The essence of the matter can be found already in Descartes's Third *Meditation,* where a rational defense of the existence of God takes its bearings from an experience of our human condition as being fallen into error, so that the task of thinking about God is immediately defined by an effort to trust and welcome that which transcends all error. Where it has avoided sheer reductivism, modern philosophy of religion has not departed from this basic sensibility, even while the esteem of modern rationality has risen and fallen any number of times.

The difficulty of welcoming God into reason may be construed as a call to reinstate harmony between a mode of living and thinking fallen from God and therefore prone to error, and a mode of living and thinking in which fallenness and error have been transcended. Historically, this construal was elaborated first by Augustine, who thought that the distinction itself must indicate the hidden presence of some normative standard (*veritas redarguens*) that could only have been infused from beyond the limitations of human error.[1] Descartes has revived this thought,[2] but now in the considerably different context of a theory of knowledge centered, as we have just noted, on discerning the formal basis of meaning in individual consciousness. The importance of this difference for philosophy of religion comes into view in the metaphysics which preserves a distinction between thinking-being, *res cogitans,* which has been determined immune from hyperbolic doubt, and thought-being, *res cogitatum,* which thus depends on thinking-being for its foundation. Among scholars of Descartes, Jean-Luc Marion has been most effective in showing precisely how this makes philosophy into "onto-theology"—a theory whereby all things are ontologically dependent on a single one of them. This is specifically a matter of Descartes's definition of self as "substance," which is to say as the particular form of being that, among all beings, thinks—and thus founds, by providing the formal basis of its meaning—everything else. According to Marion, such a theory is not merely a reduction of all things that may be thought to ultimate dependence on the one thing that can think, but the enclosure of all beings in a circle of mutual foundation: "being-as-thought [*res cogitatum*] grounds the being-par-excellence [*res cogitans,* that being which knows itself as thinking being], which in turn produces the thinking of each thought."[3] The mutual foundation of the totality of beings and a single one of them renders the closure of metaphysics consistent with the exclusion of a properly transcendent God.

Perhaps, as some have urged, it is possible to exploit other elements of Descartes's work to contest this onto-theological position,[4] but the latter has nonetheless persisted wherever modern thought, distinguishing itself from everything that had come before, argues for the existence of God as the essential foundation of knowledge. This would appear to be the case above all in the philosophy of Leibniz, who developed the final implication of his "principle of sufficient reason" whereby it is asserted simply that there is a reason for every fact: "Thus it is necessary that sufficient Reason [. . .] be found in a substance, which is a cause, or which is a necessary Being, carrying within itself the reason for its existence; otherwise one would not yet have a sufficient reason in which one might finish. *And it is this final reason for things that is called God.*"[5]

It is well known that this sort of argument both reduces the concept of God to *causa sui*, and functionalizes that concept in the search for an assurance that its own form of reason, modeled on modern science, is coherent and reliable. The evident telos is noticed less frequently: the submission of the concept of God to the principle of sufficient reason, the transformation of philosophy into onto-theology, and the closure of metaphysics within the reciprocal foundation of all beings and a single being par excellence are all generated by the pursuit of an all-encompassing unity.[6] Once it has adopted the premise that there is a reason for every fact, thinking inevitably seeks a reason even for the "fact" of the existence of God, and when it discovers this reason in the unique self-sufficiency of a God who is beyond every constraint, it considers itself to have confirmed that premise in the description of a well-ordered and intelligible universe. Needless to say, such a drive for unity and order is not content to assemble everything amenable to its task, but constantly denies the possibility that anything resisting it can thus have a fully positive meaning. If a phenomenon does not receive the dignity of a fact until a reason for it has been discovered, and the discovery of a reason immediately assimilates a fact to the totality of other facts, then what reveals itself to lie outside or beyond that totality must be considered, precisely, not yet a fact—not yet known by an anterior reason that one expects to find conjoined to other reasons. Something like this very sense of the principle of sufficient reason led Schopenhauer to suppose that its argument for the existence of God in fact has almost nothing to with God, whose ground would instead locate in a historically and culturally specific revelation.[7] And this comes close to explicitly stating a problem that troubles the whole of modern philosophy of religion: once a certain form of thinking has detached its starting point from an essential relation with the absolute—from a religious horizon for everything it thinks and says—it is no longer evident that that relation can be readmitted to its field of possibilities.

The two great temptations awaiting efforts to rescue religion from this difficulty would have to be the dualisms risked by pietism, on one hand, and the theory of Schleiermacher, on the other. These are truly not the same position: whereas pietism tends simply to oppose a faithful heart in communion with God to a godless reason that gains emprise over the things of this world, Schleiermacher is intent on getting beneath the godless reason of modern culture to a fundamental sentiment that rings with the absolute. Yet both seem to press their operative distinctions so far that it becomes unclear just how much rationality could still be present in either the faithful heart or religious sentiment. If the question at hand since Descartes and Leibniz asks how we might readmit a relation with the absolute to the field of possibilities available to reason in its present state, then it is necessary to add the following nuance: what is at stake in all of this, is the rationality specific to the life and thinking opened to that relation. What is at stake, in other words, is the rationality specific to religious experience—when confronted by a metaphysics determined by the principle of sufficient reason.

It is at such a point as this that some will ask why religious thinking does not simply refuse the entire modern adventure, and remain committed to the classical sources and worldview it would have us leave behind. Plainly, at a certain level of speculation, this is precisely what must be done, and indeed is often done, yet by itself it says little or nothing to the many for whom religion has become synonymous with one or another version of the modern theism that we have come to recognize as onto-theology—*and which is itself increasingly implausible* (see the condensed statement to this effect that opens Ignace Verhack's essay in this volume). And so the effort to retrieve classical insights from the dustbin of modern renovations is often paired with an effort to reach beneath the metaphysics that accepts as a fact only that which discloses some anterior reason. Perhaps this now brings us to the juncture where, for many of us, it is clear that we are not yet done with reading Heidegger, and above all when he gestures beyond the order of reason and its ground. Of course, it is usually here, where Heidegger is invoked as a critic of modernity (and a good deal else), that we are reminded of just how embedded in the modern constellation his own thinking happens to be, even while he attempted to twist free of it.[8] Yet we also know that the style of Heidegger's thinking never permits him the luxury of criticizing from an external vantage point, according to a wholly different form of thinking, or with the intention merely to negate what appears questionable. With regard to the modern thinking received from Descartes, Kant, and Husserl, this involves an immanent critique that knows itself to employ at least some of the tools of the thinking put in question, with the aim of laying bare the manner in which the very ground for that thinking becomes available for questioning. To the degree that this implies the possibility of asking further—or of thinking deeper—about the source for the ground of modern thought, Heidegger seems to offer a way beyond the principle of sufficient reason and its accompanying metaphysics. However, there is nothing in Heidegger's texts to suggest that this way leads purely and simply to a new and sustainable thought of God. After Heidegger, discussion of religious experience can once again take place beyond the range of the principle of sufficient reason and outside onto-theology, but there is still no assurance of a reinstatement. Indeed, according to Heidegger himself, the task of studying the essence of ground has not been completed when thinking comes before a notion like *causa sui*, but must also ask about the manner in which the possibility of that very notion presupposes its coming forth in the unconcealment of *Sein*, understood as nothingness of beings. For Heidegger, *Sein* and not some being-par-excellence is ground, and in a more primordial sense than the "popular metaphysics, which deals with some being behind the known beings."[9] Whereas this popular metaphysics inquires no further than to the Being of beings, truly fundamental thought is guided by the question of Being as such.[10]

Would this thinking that seeks the meaning of Being as such—of Being beyond the Being of beings, including the being par excellence—thus represent the overcoming of metaphysics as onto-theology *and* the further extension of a thinking that knows no relation to God? One can certainly think so without also supposing that its path is immune from critique. Enough has already been said here to cast doubt upon whether the whole of metaphysics in all its richness can be dispensed with under the auspices of a challenge specifically to an onto-theology framed in the principle of sufficient reason, and indeed several of the essays included here challenge such a notion vigorously. However, before entering that discussion, one might simply note that precisely when Heidegger himself is immersed in this entire matter of sufficient reason, ground, and metaphysics, his central concern is to isolate them in their "primordial occurrence" (*Urgeschehen*), the sheer fact of their appearing—and this points back not to the constituting activity of an autonomous subject, and also not to the creating activity of a self-sufficient God, but to the originary temporality of Dasein.[11] *Being and Time* has shown us the proper depth of this claim: just as our being-there is anterior to our natural existence caught up in causal relations, so the temporality of the former is anterior to the temporality of the latter, which charts the movement of causes and effects. This means, principally, that Dasein itself does not rest on some prior cause, but comprehends causal relations—and for that matter any appearance of principle or ground for them—in a situation of what Heidegger calls the "abyss of ground." Such a position evidently does more than resist modern rationality and its onto-theology, even if a need to expose the superficiality of the latter has been Heidegger's pretext for working it out. His later work makes the full scope of the claim unmistakable: *any* ground or principle must be grasped first in its "occurrence," and this will *always* lead back to the originary temporality of Dasein. In other words, from the perspective of this thinking capable of reaching deeper than metaphysics as onto-theology, the primordial features of our being-there represent the irreducible and inescapable horizon in which anything or anyone can appear and have meaning.

What does this imply for the encounter with God, the divine, or the absolute? Can such an encounter still be thought without considering it an example of the "occurrence" that Heidegger traces back to the temporality of Dasein? According to what conditions? And with what impact on our understanding of the human condition in which we would undergo that unique encounter? These questions, raised explicitly in the presence of Heideggerian thought, open much of the field of investigation for the essays collected here.

Jeffrey Bloechl

II

While the sorts of questions Heidegger bequeaths to theology and philosophy of religion can be compressed into a single call to re-examine the familiar category of religious experience, it is also possible to break down the category of religious experience in a different way that touches many of the prominent contemporary approaches to the problem.

(1) Let us first recall the many claims to describe an event in which all the strata of experience itself would be placed into question by the arrival of what wholly transcends them. What distinguishes this sort of effort—one thinks first of Emmanuel Levinas—from the classical interest in hierophany or Kant's reflections on the sublime is the need to reinstate claims for such encounters in the wake of all the new sophistication about our sense of subjectivity or selfhood achieved by modern thought. We are never far from worries that the new theologies and philosophies of religion concede too much to the modernity they generally resist, but we are also hard-pressed to deny that concessions are indeed in order. Unless one rejects modern thought and culture wholesale, there is no escaping the task of assigning positive value to new developments that challenge older premises. This effort would consist not in flatly reducing the structure of experience to an expression of pure egocentrism, but instead in seeking the features of our condition that seem to disrupt the egocentrism which likely does shape a great deal of our experience. A prominent feature of this effort is a turn to the language of appeal and response, rather than that of appearance and constitution, where the subject or ego remains more firmly in place as the locus of what shows itself. The shift is not without immediate difficulty, for if what appeals does so from beyond the entire range of phenomenality—as must be supposed for God or the absolute—then what appeals is also, considered in itself, on the verge of unintelligibility. It would be too easy to conclude that this signals nothing more than a hermeneutical mistake, as if concepts such as *infinity, absolute* or *the Transcendent* have been shifted from their role of interpreting an experience to define it actually in advance. This may well be the case in some theologies and philosophies, but it that fact does not yet explain how a certain hermeneutics could have gotten itself into a situation where that kind of mistake becomes possible. Ben Vedder's essay, "The Disappearance of Philosophical Theology from Hermeneutic Philosophy," offers us some of that missing explanation, with a look at the movement from Schleiermacher through Dilthey and Gadamer, each of whom struggled with the realization, essential to the hermeneutic enterprise, that the finitude of our understanding makes all knowledge of God temporary. There is, as Vedder notes, no hermeneutic experience of an infinite God, and Heidegger seems to have accepted this fact early. From this perspective, the interest of his 1921 course on Augustine appears to go beyond the attempt to grasp a dis-

tinctly Christian form of being-in-the-world, to the thought that the concrete life of faith, of being-toward-God, is prior to the intellectual concepts meant to clarify it.

Much of this is quickly left behind in what at least aspires to a neutral pursuit of the question of the meaning of Being. And it is true, of course, that the form of thinking that takes shape on this path, a thinking that memorializes and responds (*ein andenkendes Denken*) to what shows itself from beyond the showing, is fundamentally receptive and even self-effacing. But it is also true that these features of Heidegger's philosophy remain anchored in the affective tonality of Dasein, whether this is manifest in anxiety, boredom, or serenity. The early Heidegger focused on anxiety, in which the call of Being is heard in the voice of conscience. This is also the period in which Being as defined as nothingness of beings, which is well in agreement with the notion that it is in anxiety—by definition an attunement to nothingness—that its call would be heard. This way, in which a mood that discloses Being and a definition of Being that points directly to a single mood reinforce one another, opens Heidegger's early argument to a two-fold interrogation. One might oppose the privilege granted to anxiety, and one might also test the adequacy or depth of the definition of nothingness. Needless to say, when it is a matter of religion, either of the two possibilities would appear urgent. In "Rethinking God: Heidegger in the Light of Absolute Nothing, Nishida in the Shadow of Onto-theology," John Maraldo engages both of these at once, and from the salutary distance provided by a deep understanding of the Kyoto School, where—and these are only apparently clichés—the mood is different and the nothingness otherwise. Freeing himself from the negation by which Heidegger famously opposes beings and Being conceived as Nothing, Nishida envisions a To-Be that can not be contained by either beings or Being/Nothing. Maraldo's questions are provocative: would Heidegger have forgotten true Nothingness? If so, should we not therefore revisit the way his thinking banishes reflection on God in the name of thinking through the onto-theological constitution of metaphysics? And would that not mean another outcome than Heidegger's celebrated notion of waiting for the gods?

The essays by Emilio Brito and Jean-Yves Lacoste press Heidegger on points recognizably near this theme of a thinking that opens itself and responds to what shows itself from beyond comprehension. Brito's essay on the Heideggerian interpretation of the Sacred is intent on isolating what it genuinely offers: religious reflection. The results would appear to underwrite considerable reserve. With this approach, Heidegger would have been creatively violent in his reading of Hölderlin, regrettably narrow in his working account of classical metaphysics and the Judeo-Christian tradition, and fundamentally ambiguous in some of his operative epistemology, so that, most seriously, a powerful thinking is shackled precisely when it turns toward an experience by which its central aim—to think Being as such—is to be confirmed in its claim to succeed precisely without religion. In the end, for Brito, the very

7

things about biblical monotheism that Heidegger's concept of the Sacred leaves aside—its link to a personal God, the importance of the act in which it enters experience, its communal dimension, and its ethical moment—would belong essentially to the more adequate conception preserved in classical metaphysics.

In "The Work and Complement of Appearing," Lacoste finds that Heidegger's interpretation of the work of art has considerable promise for theology and philosophy of religion. Not that there is any question of confusing the experience of art with the events of "liturgy," the logic of our relation with the absolute: the interest and importance of the work of art lies in the exemplary manner in which it permits us to see how what appears depends on its own appearing in order to enter experience, and according to Lacoste this provides us with useful clues for how to think about religion. If we open ourselves to a painting in the manner of Heideggerian meditation, we do not merely come into the presence of what the artist wishes to show or stage for us, but may also glimpse the very working of appearing to bring something to light. In this way, great art permits us to think through appearing toward the non-appearing of what exceeds its own appearing. Developed in this way, Heidegger's essay on the work of art sets a course beyond the screen and filter of experience that theology, for its part, can emulate in its own attempt to open itself—not to Being, which remains Heidegger's final intention, but—to God. Both the work of art and what Lacoste calls the "liturgical event" exercise an appeal that disrupts and contests the rule of light and phenomenality over the meaning of existence and experience, even if the respective dimensions thus announcing themselves are of course significantly different. And their difference indicates the complexity of an existence open to more than one appeal from beyond the limits of our being-in-the-world.

(2) After Heidegger, philosophy has sometimes paid so much attention to religious experience as an event that would verify claims for a relation with God, that one can feel—often mistakenly, to be sure—that there is no longer much concern for the sense in which religious experience animates and orients an entire way of life. Yet neither theology nor philosophy have ever lacked interest in that other sense, as readers of Augustine or Gabriel Marcel certainly know. In this volume, three such readers—Lacoste, Adriaan Peperzak, and Verhack—attend closely to this matter of religious experience as a way of being in the world. Lacoste's essay does not hesitate to broach the question of a fundamental mood in which liturgical experience is undergone, and his work elsewhere has already prepared descriptions of an entire worldview animated by it.[12] Peperzak's essay "Affective Theology, Theological Affectivity" repeats the key concepts put in play by Lacoste, though perhaps under a slightly different understanding. Peperzak attempts first to disclose the lineaments of a distinctly religious mode of existence, but comes quickly to the matter of desire, and thus movement. "Desire," he writes, "is the motor of all we do, but

it would not move us were it not awakened by a call from elsewhere." One recognizes in this the very cornerstone for theological conceptions of speech and community but also, by unmistakable implication, responsibility and justice. No less than Brito, Peperzak is willing to suggest that certain theological determinations may well entail a view of life that holds the answer to any number of riddles confounding our secular thinking.

Verhack's essay on "Immanent Transcendence as Way to 'God'" represents something of a turning point in this collection, insofar as it carries on the discussion with Heidegger but also opens up debate with and among those who criticize him in the name of religion. In this case, the critic is Jean-Luc Marion, and Verhack plays him off Heidegger with the specific aim, still in line with Peperzak and Lacoste before him, of defining a religious dimension of human being in such a way that it is capable—and perhaps uniquely capable—of understanding what motivates human movement, in the existential sense. It is an interesting feature of Verhack's essay that his concern with "movement" can make Heidegger's search for a more divine god than ontotheology would permit and Marion's thought of a God more transcendent than any idolatry could contain appear equally unsatisfactory—as well as considerably closer together than one is often led to think. In the most brutal terms, there is too much (religious) transcendence in both conceptions of God, so that the argument, most visibly in Marion's case, often flirts with a dualism in which the Wholly Transcendent occasionally breaks into the immanence that is otherwise severed from it. Needless to say, the thesis of a life completely immersed in the sphere of immanence makes desire and its movement a conundrum. As Verhack shows, the move to avoid this difficulty is also a move to rediscover the excluded "middle" that, binding finite and infinite, is itself the very definition of the religious. For only thus, he contends, can it be said not only that we desire beyond ourselves, but also that there is indeed an intelligible relation with the aim of that desire.

(3) The themes of speech and language, community, and ethics will have been present in this volume from the beginning. If they are never far from Vedder's concern with the hermeneutic tension between finite and infinite, Brito explicitly criticizes Heidegger for leaving at least the latter two underdeveloped. Among philosophers and theologians debating the question of religious experience after Heidegger, the most refined discussions of speech and language have returned all the way to the founding text of phenomenology, Husserl's *Logical Investigations*. The protagonists have been, first, Levinas and then later Marion, in contention with Jacques Derrida. Until recently, it has generally been thought that whereas Levinas and Marion have criticized Husserl and Heidegger alike according to some deep religious affinity—the one Jewish messianism, and the other Christian Neo-Platonism—Derrida deconstructs phenomenology by exposing buried oppositions and repressed decisions that have become axiomatic. The different results of these two opera-

Jeffrey Bloechl

tions can be seen, among other places, in the way each treats Husserl's theory of signs. Again, until recently it has been generally accepted that whereas Levinas or Marion seek to wrest signification from the subject–object correlation that seems inadequate to the advent of superabundance, Derrida submits that correlation, under various guises (subject–object, interiority–exteriority, time–space, etc.), to a deconstruction that calls attention to their mutual supplementarity. The prevailing impression, then, has been one of arguments for absolute otherness, on one hand, versus an argument for original difference, on the other. However, this situation has become immeasurably more complicated in recent years, with rumors of a Levinasian turn in Derrida's recent work, and a series of books and essays in which Derrida himself extols the messianic character of deconstruction. In "Derrida and Marion: Two Husserlian Revolutions," John Caputo gives us reason to think that this prevailing impression may be misleading when, or if, it assumes that a philosophy of original difference is strictly opposed to any positive relation to religion. Building on lengthier work elsewhere, Caputo's essay is at once an argument that Derrida's reading of Husserl is more convincing than Marion's reading, and an assertion that what Derrida does with Husserl's theory of signs—unlocking the possibility of a signifier without a fulfilling intuition—is consistent with his more recent emphasis on the eschatological and prophetic nature of speech itself, insofar as it is always already open to what may come from wholly beyond anticipation. It is not necessary to go into Marion's comparative phenomenology of idol and icon to recognize Caputo's implication: from the perspective of Derrida's "messianic eschatology," the moment Marion determines what comes to experience from wholly beyond, the moment he associates it with God or *hyperousios*, he returns his own position to the sort of metaphysical restrictions (read: onto-theology) he professes to escape.

If the thought of a difference more original than any identity can be taken to disrupt any movement to totality, then it begins in rough agreement with Levinas's defense of an ethical plurality than not even Heidegger has managed to respect properly. Where Heidegger describes a spontaneous tendency of experience and thought to impose unity and wholeness on whatever it meets,[13] Levinas sees the first step toward totalization: each person will be defined first by his or her place in a panorama commanded by the ego. To be sure, Levinas does not contest the idea that such a tendency is indeed spontaneous and in that sense natural, but instead argues that the fact that each of us, left alone, exhibits it seems to indicate a plurality of individual existents that Heidegger's concept of Being, as their common horizon, immediately cancels. This plurality, irreducible to any totality, represents the first great theme of Levinas's philosophy, even before its better-known descriptions of the face as trace and trauma, which are intended as an effort to verify the fraternal relation between each separated subject and its neighbors. Above all, Levinas is thus opposed to the sort of recourse to roots or starting point from which that plurality could be qualified, or worse, defined by some ulterior viewpoint.[14] And the difference that this makes shows up, as Richard Cohen points out, in the contrast between the "abstract universality" in what matters most about each particular must be found in the elements it shares with all others, and the "concrete universality" capable of respecting the unique value and identity of each particular. Of course, since this "concrete universality" is found pre-eminently in Jewish thought—or, as Cohen contends, a form of thinking that Judaism has only sometimes recognized in itself—there is no avoiding the question of just how universal the vision of a particular tradition can be. "The Universal in Jewish Particularism," we are told, is concentrated in its commitment to "ethical monotheism," to the idea that there is no contradiction between the plurality of radically separate individuals and the oneness of their integral relation. In the philosophy of Levinas, this thought conducts transcendental descriptions of interpersonal relations to a religious conception of subjectivity that we are perhaps more accustomed to find in prophetism. In *Totality and Infinity*, care for the other person is also redemption of the world,[15] and this, Cohen notes, defines the human community by an ethical and religious task that we can only hope against hope may one day be completed.

The theme of an eschatological community is also taken up by Kevin Hart, in what is probably the most recognizably Christian theological essay in this volume. For all of his engagement with the most speculative of the major theological concepts, the Trinity, Hart also opens his account of community to some crucial help from Derrida. Specifically, this involves the notion of *aporia*, which Derrida develops, in a Kierkegaardian moment, as the site where resolution is logically impossible and therefore achieved only in the freedom of an act without prior assurance. This notion, Hart contends, not only clarifies the predicament of a Christian caught between a Trinitarian theology "from above," whereby God is fully revealed in the Son, and a Trinitarian theology "from below," whereby faith in God's salvific action is realized through hearing the message of Jesus among us. And from this "impossible place" (Hart), the believing Christian is also caught between a vocation to the work of the kingdom (βασιλεια) already arrived and an eschatological hope for the kingdom that breaks into this world and redefines it. Thus bound together, the Kingdom and the Trinity are nonetheless withheld from human grasp; instead, they are available only in the life that reaches toward them, which Augustine knew was proof that they have already touched us, or that we have already tasted them. Were they less present than this, there could be no desire or hope. Were they more present, both desire and hope would be all too easily satisfied. At this point, Hart's essay folds back into the concern with "movement" also addressed by Peperzak and Verhack.

(4) Joseph O'Leary's "Ultimacy and Conventionality in Religious Experience" is best read at the end of this volume first because one gets the impression that its "turn east" to Buddhist thought responds to features of "western" thought that have emerged only quite recently, and second because it argues

Jeffrey Bloechl

for an intimate relation between the themes of speech and language, plurality, and properly religious experience. O'Leary's interest in language is linked to an interest in specifically mystical religious experience at the point where attempts to express the latter always qualify every utterance by insisting on a sense of the "mysterious" and "ineffable." Does this mean that mystical experience entails contact with what is beyond words? Or should we rather insist, in the manner of a Steven Katz, that at some level language actually does shape the experience? O'Leary prefers to reject the opposition between these two and simply ask, with the help of some Mâdhyamika thought, whether both the conventional language of the religions *and* the ultimacy which they express/ shape are culturally context-bound and therefore plural. Plainly enough, this situates his work somewhere outside the range of the more encrusted metaphysics targeted by Heidegger, Derrida, and others, but the effort to make ultimacy and conventionality call one another into question within the historical and cultural context where a mystical text has been written aims to invite a thought of emptiness beyond all contexts that few, if any, in our biblical and Greek traditions have managed to articulate. It is unclear whether O'Leary's argument requires him to free his notion of "emptiness" from the historical and cultural context in which it first entered thought—and unclear, for that matter, whether this is possible—but in any event it is obviously a promising lens though which to read all the texts of the classical theologians and great mystics. O'Leary himself provides an elegant example in what is at once a study of Augustine from the standpoint of emptiness and a brief exercise in *lectio divina.* Two features of the reading seem inevitable: apophansis is radicalized until negating even the reference to any particular "ultimate," since there is no ultimacy that is not still a feature of conventionality; and subjectivity is said to be capable of complete illumination, its narcissistic and erotic proclivities notwithstanding. With regard to the naming of God or definitions of the absolute, what results from this argument is a restored sense of ultimacy in its "adjectival" sense, as the tint or angle of a specific vision, rather than the self-subsisting aim. With regard to the definition of metaphysics, what results is an image of vibrant plurality rather than a fixed unity. And with regard to the question of religious experience, what results is a horizon in which claims or arguments in its favor can appear plausible without depending on some prior foundation.

NOTES

1. Augustine, *Confessions* X, 23.
2. R. Descartes, *Meditations on First Philosophy* III, 24; IV, 17; V, 16, and so on.
3. J.-L. Marion, *Sur le prisme métaphysique de Descartes* (Paris: P.U.F., 1986), p. 110.
4. Cf. E. Levinas, *Totality and Infinity* (Pittsburgh: Duquesne University Press, 1969), pp. 48–54; J.-L. Marion, *Questions cartésiennes. II. Sur l'ego et sur Dieu* (Paris:

P.U.F., 1996); pp. 3–47; M. Henry, *Incarnation. Une philosophie de la chair* (Paris: Seuil, 2000), pp. 86–102.

5. G. W. Leibniz, *Principes de la Nature et de la Grâce*, §8, in *Philosophische Schriften*, vol. VI, ed. Gerhardt, p. 602 (emphasis added). Cf. also *New Essays on Human Understanding*, II, xxi, §13. It is, therefore, no surprise that Marion, in his philosophy of religion, cites this very passage and others like it whenever he discusses the early modern constitution of onto-theology. Cf., e.g., J.-L. Marion, *The Idol and the Distance* (New York: Fordham University Press, 2001), pp. 12–13, and *God Without Being* (Chicago: University of Chicago Press, 1991), pp. 33 and 64.

6. A great consistent exception is the work of Stanislas Bréton, especially *Du principe* (Paris: Aubier Montaigne, 1971), which meditates on the inner principle of this tendency, the "projection" of that principle into philosophy and theology alike, and the fate of a thinking that claims to get free of it.

7. A. Schopenhauer, *The Fourfold Root of the Principle of Sufficient Reason*, §34.

8. Cf., e.g., L. Cahoone, *The Dilemma of Modernity* (Albany: SUNY Press, 1988), pp. 173–174, and Chapter Six, passim.

9. M. Heidegger, *The Basic Problems of Phenomenology* (Bloomington: Indiana University Press, 1988), p. 17.

10. Cf. M. Heidegger, *An Introduction to Metaphysics* (New Haven: Yale University Press, 1959), pp. 17–19.

11. M. Heidegger, "On the Essence of Ground" (1929), in *Pathmarks*, ed. W. McNeill (Cambridge: Cambridge University Press, 1998), pp. 133–35. My subsequent reference to Heidegger's "abyss of ground" is taken from these same pages.

12. Cf. J.-Y. Lacoste, *Expérience et Absolu* (Paris: P.U.F., 1994) §§9–38.

13. Cf., among numerous places, "On the Essence of Ground," in *Pathways*, pp. 111–112.

14. For this reading of Heidegger, see E. Levinas, "Heidegger, Gagarin, and Us," in *Difficult Freedom* (Baltimore: Johns Hopkins University Press, 1997), pp. 231–34.

15. E. Levinas, *Totality and Infinity* (Pittsburgh: Duquesne University Press, 1969), pp. 89f.

The Disappearance of Philosophical Theology in Hermeneutic Philosophy

Historicizing and Hermeneuticizing the Philosophical Idea of God

Ben Vedder

In this essay I present a number of perspectives that are, in my view, typical of a hermeneutical approach to the "philosophy of God." What is implied in such a hermeneutical approach? The simple fact that the hermeneutical task is by definition endless already brings some special problems to the philosophy of God. From that endlessness, as developed in the work of Schleiermacher, Dilthey, Heidegger, and, joined specifically to dialogue, Gadamer, there arises the immediate question of whether the philosophical idea of God as "highest being" has not passed over into a sense of God as withdrawn or withdrawing precisely because of the transformation of philosophy itself by or even into hermeneutics. To be sure, a negative theology and mystical approach to God have long remained attentive to a sense of God as withdrawn or withdrawing from thought, but this fact only improves my question: could it be that the current popularity of those approaches in theology and prayer in fact depends on the contemporary hermeneutic turn in our thinking? This is, at least, a suggestion I wish to entertain here.

Strange as it may at first seem, one could argue that Spinoza is among the first modern thinkers to develop a theory of hermeneutics.[1] As the proponent of a philosophical conception of God, Spinoza defines the absolute as "infinite substance" in a way that involves a sharp distinction between knowledge and faith. Real truth of God is to be reached only in rational knowledge. A believer is unfamiliar with what it is to think in Spinoza's sense of thinking, and must therefore seek a true life not in intellectual insight into the truth, which is beyond the capacities of the believer, but instead simply in obedience. Furthermore, reading and interpreting the Bible is good for such believers only insofar as it educates them into a way of life that is in agreement or at least harmony with reason—even if, again, the believer does not understand reason. It is this lack of rational knowledge in the believer that leads Spinoza to describe a hermeneutical approach to the Bible that today can seem rather modern. However, it is important to keep in mind that it is indeed precisely the notion of a lack of rationality that brings Spinoza to this hermeneutical approach.

Spinoza thus marks a distinction between philosophical knowledge of God and the hermeneutic approach of believers. For Spinoza, the philosophical approach is the most important of the two; rational knowledge is knowledge apart from words and independent of historical situation. Today, of course, things are virtually the opposite: it is the hermeneutical approach that seems to us the most "reasonable" way to God. Knowledge, we now think, is possible only through words and in finite, historical situations. Just what is this hermeneutical way, and what consequences follow from it? Does the God of hermeneutics not have some specific features that ensue from the hermeneutical approach as such—just as the traditional philosophical idea of God as "highest being" has features that ensue from the traditional philosophical approach? In what follows, I sketch the development of this hermeneutical approach, together with what is presupposed in relation to the philosophical approach to God. My starting point is the work of Schleiermacher.

I. The Feeling of Absolute Dependence

In Schleiermacher we find the origin of the separate paths of philosophical theology and hermeneutical theology. Strictly speaking, Schleiermacher rejects the philosophical approach to God. Philosophy is not an avenue to God. In Schleiermacher, the endless interaction of thinking and speaking, and of dialectic and hermeneutics, is a consequence of the impossibility of absolute knowledge and the limitation of knowledge to the province of finitude and history. This limitation, further, is based on the finitude of the human subject, which cannot constitute itself, but feels its absolute dependence in immediate consciousness. A human being cannot think the whole of the universe, because he or she uses thinking as the path or avenue to that task. Thinking is thus not a help but a hindrance. "The reason for this failure of our enterprise," writes Schleiermacher, "is given by the fact that we wish to think the transcendent" (D 270).[2] *Thinking* will never give us the whole of contact with the universe. Accordingly, Schleiermacher rejects the philosophical and rational approach to God; it is *feeling* that brings us to God. However, because feeling is not an instrument of thinking, this approach must be aided by dialogical and hermeneutical reflection.

The question of how to "think" God is the central theme of Schleiermacher's philosophy of religion.[3] According to Schleiermacher, that fact that we are aware of our dependence indicates that self-consciousness is not the beginning. In this respect, Schleiermacher is not a modern thinker. Self-consciousness itself is there as a feeling of absolute dependence. The unity of consciousness is not an act of the thinking subject but is given to it. This characteristic of *giving* is open to us in and by feeling. Unlike the consciousness that is related to objects, this immediate self-consciousness is not given with thinking and willing. For Schleiermacher, thinking is not the highest of human capacities (R 45). The capacity to give a subject unity lies with and belongs to feeling. Feeling would thus be pure susceptibility, something beyond the power of the human subject, in contrast with (the objects of) willing and knowing.

This self-consciousness that is aware of its susceptibility and openness to the universe Schleiermacher calls "absolute dependence" (*schlechthinnige Abhängigkeit*). In this susceptibility the subject is aware that he or she is determined by others. Absolute freedom, or absolute subjectivity, is not possible to a subject that does not make its own existence. The feeling of absolute dependence is the first stage of the finitude of the subject. For Schleiermacher, the understanding of human being as a finite being belongs to the domain of religion. It is not a matter for thinking or philosophy.

Nevertheless, we can distinguish between a religious attitude and a philosophical attitude toward the feeling of absolute dependence. In the religious attitude toward this feeling, one sees a revelation of the whole universe in each and every particular thing. For Schleiermacher, Spinoza was the great hero of this religious view (R 54–55). Yet what for Spinoza was possible through rational thought is for Schleiermacher possible only through feeling. Religion means grasping the separate individual as a part of the whole. And in the whole universe, everything, each finite being, remains each in its proper place. All is one and all is true. The infinite shines forth from each and every single thing. This religious attitude is one of calm and tolerance. Each of us has his or her own relationship with the whole universe. It is the feeling of calm that dominates the religious attitude.

According to the philosophical conception of the feeling of absolute dependence, one is aware of a ground that one cannot reach or attain. The philosophical, rational approach even weakens that feeling: the ground is said to be beyond thinking; it is therefore a transcendental ground to which we can apply the word *God*—whose content is never certain to us—only in a provisional way. The rational approach divides the feeling of absolute dependence between a subject and an object, with the result that we have lost the original whole. We are therefore to avoid reducing the religious consciousness of the whole to the knowledge or idea of God. The feeling of absolute dependence is more fundamental than knowing and thinking. Thinking, in turn, always comes "after" the experience of dependence. The whole that we *feel* cannot become an object of pure knowing. Religion is therefore always individual and historical (R 100). This is why Schleiermacher considers the plurality of religions to belong to the essence of religion (R 240).

The word *God* is the indicator of a feeling of absolute dependence in reflective, rational consciousness. It is a finite expression of (the) infinity and, as a finite expression, belongs to object-consciousness; at the same time, as an expression of the intended infinity, it is not an object of knowing, but a manifestation of feeling. But what is the function of feeling in relation to thinking and knowledge? For Schleiermacher, because there is a gap between feeling and thinking, it is impossible for the philosopher ever to undo the feeling of dependence. As he says in his *Reden über die Religion*, thinking is unable to replace feeling as the specific domain of religion. In the notion of God as "transcendental ground," that which by definition cannot be an object of thinking nonetheless receives objective form and becomes an object of reflection. In this way, the experience of the whole universe that defines feeling is made to withdraw (R 75). It is by this withdrawal that the subject acquires a consciousness of objects, of the world as an assembly of objects, and—not least—of itself, as self-consciousness.

Subject and object are surrounded by language, and language thus becomes the primordial defining feature of human being. The origin of language is an act of the individual human insofar as he or she invents a word to indicate the feeling of absolute dependence. But this never completes a bridge over the gap between thinking and the intended matter of thinking: infinity. For the experience of the whole universe withdraws at the very moment and in the very process of thinking and verbalizing it. In this sense, the word *God* is a testimony to human finitude. The fact that we must invent words for this ground represents the very origin of anthropomorphism and mythology, because the transcendental ground can be present in language only as the condition of finitude and object-consciousness. Immediate consciousness of self is present only as consciousness of an object. It is present only in language and history, because its presentation as an historical object is due precisely to its absence from language. "Nothing we say about the highest being is completely right, everything stays imaginary . . ." (D 297). With this, the rational approach to God moves close to becoming a hermeneutical approach.

The meaning of the feeling of dependence can be discussed only if the feeling is expressed in object-consciousness. If this does not happen, we cannot speak about it. It must be expressed on the level of words, language, and texts. But in a meaningful text, the immanent character of the letter and the transcendental character of the meaning are united. Consciousness of God, to the degree that it does exist in language, has the character of a text, but certainty about the question of whether the word is related to the intended matter can only be attained by a jump—into a religious attitude, and thus in feeling, not thinking.

The word "God" is the primordial text which is made by a human act to represent the transcendental ground, and which is a result of an interpretation of the feeling of dependence. This primordially given dependence must be interpreted, and as such this interpretation must be in tune with what is thought in it. But this primordial difference is gathered into a provisional identity. The making of the word, in tune with the matter that is thought, is a response to the feeling of dependence. The origin is that dependence and it will always be expressed in a finite way, because the infinite withdraws.

This priority of dependence is a justification of the need for hermeneutics, because the feeling of dependence can enter awareness only as an object, which is to say in our object-consciousness of God: by words, signs, and texts that demand interpretation. In the end, it is the finitude of the subject that provides the necessary impulse toward deriving a hermeneutics from the notion of a feeling of dependence. Moreover, since the subject is dependent, and has an unrepeatable original susceptibility that enters human understanding through the mediation of signs and human activity, Schleiermacher correlates this hermeneutics with his philosophy of religion.[4] In other words, this hermeneutics not only develops a philosophy of the subject but also founds it on a philosophy of religion.[5]

Absolute knowledge is possible only beyond finitude, in the feeling of the whole universe, but this is not hermeneutics. The philosophical approach is a hermeneutics approach, and it yields only temporary knowledge of God. This is because the feeling by which we feel the whole universe withdraws from thought the moment we begin to think. Is this not the moment in which the withdrawal or withdrawing of God appears on the philosophical stage? God withdraws with the rise of hermeneutics.

III. Dilthey

In Dilthey's work, hermeneutics is developed more explicitly as a philosophical approach. Dilthey also makes the temporary character of hermeneutics more explicit than had Schleiermacher before him, but he does this against the background of a certain metaphysical presupposition. For Dilthey, hermeneutics, introspection as self-contemplation, and worldview are all involved in endless process. It is important to recognize the reason for this endlessness: Dilthey speaks of a metaphysical feeling in us; I hope to demonstrate that this metaphysical feeling is directed toward the infinity of the universe, which cannot be expressed in words, reflection, and worldviews. Every attempt to grasp the whole of life must necessarily fail because of the primacy of the infinite universe, which was Dilthey's foremost concern throughout his life.

It is well known that Dilthey rejected metaphysics as an outmoded way of thinking. Metaphysics is considered to be directed at an independent objective reality unrelated to human subjectivity and existing without any relation to historicity. It seems as if the ideal of knowing reality as an objective totality having its own validity does not exist for Dilthey. In his view, what is left out of the usual metaphysical theory is an account of metaphysical mood. This basic metaphysical mood, or feeling, depends on the immeasurability of the universe, and is a symbol for infinity. Yet this feeling is not capable of proving the validity of its own truth-claims. As a "logical" system, metaphysics falls silent (I, 364).[6]

However, for Dilthey this gesture of pointing out a mood as a remnant of metaphysics is not intended negatively, as depreciation; rather, it is this gesture that keeps alive the relationship of thought with the totality of life and reality. For him, it is an important mood as the point of departure from which the totality of life and world form a unity. The world, he says, is carried by the mood: "As living Whole, as creation of a person, in which the concept of this All becomes an ideal, it is borne by a basic feeling (*Gemütsverfassung*), a fundamental attunement (*Grundstimmung*)" (VIII, 33). What remains, after the disappearance of abstract and substantial essences as the ground for metaphysics, is the mood from which every ego forms a unity with its world.

After the loss of metaphysics, Dilthey poses a new philosophical question: How is scientific knowledge of individuals possible? Is such knowledge indeed possible, and how can we achieve it? (V, 317). For Dilthey, the question of the possibility of understanding the individual is the key problem of hermeneutics, and is relevant for the whole of the humanities. The possibility of a general valid interpretation of individuals can be deduced from the nature of human life, where the interpreter and the person interpreted are not unfamiliar to each other since both have formed themselves on the basis of a same general human nature. This general human nature makes possible both the understanding of the other and the understanding of the human as such. However, according to Dilthey, this does not result in a final, complete understanding. At this point, I would like to ask precisely why understanding is indeed incomplete. After all, following this line, it should be possible, on the basis of a few words and their connections in sentences, to arrive at an understanding of the whole work. From this angle, it would have to be said that the whole is not definitively determined simply because one has not yet grasped it. This could also be said with respect to individual expression: the individual is incapable of complete self-expression in and through signs he or she has made.[7] "Theoretically, we are here at the limits of all interpretation; it can only fulfill its task to a degree: thus all understanding always remains relative and can never be completed: Individuum est ineffabile" (V, 330). Due to the unspeakable individuality of nature, in the end hermeneutics does not succeed in gathering complete knowledge. This is the first reason why hermeneutic knowledge is only temporary.

We come to the second reason as follows: Dilthey speaks of philosophical hermeneutics as a process of self-reflection, which ultimately takes the form of a biography. Writing the history of countries, people, cultural systems, organizations, eras, and finally universal history is, in the final account, a biography of humankind (VII, 250). In hermeneutics and the humanities, one is always absorbed in a process of self-reflection according to the model of biography. However, it remains questionable whether true self-knowledge is possible, since an understanding of other individuals is definitively impossible. After all, none of us could finish his or her own biography. And every autobiography must remain provisional, since all self-reflection is incomplete.

Through this process of self-reflection, life, experience of life, and the humanities have inner connection and interaction. Life understands life. And, furthermore, the construction of the concepts of the humanities in history and social science is determined by life itself (VII, 136). However, the immediate relationship between life and the humanities leads to a struggle between the tendencies of life, on one hand, and the scientific goal, on the other. Through a self-understanding of life, the scholar subjects it to him- or herself and wants to act on it. The scholar is always surrounded by his or her own historical time and place, and yet also keeps to a kind of universality. This requires an increasingly critical approach to the subject of study (VII, 137). Understanding penetrates ever greater depths of life. With all of this, Dilthey comes to see the humanities as absorbed in a process of self-reflection by historical man. And he sets for himself the task of a critical and rigorous elaboration of the objectivity of the humanities (VII, 138).

All that is living, even where the highest level of reason emanates from it, has a finitude that involves a darkness and illusion which renders life invincible. That finitude appears in the endless process of understanding, from which it appears than one cannot gain a clear understanding of one's own life or of life in general (VII, 150–151).

In theoretical reflection on humanity, based on the human sciences, we see a circular movement resembling individual reflection moving toward its own unreachable individuality, making theoretical reflection an endless task. In its orientation to a unique event, self-reflection works through the humanities to the whole of reflection on humanity. In its orientation toward the whole, it moves in an interaction between the universal and the particular (VII, 146). This is an interaction without end; a round and total self-understanding of humankind remains an ideal beyond reach. It thus seems that, in the end, the interpreter makes no real progress in his or her pursuit of knowledge of other individualities or in his or her process of self-reflection.

The most important reason why Dilthey rejects metaphysics is that for him historical consciousness in fact lies behind the metaphysical system. This historical consciousness objectifies the actual existing contrasts of metaphysical systems. Historical consciousness, in other words, sees that one has not progressed to a balanced system. And the contradictions in the systems and between the systems are based ultimately on life and the experience of life. In a historical survey, different types of worldviews become visible. In such a survey, experience of life is seen as the result of positions that one has or may have in relation to life, in relation to birth and to death. For Dilthey, birth and death are aspects of life toward which one has a position. This position opens up certain aspects of life. Historical research shows us the coherence of life within a worldview. The point of departure for this analysis would thus be the thought that every philosopher unravels the mystery of life from a certain viewpoint or perspective (VIII, 99). Life is always the beginning and end of the thought-process; thought arises from it and returns to it insofar as it always tries to understand it. And since life is given as the first and last principle beyond which we cannot go, we are caught up in an endless task. Hence, one again, the project of a worldview is always temporary.

In the foregoing, I have referred to the endlessness of hermeneutics, self-reflection, and worldviews according to Dilthey. It remains to ask how we can understand this endlessness as an ongoing, continuing endeavor. After Dilthey had eliminated universal truth-claims in metaphysics and had made herme-neutics the central avenue toward access to life, metaphysics was only one possible interpretation of life and its problems. In short, metaphysics disap-peared into historical anarchy. Still, according to Dilthey efforts to reach understanding and self-reflection, as well as to conceive a worldview, must not be abandoned, since there is always something eternally metaphysical in hu-mans. What is the place of this eternal metaphysical element in relation to self-understanding? Dilthey highlights the metaphysical in us at several points in his work:[8] "However, the metaphysical of our life, as personal experience, that is as moral-religious truth, remains" (I, 384). After the loss of the indepen-dence of metaphysics, the metaphysical in life is approached through the personal experience from which it receives personal and historical expression. "After this independence has become untenable, there still remains a deeper and farther reaching metaphysics: "the inner metaphysical consciousness is undying" (II, 498).

This eternal metaphysical element, however, is never represented as an idea, symbol, or image in history. Yet it is precisely this which, as the whole of life, must be expressed. Dilthey is aware of having posed an unsolvable prob-lem. But he understands its appearance as belonging to—and peculiar to—us humans, as we try to come to self-understanding in hermeneutics. Traces of this can be found in his continuous effort to bring an end to criticisms of historical reason. Dilthey's project, in other words, has an incompleteness that follows from the nature of his own presuppositions. Hermeneutics as a process of appropriation in self-reflection and the interpretation of life remains un-finished in relation to the whole of life.

The fact that Dilthey himself has seen this incompleteness appears ob-vious in his letters to Count Yorck,[9] to whom he writes: "We all work in a certain sense pro nihilo" (B 146). Dilthey always has the impression that the subject he seeks to comprehend is endless. To express this, he employs the image of the sea, speaking of a "See von Folianten" (B 147) and of his head as completely submerged in a "See von Arbeit" (B 170). It is therefore unsur-

Ben Vedder

prising that he envies the lumberjack who "sees results each day, each week" (B 39). He doubts whether he can "produce significant secure results" (B 181). And he expresses his project very strikingly as the result of a dream he once had, reporting that in the dream he looked at a painting from Rafael's school in Athens: the figures, old and modern philosophers alike, suddenly came to life, and began discussion in groups formed along lines similar to how Dilthey had described their relationship in his philosophy of worldviews. Nevertheless, he is sorry to see that in the dream the groups were separated: "A strange anxiety overcame me, one that was philosophically engendered, caused by seeing philosophy divided and torn in three or even more directions. The unity of my very being was torn asunder, for I was deeply attracted now to one group, now to another" (VIII, 221). As Dilthey awakened, he saw the stars through his window and was struck by the immeasurability and impenetrability of the universe; he remembered the anarchy of thinking that results from the historical determination of systems, but also experienced a feeling of freedom. Worldviews are based on the nature of the universe and on the relationship of the understanding spirit to that universe. "Thus does each worldview express within its limits one aspect of the universe. In this respect each is true. But each is one-sided. To contemplate all the aspects in their totality is denied to us. We see the pure light of truth only in various broken rays." (VIII, 224). Dilthey's understanding of human finitude and the finitude of hermeneutics must be understood in light of the inexpressibility of what is beyond history: the eternal universe. The one whole life can only manifest itself historically in many different ways—in fragments and in streaks.

However, this concept of finitude is dependent on Dilthey's ideal of the unity of the universe and life, which finally had to be understood. Human finitude is understood in terms of the infinite universe. The reason for the eternity of metaphysical consciousness comes from the unity of life, which is experienced in a mood as unity, but which can be presented only in a limited and incomplete way. The ambition to overcome finitude arises from consciousness of the eternal metaphysical element in which we contemplate the totality of the universe. In other words, Dilthey, who is himself motivated by the infinity of the universe—and this is the classical metaphysical ideal of knowledge—must move to the endlessness of hermeneutics, self-reflection, and worldviews, because of the temporary and provisional inaccessibility of the infinite universe. But this touches on work taken up only by those who would come later.

IV. Gadamer: Endless Discourse

Since in my view Gadamer is more tributary to Hegel and Dilthey than is Heidegger, I will address his work before that of Heidegger even if he was a disciple of Heidegger. Gadamer is more loyal to western philosophical conceptuality than is Heidegger, as we see when he tries to work out human finitude in terms of historicity in human science. For Gadamer, the world is a hermeneutic phenomenon. The temporary character of our knowledge of the world is determined by the finitude of our historical experience (TaM, 457).[10]

Gadamer broke with philosophical theological conceptuality and its metaphysical presuppositions. For him, language has a metaphorical structure. This means that a word is no longer the perfection of the species, as medieval thought held. When a being is represented in the thinking mind, this is not the reflection of a pregiven order of being, the true nature of which is apparent to an infinite mind (i.e., that of the Creator). But the word is also not an instrument, like the language of mathematics, that can construct an objectified universe of beings put at our disposal by calculation. Language has a metaphorical structure by which a word is a revelation of the world we live in. It is the medium of language alone that, in relation with totality of beings, mediates the finite, historical nature of humans to themselves and to the world (TaM 457).

This means that all human speech is finite. But for Gadamer, this is the case in such a way that there lies within it an infinity of meaning to be explicated and laid out. "If there are basically no bounds set to understanding, then the verbal form in which this understanding is interpreted must contain within it an infinite dimension that transcends all bounds" (TaM 401). Humanity is faced with an endless task that corresponds to the infinity of meaning to be explicated. But we will always fail at this task. "The most fundamental principle of philosophical hermeneutics says that in whatever manner I think from myself (and this is therefore a hermeneutical philosophy), we cannot say everything, and this fact can be said. For we are always just behind, and cannot say everything, as in fact we would have liked."[11] This is why the hermeneutic phenomenon can be illuminated only in light of the fundamental finitude of being, which is wholly verbal in character. Yet in this finitude there can also be glimpsed a utopia of infinity (TaM 458). This is an infinity that can never be surpassed and will always be anticipated.

However, the experience of this utopian infinity cannot be verbalized with classic philosophical statements. Gadamer compares this attempt with what transpires in a police interrogation. Anyone who has experienced an interrogation—even if only as a witness—knows what it is to make a statement and how little it is in actuality a statement of what one means. In a statement, the horizon of meaning of what is said is concealed by methodical exactness; what remains is the pure sense of the statements. And it is this that goes on record. Meaning is thus reduced to what is stated, and this reduction is a distortion. The methodological way to think and reach knowledge does not see its own shadow and unspoken presuppositions.

Similarly, to say what one means—to make oneself understood—is to hold what is said together with an infinity of what is not said in one unified meaning, and to insure that it is understood in this way. Someone who speaks in this way may well use only the most ordinary and common words and still be able to express what is unsaid and what is to be said (TaM 469). To speak is to

Ben Vedder

behave speculatively, because words have the character of a proposal. Words do not express fixed beings, but rather a relation to the whole of being. In this speculation, the interpreter is aware of the unsaid; one is aware of not saying the whole; every word functions as a proposal in a dialogue. As is also the case with Schleiermacher's dialectical approach, the truth is found here in a dialogue in which every statement is a proposal related to the matter spoken about. In the same way, hermeneutics has the task of revealing the world by verbalizing the meaning of the perspective one has on the world (TaM 471).

One might have the impression of a parallel with Hegel, but any such parallel would fail to take account of the real nature of the hermeneutical experience and the radical finitude that is its basis. It is true that interpretation must start somewhere, but it is not true that it starts just anywhere. There is no absolute beginning. The hermeneutic experience always includes the fact that the text to be understood speaks in a situation already determined by previous opinions. When we begin our interpretation, we can do so only because we and the world are already interpreted. The apparently thetic beginning of interpretation is in fact a response to a foregoing interpretation (TaM 472).

Hegel's dialectic of beginning and end is quite different than consciousness effected by history, which would include hermeneutical experience. Hermeneutic experience knows about the openness of the event of meaning in which it shares. Here, too, there is certainly a standard by which understanding is measured and which it can meet: the content of the tradition itself is the sole criterion, and it expresses itself in language. But there is no possibility of infinite consciousness because of the historicity of understanding, in which any traditional "subject matter" would appear in the light of eternity. Every appropriation of tradition is historically different, which, however, means more than simply that each one represents only an imperfect understanding of it. Rather, each appropriation is the experience of an "aspect" of the thing itself (TaM 472–473).

The whole of meaning is something announced (TaM 475). This means that meaning is not given completely; we must wait for it. Yet this is not the way Gadamer works the matter out. If we start from the fact that understanding is verbal, he emphasizes, on the contrary, the finitude of the verbal event in which understanding is always in the process of being concretized. The language that things have—whatever kind of things they may be—is not the *logos ousias,* and it is not fulfilled in the self-contemplation of an infinite intellect; it is the language that our finite, historical nature surrounds, bit by bit, as we learn to speak (TaM 476).

The philosophical idea of God presented in Hegel's philosophy of infinite knowledge is discarded in the hermeneutical approach. The universality of the hermeneutical experience would not be available to an infinite mind, for the latter develops all meaning, all noeton, out of itself, and thinks all that can be thought in perfect contemplation of itself. The God of Aristotle, as well as the Spirit of Hegel, left "philosophy" where and when philosophy became hermeneutics. Hermeneutical knowledge gains us the experience that that which is won will also be lost again. Thinking can also be an expectant and hopeful opening up to the things that one cannot appropriate at will, but which must be offered to and conferred on a person as an insight. With Plato, eros developed into a thinking that opens up, full of expectation, to receive what may suddenly appear. There is no hermeneutical experience of an infinite God.

V. Heidegger's Provisionality

As opposed to what we have seen in Spinoza's philosophical theology, we have found the hermeneutical theories of Schleiermacher, Dilthey, and Gadamer a notion of temporariness (*vorlaufigkeit*) which, however, appears only against the background of the idea of infinity. Heidegger, in turn, develops a hermeneutic without that horizon of infinity. In Dilthey we saw that every effort to interpret and understand another was temporary because it is seen from the perspective of the totality of life not yet expressed in a realized interpretation or understanding. In that respect, every interpretation is provisional. Now Heidegger has drawn attention to the fact that Dilthey's works were not finished, or fragmented. Each work seems to be no more than a sketchy presentation of the whole. But in Dilthey this notion of temporariness or provisionality has something to do with his concept of the whole of life that will someday be understood. The notion of infinite universe determines Dilthey's concept of temporariness.

In Heidegger, the notion of provisionality is very important, and in a way in which the difference from the notion in Dilthey exemplifies the difference between their two philosophies as a whole. Heidegger spoke of this provisionality as early as the winter of 1923: "As far as I am concerned, if this personal comment is permitted, I think that hermeneutics is not philosophy at all, but in fact something preliminary [*vorläufig*] which runs in advance of it and has its own reason for being; what is at issue in it, what it all comes to, is not to become finished with it as quickly as possible, but rather to hold out in it as long as possible."[12] This remark, which Heidegger made more or less indirectly, is quite strange. It is virtually incomprehensible from the usual perspective: staying with something temporary, instead of leaving the temporary as soon as possible. Hermeneutics, it would seem, therefore has to remain for a long time in the temporary. How does it do so?

The unfolding of the question of being, argues Heidegger, happens on the basis of an understanding of being already given in Dasein. This means that the analysis of Dasein must precede an elaboration of the question of the meaning of being (GA 29, 201–202).[13] However, the understanding of being is still indeterminate. This indeterminateness of understanding has its origin in the possibility of death, which is not to be outstripped. Because of this, that indeterminateness becomes something belonging to temporality. The moment of death is indeterminate. The analysis of Dasein that is explained in terms of its understanding of being is therefore always a provisional concept. "Dieses Seiende soll vorläufig genauer gewonnen werden"[14] (GA 20, 199). Interpretation and hermeneutics always happen in anticipation of a horizon given as indeterminate and preceding every explicit formulation.

Explaining and interpreting always happen through anticipation, a running ahead of things. Heidegger has said precisely this in his lecture on *Der Begriff der Zeit*"—the concept of time.[15] In anticipation, Dasein runs ahead of itself toward its bygone (*Vorbei*). "Der Vorlauf ist, sofern er die äußerste Möglichkeit des Daseins ihm vorhält, der Grundvollzug der Daseinsauslegung" (insofar as it holds before Dasein its extreme possibility, running ahead is the fundamental way in which the interpretation of Dasein is carried through) (BZ 18). This running ahead toward its bygone is Dasein's rootedness in its own historicality, the historicality of its own understanding. This is the first principle of hermeneutics.[16] This provisionality not only means that the interpretation runs ahead or anticipates what comes before it, but also that the interpretation is temporary or, in other words, passing. These characteristics of hermeneutics are also evident in Heidegger's later conception of thinking.[17] Dasein is temporary in its running ahead; only in anticipation (*vorlaufen*) is it passing (*vorläufig*), and without this it could not be historical.[18] More radical than Gadamer and Dilthey, Heidegger sees hermeneutics as a project of finite historical being.

In *Being and Time*, Heidegger shows that every understanding and interpretation, including understanding and interpretation of texts, is always carried out in a hermeneutic situation. Understanding is always anticipation of a meaning that announces itself as a possibility. This anticipation develops in the interpretation; without this "running ahead," it would not be possible to read in the sense of interpreting. The reader and the historian are part of the whole of the hermeneutic situation. The historian is related to a meaning that announces itself from the future, a future that the historian cannot survey and that the historian does not control. The thinking dialogue with the text will therefore never end, for history is never a surveyable totality. This means that every insight into the text is provisional, in the two-fold meaning of "running ahead" (*vorlaufen*) and "passing" (*vorläufig*); as an anticipation and interpretation, it is passing.

If we see the whole, in principle, as a closed totality that can be surveyed in the end—and this was the case for Dilthey and some idealistic philosophers—then an exhaustive interpretation is possible. Such an understanding of the whole is rejected by Heidegger because the reader, the historian, and the interpreter are always temporal. From the beginning of his teaching, Heidegger criticizes every attempt of philosophical theology to present God as a highest being. In that beginning, he analyzes Augustine from the perspective of hermeneutic facticity. For Heidegger, classical conceptuality hinders an understanding of the facticity of life. This also applies to Augustine's philosophical idea of God.

VII. Heidegger's Interpretation of Augustine

An excellent example of Heidegger's argument that classical conceptuality hinders an understanding of facticity can be found in his analysis of Book 10 of Augustine's *Confessions*. This analysis was part of a lecture course given during the summer semester of 1921, announced as "Augustine and Neo-Platonism" (GA 60, 160–299). According to Heidegger, Augustine wishes to approach life from the perspective of facticity.[19] The *beata vita* (beatific life) is seen by Augustine from the perspective of actualizing the search for it. Augustine changes the question of how we may find God into how we may find the beatific life. This is possible for him because he sees the beatific life as the real life, and the real life is the true life, which is God. For most people, the relation to this beatific life consists in looking forward to it and hoping for it.

While Augustine approaches the quest for God from the facticity of life, he also exhibits a tendency to move away from facticity. This, however, as we will see in a moment, is part of Augustine's facticity. According to Heidegger, Augustine, in his facticity, does not radically question the search for God because his situation is such that he is oriented to an objectifying way of knowing (GA 60, 194). Nevertheless, Augustine knows that the beatific life is not present in the way that, for instance, the town of Carthage is present for someone who has been there and now has a certain mental picture of it. The beatific life is present in such a way that we have a certain understanding of it that makes us want to make it our own. But it is difficult to be in the right position with respect to this authentic truth to which we look forward. In his *Confessions*, Augustine explains why this is so difficult, even though the quest for truth seems to come easily and naturally. In factical life, people live according to their own self-evident opinions. These are determined by tradition, fashion, ease, and fear of emptiness. Thus, truth is hidden from us because we flee from it. Yet, on the other side of this flight Heidegger sees a concern for truth, though one which is for the most part hidden. This concern, typical of factical life, is actualized within a horizon of expectations. For Heidegger, the most important element is the fact that this care is actualized historically (GA 60, 207). The human self is seen from the perspective of historical experience, because care is in itself historical. But, at the same time, in the tendency of care there is also always a danger of falling into inauthenticity. And this means that one is not directed towards God as the true beatific life.

Heidegger sees a Neo-Platonic influence in Augustine especially in the theme of enjoying oneself, which shows up where Augustine considers beauty to belong to the essence of being. Something is a pleasure and provides enjoyment if it does not refer to other things and if it is chosen because of itself. This pleasure is directed toward eternal and unchangeable goods. This results in a position in which peace and quiet are the aims of life; the true life would then be the realization of peace and quiet. However, this would be actualized in a historical manner, since life actualizes itself in the direction in which expectations are already moving. Nevertheless, it is difficult for one to actualize one's life in an authentic way because it is difficult to distinguish the tendency towards the true beatific life from the tendency towards other kinds of pleasure and enjoyment. To solve this problem, Augustine tends to construct an order of values that is rather theoretical and, as Heidegger sees it, Greek in origin.

The basic orientation of these values is connected with Neo-Platonism and the doctrine of the *summum bonum*, and this Greek theoretical approach is joined to the Christian message. Heidegger points out that the Pauline words registered in *Romans* 1:20 are in fact the foundation of all patristic thought. Those words secured Christian doctrine within a Greek philosophical framework even until today. And it is from them that the motivation for a Greek foundation for Christian dogma is derived. Accordingly, it is impossible to deny the influence of Platonic philosophy, taken up by Paul, on Augustine the reader of Paul; moreover, it is a misconception to think that we can arrive at an authentic Christianity (= pre-Greek Christianity) simply by going back to Augustine. The Pauline verse reads: "Ever since the world began his invisible attributes, that is to say his everlasting power and deity, have been visible to the eye of reason, in the things he has made." This means that human beings can know the divine world by transcending the visible world to the invisible (GA 60, 281). This affirmation of the truth of Platonism, as formulated by Paul, makes its influence felt even today.

Due to this Greek influence, there is an ahistorical understanding at work in Augustine's quest for the beatific life. Still, Augustine is aware that, in a certain sense, the *beata vita* cannot be found in things that a person finds easy to believe. It is not among our "easy" tendencies that the beatific life is to be found. With respect to the quest for the true *beata vita* and the danger of following easy tendencies, one must answer the question of who one is. This question becomes urgent when one sees oneself doing things one does not want to do, and wanting to do things one does not in fact do. There are also inner processes over which one has no control. This puts a certain burden (*molestia*) on us, and that burden is part of the facticity of our existence. According to Heidegger, philosophical activity should start from this facticity and not from theoretical notions like body and soul, sense and reason, *summum bonum*, God, and so forth.

The self is completely historical; it is not a quiet and theoretical moment, but historical actualization. In this quiet and theoretical approach of a certain philosophy, Heidegger sees a human tendency to fall into enjoyment and the pleasures of obvious things. Augustine describes three kinds of tendencies in us: (1) *concupiscentia carnis*, (2) *concupiscentia oculorum*, and (3) *ambitio saeculi*. The first two of these three are important in the present context. In the quest for truth and the *beata vita*, one must question oneself. But in the very process of questioning myself I am always in danger of not really doing that but instead enjoying the pleasure I meet during my quest—as can happen when someone sings praises to the Lord, and then while singing forgets the praises and begins to take pleasure (*concupiscentia carnis*) in the singing, in the beauty of the tones and song. This sort of weave of carnal life and true life in factical life explains how one is always in danger of turning or falling toward something other than the true life. Against this background, there is a long tradition in which God is seen as the highest life and the highest form of self-possession, and in which God is joyfully witnessed as the highest beauty. These beautiful Greek things hinder our understanding of factical life. Because of the Greek origin of philosophy, the theoretical approach in the Christian thinking of someone like Augustine is unable to destroy its framework and begin to truly understand factical life (GA 60, 257). But inasmuch as God is experienced in the actualization of the quest for God, this happens in a way in which one is initially moving *away* from the "highest light" that is God. In the quest for the true life, the distance to the "highest" God, as beauty, as if a place within a conceptual framework, never ceases to grow. The quest for the *beata vita*—which must not be seen as beauty in a thing (*in re*)—is directed towards something we hope for and that we do not have in our grasp. For Augustine, the question is how to gain access to God. God is "present" in the concern and care for the quest for life of the self (GA 60, 289). We must avoid every cosmic metaphysical representation of God as a "thing." But in Heidegger's view, Augustine's explication of the experience of God is still Greek in the sense that all philosophy is still Greek (GA 60, 292).

The second tendency identified by Augustine, *concupiscentia oculorum*, is—as the expression states—pleasure of the eyes. As we have just seen, singing praise to God can decline into a pure enjoyment of tones and melody. Something similar can happen with our eyes. Pure seeing as such can, out of sheer curiosity, dominate the quest for truth. This seeing is a mere looking-at, a witnessing, informing, and objectifying. There is an analysis of this eye-pleasure in section 36 of Heidegger's *Being and Time*.

In this context, we must introduce an aspect of understanding that Heidegger associates with the preference for seeing that defines the western constellation of knowledge. This preference for seeing brigs with it an ontology all its own. Heidegger begins his analysis of seeing and the ontology belonging to it with a look at the beginning of Aristotle's *Metaphysics: pantes anthropoi tou eidenai oregontai phusei*, which he translates as "The care for being is essential to human being" (*Being and Time*, 215). As a result of this beginning, in western philosophy the thesis applies that primordial and genuine truth lies in pure observation. Following in Augustine's footsteps, Heidegger calls this phenomenon "curiosity." This curiosity seeks novelty only in order to leap from it anew to another novelty. Curiosity wants to make things present; it cannot endure absence. Heidegger connects curiosity to "falling," which means that it is connected to presence. The intellectual approach to God in philosophy thus belongs to inauthenticity. And it is not aware of the historicity of every human attempt to understand "God."

Ben Vedder

NOTES

1. See B. Vedder, *Wandelen met Woorden, een weg van de filosofische hermeneutiek naar hermeneutische filosofie* (Best: Damon, 1997).

2. F. Schleiermacher, *Dialektik,* Im Auftrag der Preußischen Akademie der Wissenschaften auf Grund bis veröffentlichen Materials herausgegeben von Rudolf Odebrecht (Darmstadt: Wissenschaftlichen Buchgesellschaft, 1988). Henceforth cited only in the body of this text, abbreviated as D.

3. F. Schleiermacher, *Über die Religion. Reden und die Gebildeten unter ihren Verächtern,* ed. H.-J. Rothert (Hamburg: Meiner, 1958) (Ph.B. 255). Henceforth cited only in the body of this text, abbreviated as R.

4. See R. Rieger, *Interpretation und Wissen. Zur Philosophischen Begründung der Hermeneutik bei Friedrich Schleiermacher und ihrem geschichtlichen Hintergrund* (Berlin: de Gruyter, 1988); and M. Frank, *Das individuelle Allgemeine Tekststrukturierung und -interpretation nach Schleiermacher* (Frankfurt: Suhrkamp, 1985), pp. 91–114.

5. See M. Frank, *Das individuelle Allgemeine Tekststrukturierung,* p. 94.

6. I cite Dilthey's *Gesammelte Schriften* between parentheses in the body of this text. The Roman numeral indicates the volume, with the page number(s) following.

7. Cf. J. C. Maraldo, *Der hermeneutische Zirkel. Untersuchungen zu Schleiermacher, Dilthey, und Heidegger* (Freiburg/München: K. Alber, 1974), p. 74.

8. See also T. Nenon, "Systematic Assumptions in Dilthey's Critique of Metaphysics," *International Studies in Philosophy* 22, no. 3 (1990): 41–57.

9. See *Briefwechsel zwischen Wilhelm Dilthey und dem Grafen Paul Yorck v. Wartenburg. 1877–1897* (Halle: Niemeyer, 1923), p. 23. Henceforth cited only in the body of text, abbreviated as B.

10. H.-G. Gadamer, *Truth and Method,* 2nd, revised edition, trans. J. Weinsheimer and D. G. Marshall (London: Sheed and Ward, 1989). Henceforth cited only in the body of text, abbreviated as TaM.

11. H.-G. Gadamer, *Gesammelte Werke,* Bd 10 (Tübingen: Mohr, 1995), p. 274.

12. M. Heidegger, *Ontology—The Hermeneutics of Facticity,* trans. J. van Buren (Bloomington: Indiana University Press, 1999), pp. 15–16.

13. The text in question here is Heidegger's 1926 lectures later published as *Prolegomena to the History of the Concept of Time.* I cite the German text, which has appeared as a volume of Heidegger's *Gesamtausgabe,* abbreviated as GA and followed by volume and page numbers. This pagination is also provided in the English translation.

14. The English translation (p. 147) does not bring out this notion of *vorläufig:* "For now, this entity must be secured more precisely."

15. M. Heidegger, *Der Begriff der Zeit* (Tübingen: Niemeyer, 1989); translated by W. McNeill as *The Concept of Time* (Oxford: Blackwell, 1992). Henceforth cited only in body of text, abbreviated as BZ.

16. W. McNeill, "The First Principle of Hermeneutics," in T. Kisiel and J. van Buren, eds., *Reading Heidegger from the Start* (Albany: SUNY Press, 1994), p. 407.

17. See M. Heidegger, *Was heisst Denken?* (Tübingen: Niemeyer, 1971), p. 161.

18. See also B. Vedder, "Die Faktizität der Hermeneutik: Ein Vorschlag," *Heidegger Studies* 12 (1996): 95–107.

19. I am following Heidegger here; the references are not to the work of Augustine.

Rethinking God

Heidegger in the Light of Absolute Nothing, Nishida in the Shadow of Onto-theology

John C. Maraldo

The following engagement with the thought of Nishida Kitarō (1870–1945) and Martin Heidegger (1889–1976) puts the two in confrontation with each other and certainly in a place they never met, despite their acquaintance with each other's work. Out of the enormous corpus that each produced, the following meditation confines itself to parts of only four texts. It casts Heidegger in the light of Nishida's Absolute Nothing, and sets Nishida in the shadow of Heidegger's ontological difference. It places them together, however, to undergo a single quest: for a new, or rather an other, way of speaking and thinking God.

At the beginning of Nishida's attempts to globalize philosophy, and not only his own philosophy, we find a statement of difference that defines his worldview and that of his Kyoto School followers. In expanded translation, this statement reads, "Looking at the [classical] forms of culture of East and West from a metaphysical standpoint, how shall we distinguish them? I think that we can differentiate them [by saying that the West] thinks of being 有 as the ground 根底 of reality, [whereas the East] thinks of the Nothing 無 as the ground of reality. We could call these [reality as] having/being form 有形 and [as] formless 無形."[1]

Nishida's alignment of being with Western metaphysics seems to confirm Heidegger's contention that being is at base the sole concern of metaphysics. The sheer breadth of Nishida's generalization may remind us of Heidegger's sweeping claim that all metaphysics, indeed all philosophy (at least since Plato) is onto-theology. The resemblance in scope, however, soon turns to divergence in detail. Just as Heidegger's description overlooks traditions such as skepticism and ethical-political philosophy that many philosophers see as independent of metaphysics, so Nishida's characterization seems to disregard the traditions of "the East" that are not guided by the thought of the Nothing, and to overlook the deep similarities he himself often finds with the thought of nothingness in "the West."[2] Heidegger would further distinguish his own contribution as a thinking on the way to overcoming onto-theology. Nishida's essay proceeds to distinguish not his own thinking but rather Japanese culture, in a manner that both celebrates its unique contribution and clears a space for the formation of a pluralistic world culture. A "metaphysical standpoint" opens the space for Nishida's comparisons and contrasts of forms of culture, where metaphysics is broadly conceived as "the question of reality" and of "human life." For Heidegger, metaphysics—the question of being as such and in its entirety—is a great divide, defining philosophy exclusively and thus separating it from thinking, separating the occident from the rest of the world, and Heidegger from the (occidental philosophical) tradition. Heidegger is blatant in his refusal to recognize philosophy outside the Greek tradition and its heirs.[3] Nishida is circumspect and recognizes that metaphysics as a science or discipline is the contribution of Greek and Western culture, while what underlay traditional Eastern cultures was only implicit "metaphysical thought." To be sure, there is also exclusionism in Nishida's view and expansionism in Heidegger's. Nishida's great division implies the exclusion of a true philosophy of nothingness from Western cultures; Heidegger, on the other hand, proposes that technology is the global outcome of (Greco-European) metaphysics. But in the end, while Heidegger would contain metaphysics and release thinking, Nishida would globalize philosophy and personally pursue metaphysics. Their projects follow different paths.

It is not the intent of this essay to challenge Heidegger's and Nishida's divergent mapping of the bounds of philosophy, or to expose the kinds of nationalism that these mappings entail. Even if onto-theology only partially defines the (Western) philosophical tradition, even if premodern Eastern cultures only in part developed under the sway of the thought of nothingness, even if it is a gross oversimplification to divide the West and the East at the edge of metaphysics or from its standpoint, the issue that I wish to investigate remains intact. I want to explore one place where the paths of Heidegger and Nishida do cross, perhaps at more than one juncture. The name of this place is nothingness. To site it on Heidegger's path is already to challenge

Nishida's contention that the thought of the Nothing properly belongs to the East; and to bring Nishida and Heidegger together at this place will mean to challenge the difference with being that Heidegger finds hidden in his philosophical tradition.

The contrast of Heidegger and Nishida presupposes a thematic space they share in common. That space is not delineated by a common foundation to which we could trace their respective thinking; such a derivation would itself be a fall back to onto-logical reasoning that Heidegger would overcome and Nishida would find alien. Nor is this space defined by historical influence. Although the influence of Western philosophy on Nishida's thinking is ubiquitous in his work, and the influence of Asian thought on Heidegger has been well documented,[4] there is no evidence that Nishida read Heidegger's thoughts on onto-theology and that Heidegger read Nishida or first formed his conception of philosophy as metaphysics in contradistinction to Asian thought. Yet if the Nothing names a theme they have in common, it is not an arbitrarily chosen part of their respective thought. It is the central theme in Nishida's work, and it is the ulterior side of the To Be, the central theme in Heidegger's.[5] It names, as I will appeal, a place where it might be possible to change the course of philosophy, if not to overcome metaphysics, so as to think the Absolute in a new or another way. Such recourse, if it is possible, would obviously not come from within the onto-theological tradition or at a point continuing from it. Nor would it occur in a "step back" to a ground beneath that tradition. It would come as a discontinuity of, or even an outsider's intrusion into, the path that connects metaphysical philosophy and post-philosophical thinking for Heidegger. It might well be an interruption of both Nishida and Heidegger, in that it interjects a question into Nishida's thought that he himself did not raise, and pursues an answer that Heidegger would not follow.

But let us first step back into the way that Heidegger defines onto-theology. The Introduction of 1949 added to the text of "What Is Metaphysics" (1929) offers an indication. Metaphysics is ontological in concerning itself with being as being, but in a two-fold manner: it represents "the totality of being as such with an eye to its most universal traits," but at the same time also "in the sense of the highest and therefore divine being."[6] The naming of the divine (*theion*) makes the obvious connection to theology. The lecture "The Onto-Theo-Logical Constitution of Metaphysics," (1957) elaborates: metaphysics is theology because God comes into philosophy. But how? Heidegger asks.

The To Be is fashioned as ground, and thinking as grounding. (Heidegger comments in the context of interpreting Hegel's Science of Logic, but makes it clear that he is speaking of the entire tradition that Hegel, too, has inherited.) In this sense metaphysics is logic; it is the onto-logic that seeks grounds and above all the first ground, the *prote arche* or *causa prima*. The To Be of being is represented in its ground only as *causa sui*, that is, as God. Like ontology, theology is an "ology," a logic in the sense that it gives an account of the ground of being. Metaphysics is thus onto-theo-logic. The unity of that which is thought and questioned in this onto-theo-logic is "being as such in general and as first *in one with* being in the highest and the ultimate [sense]."[7] We note that Heidegger has added *first* and *ultimate* to the designations *universal* and *highest* mentioned in the 1949 Introduction; and that ground [*Grund*] is placed in apposition not only with *logos* but also with *hypokeimenon*, substance, and subject as ways that the To Be prevails [*west*].

In the earlier essay, Heidegger writes that the theological character of ontology derives not merely from a historical fact that Christian theologians drew upon Greek metaphysics but more so from how the To Be long before had disclosed itself. Only this disclosure of primal ground and first cause allowed Christian theology to take possession of Greek philosophy . . . for better or for worse, depending on the decision of theologians.[8] Yet if the inclusion of the God of metaphysics into Christian theology is a matter of decision, then the inclusion of God in philosophy, i.e., metaphysics, is a matter of destiny. The later lecture states: Philosophy in its very essence determines that God comes in and how God comes in.[9]

These judgments—which Heidegger would rather consider discoveries— make several crucial assumptions. First, there is pregiven a philosophy into which the notion of God comes from the outside—if not yet personalized as an outsider, an intruder, then still as a foreign element. Secondly, there existed a Christian theology (and not merely a Christian faith) before the intrusion of Greek metaphysics into it. As God is foreign to original philosophy (which is not the thinking of the pre-Socratics but the formation of metaphysics), so the God of metaphysics is foreign to original Christian theology.[10] Moreover, to propose that metaphysics become theologic, an account of beings in terms of their first cause, is to propose that theology in the sense of assertions about God as highest and first replaced another original theology, "the saying of the gods." Heidegger leaves the question unanswered, does not even raise the question, of how a pre-Greek Christian thinking—clearly not a saying of the gods—can be still be called theology. He would free both *original* theologies from metaphysics—both the saying of the gods and the "theology" inspired by Christian faith. For *later* Christian theology is it too late—that is, perhaps, unless we overcome metaphysics, the thinking of being in terms of ground and the thinking that is grounding. This judgment, it seems to me, implies that to think and speak of God in a way freed from Greek metaphysics is not merely to reformulate theology but also to give up theology.[11] I am not punning: I do not mean to release theology into another manner of speaking and thinking, but rather to abandon it. Similarly, Heidegger's historical account of metaphysics aside, to give up the thinking that grounds, the reasoning that seeks justification, is to abandon philosophy in the minds of most contemporary philosophers. Again, Heidegger's reading of the history of theology aside, to free theology from philosophy is to give up an account of God, of what God is or isn't or how God is or is not, or even of how God gives. That is, in fact, the position in which Heidegger ends up, simply waiting for a word from the gods.

That God, the divine, the holy, might come not in the form of the word seems not to occur to Heidegger, lest it be in his thinking of the fourfold [*das Geviert*] and the earthly flashing of immortals in ordinary (non-technological) things. Perhaps a logo-centrism affects Heidegger's waiting for the gods as well as his reading of theology. That some deliverance, not so much from the plight of technology as from the lock of metaphysics on God, might come from a non-traditional source such as Buddhism, is a thought that Heidegger expressly rejects.[12] It is, however, a possibility that many theologians engaged in Buddhist–Christian dialogue take seriously.

In the traditional Buddhism that inspired Nishida, there was no speaking of God as ground, or of God as word from elsewhere; nothing was said of God at all. Nishida's early encounter with Christianity and Western philosophy, however, convinced him that there was no getting around the notion of God if one is to think philosophically. He seems here to comply with Heidegger's conviction about the destiny of philosophy as metaphysics. Yet Nishida takes advantage of his heritage outside this history, and of the absence of the thought of God in traditional Buddhism, to think of God in terms of Absolute Nothing. The Western tradition is also part of Nishida's inheritance; yet he seems to inherit the notion of "God" emptied of its metaphysical definitions as first cause and highest being, as any being, whether substantialized and made subject—or, for that matter, personified and made a "Thou." Nishida's God is clearly a God of philosophy, to whom no one can pray or sacrifice, before whom no one can fall to his or her knees in awe or play music and dance.[13] Heidegger would find it difficult to believe, but Nishida's philosophical God seems unaffected by onto-theological destiny. As we shall see, Nishida's God is related in terms that defy both identity and difference, both identification and differentiation. The striking similarity with the Western mystical, apophatic tradition did not escape Nishida's notice, although he considered it insufficiently dialectical and still rooted in a notion of God as underlying subject.[14] Before we look directly at Nishida's thinking of God, however, we need to see how his differentiation of East and West, nothing and being, is still cast in metaphysical terms.

Recall how Nishida differentiates the classical forms of culture of East and West, "from a metaphysical standpoint," by saying that the West "thinks of being 有 as the ground 根底 of reality," whereas the East "thinks of nothingness 無 as the ground of reality." Although Nishida understands his "metaphysical standpoint" in the very broad sense of "how the problem of reality 実在 is thought of," his terms belie an unwitting adherence to the metaphysics that Heidegger confines to the West.[15] The terms of Nishida's contrast of East and West work against his division, and in several illustrative ways.

First, the very term for metaphysics in Sino-Japanese, 形而上学, is foreign to classical Eastern cultures. As a translation in modern times of the Greek and cognate Western terms, it literally means "the study of [what lies] beyond form." Although this usage of "form" is highly equivocal, the translation of "metaphysics," like its Greek original, implies the antecedent study of forms, i.e., nature: 形性.[16] In one sense, Nishida's characterization of Western metaphysics as thinking in terms of form would seem to cover both West and East: the Western thinking of things as having or being form 有形 (the glyph 有 that translates as *being* can mean *having* as well) and the Eastern thinking of the formless. Yet the formless 無形 serves in Nishida's text as an unmistakable allusion not only to the Nothing, 無, but also to Buddhist emptiness. It implies a "nothing of form" 無形 that in a specific sense will have nothing to do with form, at least with substantial form, as we shall see. Metaphysics, even as the study of what lies beyond form, will not prove a viable way to think that which characterizes the East for Nishida.

Secondly, Nishida invokes the notion of ground, the basis at the bottom of the respective ways of thinking of reality. The standard term that he uses, 根底, literally denotes the root at bottom, and not a logical foundation; as such it has nothing to do with grounding in the sense of supplying reasons. (Such reasons would be rendered 理由 in Japanese.) It seems, rather, to connote for Nishida the ground or soil beneath the surface out of which the respective thinkings of reality grew. Heidegger does employ the term *Grund* in manifold senses that include the sense of historical wellspring, but he deliberately retains the connection to metaphysics; he wants to uncover this ground so that the essence of metaphysics can be revealed.[17] Nishida's reference to a ground belies the metaphysical tendency that Heidegger identifies as the province of Greek-European thinking. It would seem inappropriate to characterize the "Eastern thinking" of the formless. This is particularly the case when Nishida, in this and numerous other essays takes 無, the Nothing, in the sense of "without ground" or uses it as a synonym for Buddhist emptiness. A defining characteristic of Nishida's own philosophy is his notion of place 場所 rather than ground. Even his original "logic of place," 場所の論理, is not reasoned discourse, or 理的論, about the place of things but rather a thinking that puts nothingness in their place. It is placemaking 場所的 rather than grounding discourse.[18]

Thirdly, when Nishida translates "being" as 有, he is as oblivious of difference from the To Be as is traditional metaphysics. His term is as equivocal and general as "being" and its Greek-European cognates. In Heidegger's perspective he would seem to remain captive to metaphysics and its oblivion of the To Be. Nishida does invoke a sense of difference, that between being and the Nothing, West and East, but it is not clear whether this differentiation of ways of thinking names an ineluctable and destining difference or a distinction. (Heidegger insists that the ontological difference is not a distinction, something that human minds construct or represent as a relation between two things.[19] It is rather an ineluctable difference that we inherit even when we lose sight of it.) Nishida's differentiation of East and West names more a historical difference of traditions than a logical distinction, but it does not imply a necessary division fixed forever for all time. Nishida will later undermine his own differentiation by placing being and nothing together in an Absolute Nothing that makes space for both. Although this Nothingness has been the province of the East, it need not remain so. The sense of difference Nishida invokes is not that of an irrevocable, irreducible, impossible to overcome ontological difference as in the case of Heidegger. If metaphysics, in Heidegger's view, has not properly thought either the Nothing or the To Be (which are hidden as two sides of the Same), then an other thinking of the Nothing may show a way out of metaphysics and its representation of God. Though the absence of the ontological difference in Nishida seems to confine him to a metaphysical standpoint in Heidegger's sense of the word, this absence may clear a space for a God of a different kind.

In Nishida's mature philosophy, God also goes by the name of the Absolute, 絶対者, a term deliberately chosen to represent the traditional notion and at the same time to undermine it. By the time Nishida wrote, the term 絶対 had become the standard translation of "absolute" (and its European cognates) as opposed to 相対, "relative." Nishida and the Kyoto School philosophers following him break with this common usage and implicitly return to the literal sense of the two glyphs in the compound term 絶対. 対 gives the sense of opposition, and 絶 in its verbal form 絶する means to cut through, break, or overcome. The Absolute, 絶対者, is that which overcomes all opposition.[20] The term for relative, 相対, has the literal sense of mutually opposing. Nishida often remarks that a supposed absolute that stands opposed to relative things (taking them as its objects) would be a merely "relative absolute," where absolute and relative mutually oppose each other. Yet in his last essay, Nishida also insists that the true Absolute is not merely something that breaks through opposition. He implies—and here I read between the lines—that such a purported absolute would be a mere all-inclusive totality, a passive harmony or, in his own words, a God without creative power, not really God at all. On the one hand, a supposed absolute that stands in opposition to something as object is not the true Absolute. On the other, that which merely breaks through opposition is not truly absolute either. The true Absolute, he says, is self-contradictory—not by now somehow going against its nature as it were and standing in opposition to relative things; and not by standing over against itself as if *it* were something, taking itself as object. Rather, it is self-contradictory in contravening itself and opposing nothing. "The true Absolute [God] is Absolute Being by opposing Absolute Nothing."[21] It is called nothing precisely because there is *no thing* that stands over against it. It must be(come) nothing, lest there be thought something other to oppose it; it has its "being" only in self-negation. The Absolute is describable as an absolutely contradictory self-identity.

Heidegger may have prepared us to hear of the Nothing as a grammatical name with a referent, and Hegel to think dialectically, but Nishida's thought of "absolutely contradictory self-identity" still seems to defy sense. Perhaps a logical clarification will help—to a point. Nishida reminds us that only things of the same nature or kind can form logical contradictories or contraries; for example, green and triangular are not contradictories or contraries. The closer the relation, he implies, the stronger the contrariety. Let us try to follow this thought. If self-identity "A is A" names the closest possible relation, it entails the strongest form of contrariety, which is contradiction. Self-identity entails self-contradiction. Note that "A" and "non-A" both refer to "A"; the identification of both "A" and "non-A" entails thinking in terms of "A." For Nishida, however, self-identity entails self-contradiction not merely in terms of semantic reference or logical entailment, but within a determining context.

Think of this sentence: "The whole world consists of only two kinds of things: apples and non-apples." Of course, only the notion of "the one, whole world" that includes both terms allows the formation of such contradictories. Now suppose we bring both the one whole (created) world and God under one thought as opposites totally other to each other. Then all is not described by the principle "either God or created being"; there is still the space within which the opposition stands. Suppose we identify God with the all, the all with God. Then there is still the matter of our standing outside to so identity it/them.[22] God and created being do not form real contradictors that exclude all else; God and world cannot form an identity that includes everything. Self-identity entails self-contradiction, and vice versa, within the space that includes both God and world, self and other.[23] Nishida names this place "Absolute Nothing." This name does not designate a ground beneath God, world, self, or other; nor does is admit of another reality beyond them. To take it this way would be to objectify it, thus placing ourselves outside it and inferring a still greater space. It cannot be grasped by objectifying thought. To speak admittedly in metaphors, it embraces every all but cannot itself be embraced by anything outside it. It embraces by self-negating. It is not something that negates itself, but the active place or rather placing of things through their self-negation. The Absolute Nothing, in a sense, names the occurrence of self-negating.

Nishida has not directly named God the Absolute Nothing 絶対無. He speaks instead of "the Absolute" 絶対者. In my understanding, there are three thoughts to consider here. Nishida's term suggests that God, too, is "placed" as "something" that is what it is only by negating itself. Moreover, if God is "Absolute Being by opposing Absolute Nothing," this dynamic stance defines God from the beginning as it were, and embraces God from the beginningless beginning. Finally, the Absolute and relative form a pair, even if not one of mutual opposition or of partial identity. God/the Absolute is not a totality of which we relative beings are parts or are lesser versions. This means the Absolute must relate to the relative without opposing it and without being reduced to it. The Absolute is not over and above or beyond all relative or contingent being; rather it does not "exist" except in the form of its particular relative expressions. It is not a remainder, once we have abstracted from all contingencies. It is not an ultimate reality that lies beyond any and all particular manifestations or expressions of it. To name God the Absolute means that God includes real difference from Godself,[24] not difference from some relative thing that is merely a part of God or a lack of God, and not opposition that differentiates by objectifying. This difference comes about through God's self-negation.[25]

Nishida himself quotes the Diamond Sutra, "The Buddha is not the Buddha and therefore is the Buddha," and his context makes it plain that he is speaking of God as well. This curious, apparently non-sensical thought is worth our attention. Nishida's follower Nishitani provides a hint we can elaborate. Nishitani quotes another passage from the same sutra: "Fire is not fire and therefore it is fire."[26] Think of fire in a broad metaphorical sense, and not as some thing, but as activity, as what fire does, what it is by be-ing fire. What is it that only fire does, that defines its singular being? Fire burns, is burn-ing. But it cannot burn itself. Of everything in the (physical) universe, only fire is exempt from burning. It is itself only by negating what it is. Nishitani counters the temptation to understand this as our own objectification: this is "not only the selfness of fire for us, but also the selfness of fire for fire itself." To use a more traditional Buddhist term, we can as easily say "no self" as "selfness" in Nishitani's sentence. Similarly, "water does not wet water"; "the eye does not see the eye"; and we could add, a knife cannot cut itself. Following his friend D. T. Suzuki and Buddhist texts, Nishida would call these examples of "the form of the formless."

Yet such examples, besides being metaphorical, also seem applicable only to things expressible as activities and only activities expressible as transitive verbs that take a grammatical object.[27] On the other hand, Nishitani's Japanese explanation that I elaborate does have the advantage of Sino-Japanese grammar. The Japanese and Chinese written languages have a connective, frequently used in Buddhist texts, that roughly translates as "is" or "is at the same time," or "*ist zugleich*" in German. But the Sino-Japanese connective 即 (pronounced *soku* in Japanese) is not a copula or a verb; it is not conjugated, and it does not functions like the "is" of identification, predication, or existential instantiation. (We note that other Japanese grammatical constructions avoid the awkwardness of expressions like "Nothing is . . ." such and such, or "the To Be is not . . ." such and such.) *Soku* can function as an elaboration, as in the phrase "God, that is, *causa sui*," but it connects terms usually taken as contraries or contradictories. The locus classicus in the Heart Sutra reads as follows: emptiness *soku* form, form *soku* emptiness. Nishida can simply write 無即有, nothing-*soku*-being. He also writes of God's transcendence-*soku*-immanence, immanence-*soku*-transcendence; self-negation-*soku*-self-affirmation, and vice versa. Some translators use the Latin *sive* for *soku*, but then *soku* is never a disjunctive "or." The translation *qua*, which indicates the aspect of a matter, is also not appropriate. Those unfamiliar with Latin usage might as well use the original *soku*.

What does *soku* indicate? Not merely a juxtaposition necessary for understanding co-dependence. Not merely the relativity of opposites, definable only one in terms of the other, e.g., outside/inside. Not a transformation of one into the other, its opposite. Not, for example, transcendent in one respect, immanent in another, which would be to take them as overlapping but not coincident parts. Rather, the simultaneous co-habitation of a space—to speak metaphorically again—a place itself hidden by the terms and revealed by following their self-negation. 超越即内在. Transcendent-*soku*-immanent: beyond yet within. Beyond because within. Beyond and at the same time within. Going beyond, starting from within. Being within by seeing beyond. Beyond by being within. None of these quite captures the sense of *soku*.

The connective *soku* can be combined with a negative, 非 (pronounced *hi*), that then is applied to a single term such as *fire*. The phrase, "fire is fire and at the same time is not fire," translates "fire *soku-hi* fire." We might also say: fire—not fire. The explanation above uses causal and logical conjunctions that are absent in the original Buddhist texts: "*because* fire does not burn itself, fire *therefore* is not fire." Nishitani's text clearly implies these conjunctions. There are other ways to understand the term *because*: not as causal, but chiasmic,[28] transpositional, equiprimordial [*gleichursprünglich*]. Transgressive of grounding logic. Co-dependent. Dependent co-origination [*pratitya samutpada*] is the Buddhist corollary to emptiness. But again, none of these quite expresses Nishida's logic.

Yet the advantage gained by Sino-Japanese grammatical construction seems offset by an explanation that ostensibly works only for terms that can be thought of as activities expressible by transitive verbs, like *burn*. How then does this logic of *soku-hi* express the nature of God? Nishida answers this question more by apposition than elaboration: he replaces his terms with terms borrowed from Christian sources. This is the logic of kenosis, he says, God's self-expression in love. It is said that God created the world out of love, but God's love must mean God's self-negation. I attempt an elaboration: To take love as the nature of God is to say God is loving, where "loving" functions as identity and not attribute. To say God loves is analogous to saying fire burns. And as fire cannot burn itself, so too God cannot love Godself. Fire is not itself except in terms of what it is not, both the not-fire that burning is and the not-fire that is the thing burned. God cannot "be" God without be-ing not-God, and without that which is loved and which is not God. Does not God love Godself through the trinity, or in the person of the Holy Spirit? Although I would not presume to venture into a theology of the trinity, the thought of the trinity evidently involves some kind of non-identity with or within a singular God.

What if we define God's nature as creator, as the only being that can truly create? Nishida's logic would propose that, as fire does not burn itself, a creating God does not create Godself. This thought may remind us of the old, onto-theological idea of God as *causa sui*, which as Hume pointed out is an ambiguous term. Does it mean that since God is self-caused God doesn't need to be created? Or that self-caused means self-created? Nishida settles the issue this way: if we say that the created world exists because there is God as creator, the reverse holds too: there is God because there exists the world as created. Nishida does not say that God and world co-create or create each other, and again he explicitly rejects pantheism.[29] Nor does he merely imply that both creator and created are logically needed for the thought of creation to make sense. He does not write God-*soku*-world. Rather: if God's very being *is* creating, then God is not creating, not being God, at the same time. Nishida thinks of God as creator, however, in his own way. He distances himself from the idea of *creatio ex nihilo*, something from nothing, which for him conveys something enacted by an arbitrarily acting God.[30] (Does he fail to appreciate the sense of gratuity in the Christian doctrine of God's creation, that is, the sense in which God is thought to create the world in freedom but in consistence with his nature as love?) Nishida's idea of creation is not causation; God is not *causa sui* or *causa prima*. Only a God that includes self-negation within itself could be creator. God's self-negation is not an addition, a supplement, a self-alienation into something God lacks but needs. It is not, as Nishida writes, an "opus ad extra." God's self-negation *is* God, and since it is, God is not God.

In Buddhist teaching, indeed everything is empty of self-subsistent, substantial being (*svabhâva* in Sanskrit, meaning roughly "own being") that could be or be explained in its own terms. Nishida's thinking shifts the negation from the nominal form *(being)* to the verbal (*be-ing*, doing whatever a particular thing and only it does, e.g., burning, creating, etc.).[31] In one sense, God's self-negating "self-nature" is no different from that of anything else: all are self-negating. In another sense, each thing's self-negation is unique: only fire burns (things), only the Absolute truly creates, and so on. We relative persons likewise are what we are by self-negating, and it is through our self-negation that we contact the Absolute. That means, Nishida says, through dying. For something relative to stand over against something Absolute means to die, to become nothing. We touch God only through death of self; we are connected to God in a contrary correspondence, 逆対応.[32]

Like *absolutely contradictory self-identity*, the expression *contrary correspondence* functions to deny both ultimate identity and ultimate difference. It applies, however, to two terms usually differentiated (not to one term, such as the world or God as absolutely contradictory self-identities), and yet is not a substitution for *soku*.[33] It seems to indicate only the "relation" between God/the Absolute and us relative human selves. It implies three things: (1) the impossibility of dissolution of one into the other, God into relative human self; (2) the necessary connection between and inseparability of the one and the other; and (3) self-surpassing, i.e., self-identity through self-negation. Nishida draws examples from the Neo-Platonists and Christian mystical, apophatic traditions, but the statement that best illustrates the term for him is from the fourteenth-century Zen master Daitō Kokushi: "[The Buddha and myself:] mutually separated for an eternity, and yet not apart even for a moment; mutually opposed the whole day, yet not opposed even an instant."[34]

The self properly relates to God only by dying to itself, to ego (a death that is *not* the same thing as the nihilation of the individual person), and so be-ing its true self. This is a clearly an obscure topic that deserves much more attention,[35] but it allows me here to make a brief connection to religious experience.

Nishida's first book thematizes "pure experience," a term he adapts from William James. Such experience takes place prior to the split between subject and object, prior to awareness of oneself as somebody experiencing something. Nishida proposes that this founding experience occurs without a subject, i.e., before its emergence, and issues into discriminative thought on its way to ever higher unities. Its intuiting, or, we should say, its *living*, of the oneness of subject and object is the heart of religious awakening; the longing for wholeness and unity is at the basis of all religion.[36] Nishida's ultimate scheme in his first essay borders on an idealism that does not differentiate the working of the divine and that of the world, and he does not thematize human death. The temptation to link pure experience and death, however, is compelling even if complicated by language. One cannot "experience" one's death, although to experience can mean passively to undergo, to have something happen to someone. In the case of death, however, there is no one left (at least not as a worldly being); in the notion of pure experience, too, the "someone" is missing. Nishida's first essay submits that the true self is the unifying intuition, the living of unity. His last essay proposes that to be truly oneself is to die, to "face" the Absolute. Yet if pure experience, understood as death, could be called a letting-go of self, this manner of speaking is cut short by the talk of "facing" or "opposing." The last essay makes space for a kind of non-unity unrecognized in the first book. Death may be thought of as a passing-over or a disruption; either way, it implies a negation. Nishida advisedly never spoke of "the experience of the Nothing"; like death, it does not enter the domain of experience, at least not the domain of a subject's (objectifying) experience.[37] It is as if religion, in the sense of contact with God, commanded the negation of experience.

The early Heidegger confronts death in the Angst that is an opening to the Nothing. After this long diversion, we may now return to his thought on that theme.

Heidegger's text "What is Metaphysics" is a meditation on the founding question of metaphysics in an attempt to uncover its hidden assumptions. The question, why being at all and not rather nothing? leaves us with two choices, either being or nothing. If we translate the thought behind this question according to the principles of logic, we are dealing here with contradictories that exhaust all possibilities; the "or" is disjunctive and the middle excluded. Furthermore, as Heidegger notes, in asking "why" we are seeking a reason, a ground. Heidegger's meditation questions our usual way of reasoning, grounding, and explaining why. It also recovers the missed third possibility: the To Be, different from being and non-being; and it exposes the middle that is mistakenly eliminated: the ontological difference, the "not" between the To Be and being. The "not" of the To Be [its not being] is no mere *nihil negativum*; the "not" of the ontological difference [the "not" between being and the To Be] is no mere distinction contrived by rational thought. The two "nots" are not identical. The distinction (as I would call it) between them would seem to preserve a space in Heidegger for a Nothing not held captive by being or by the recovered To Be. In fact, however, Heidegger calls these two "nihilative nots" "the Same in the sense of belonging together in the essential prevailing [*Wesen*] of the To Be of beings." Heidegger's unclarified distinction notwithstanding, his Nothing belongs solely to the To Be of beings.[38]

The thought of Nishida casts doubt on whether Heidegger has sufficiently recalled the Nothing.[39] Existentially revealed through *Angst*, the Nothing appears as the great abyss beneath our ground, the *Ungrund*. It renders us speechless.[40] Philosophically recovered through the thinking of the ontological difference, "the Nothing, as the other of being, is the veil of the To Be."[41] We see the veil before the face that it darkens; the nothing is the darkened way the To Be appears when beings are taken as all that there "is." As such, this nothing prevails as the doubled negation of being and the obverse of the To Be.[42] In light of the thought of the Kyoto School, perhaps we could speak of Heidegger's forgetfulness of the Nothing, or at least ask, in the spirit of Heidegger, whether he himself became oblivious of the Nothing—in spite of, or precisely in light of, his own notice: "the Nothing . . . remains forgotten," the Nothing, that is, taken as "that which is not a being," the Nothing "understood as the To Be itself." "How does it come about that when it comes to the To Be we are really dealing with nothing and that the Nothing really does not prevail [*west*]."[43] We would need to ask whether Heidegger's Nothing continually remains under the sway of the To Be, in its difference from being. An obverse of the To Be, this Nothing would seem to find its place on one side of Nishida's phrase "Being-*soku*-nothing," and thus to leave open unnoticed the space in which both are placed, which Nishida calls the Absolute Nothing: the negating not only of being but of non-being as well.

Nishida, of course, does not employ Heidegger's ontological difference, so we must attempt some translating. The negating of being [*Seiendes*] issues in non-being. The negating of non-being issues in being. The negating of the To Be, as an historically destined denial, issues in its oblivion; the negating of the To Be once recovered issues in its difference from beings. For all its distinct destined designations [*Schickungen*] as logos, *hypokeimenon, substantia*, and so on, the To Be is held in a difference from beings that is essential, irreducible, and non-transferable. The destined designations of the To Be may conceal it but they do not ever render it a being. That is why it can be perpetually forgotten, uncovered, and recovered. Though its designations change, the To Be abides in its destining sense as presencing (*Anwesenheit*). Its eternal difference from beings permits the perpetuation of being, and of not-being as its (the To Be's) own veil. Its particular historical destinings are not its own self-negations (it could not count as Nishida's God). It does not account for its eternal, essential difference, either as a self-negating or in any other way. Its difference simply "is" what it is, ungrounded but consistent. It does not provide space either for its self-negation or for a mutual negation of being and non-being. It does not translate as To Be-*soku*-being. It cannot account for a self-negating God, or any self-negating being. Seen in the light of Buddhism, it is substantialist.

God has disappeared in Heidegger's meditation on nothing. Why? Metaphysics is onto-theology, which entails a certain way of thinking God. The preeminent metaphysical question is "why being at all rather than nothing," and its common (onto-theological) answer is this: because God created the world. Why, then, does the theme of God drop out of sight in an attempt to recover the hidden ground of metaphysics, the oblivion of the To Be and its difference from being? In other discussions, Heidegger does refer to God in denying that the To Be can be another name for God.[44] But where is the theme of God when it comes to exposing the ontological difference? Of course, Heidegger wants to overcome metaphysics or onto-theology, and perhaps this requires dropping the name of God, or at least the onto-theological designation of God as the answer to "why is there anything at all?" Yet Heidegger recognizes other designations of God, the Greek gods, the pre-Greek Christian God, the holy of Hölderlin. Perhaps metaphysics is destined to live with the onto-theological God, but God—in the other senses of the name—is not the captive of onto-theology.[45] Although Heidegger's essays are framed as relentless questions that remain open, he has already given an alternative to metaphysics in the very exposure of its forgotten ground. Why does God not play a part in this alternative? Because, as he intimates, we do not yet know how to think God? Or because, as I have suggested, Heidegger himself has forgotten Nothing. In trying to keep everything in mind, Heidegger even remembers to think about letting-go [*Gelassenheit*], but what he, so attuned, awaits in the end is a word from the gods, who have become speechless. We will never know, of course, whether Nishida's thinking of God would compel Heidegger to rethink his position, but it may inspire us to think over our own.

NOTES

A senior fellowship from the Higher Institute of Philosophy, Katholieke Universiteit Leuven, Belgium, 1999–2000, made the research and writing of this essay possible.

1. *Nishida Kitarō Zenshū* [hereafter NKZ], 2nd ed. (Tokyo: Iwanami, 1965–66), vol. VII, pp. 429–30; composed in 1934. All translations are my own unless otherwise noted. See also David Dilworth's translation, "The Forms of Culture of the Classical Periods of East and West Seen from a Metaphysical Standpoint," in *Sourcebook for Japanese Philosophy: Selected Documents*, trans. and ed. David A. Dilworth and Valdo H. Viglielmo, with Augustin Jacinto Zavala (Westport, Conn. and London: Greenwood Press, 1998), p. 21.

2. Nishida's essay does distinguish between the Greek, Jewish, and Christian cultures in the West, and Indian, Chinese, and Japanese cultures in the East; and even between Confucian and Taoist Chinese culture. It also proposes various similarities between pairs, such as the religious orientation of both Indian and Jewish cultures; and it suggests aspects of Western cultures that approximate a philosophy of nothingness, for example, the negative theology of Dionysius the Areopagite. The primary demarcation, however, remains that between the being of the West and the Nothing of the East.

3. For example, [T]he style of all Occidental-European philosophy—and there is no other, neither a Chinese nor an Indian philosophy—is determined by the twofold, "beings—in being." *What Is Called Thinking*, trans. J. Glenn Gray and F. Wieck (New York: Harper & Row, 1968), p. 224 (translation modified); see *Was heißt Denken* (Tübingen: Max Niemeyer, 1961), p. 136.

4. See especially Reinhard May, *Heidegger's Hidden Sources: East Asian Influences on His Work*. Translated, with a complementary essay by Graham Parkes (London and New York: Routledge, 1996) and Graham Parkes, ed., *Heidegger and Asian Thought* (Honolulu: University of Hawaii Press, 1987).

5. I will employ the unusual translation of *das Sein* as *the To Be*, in order to mark the difference with being (*Seiendes*) vocally and to indicate the difference between the infinitive form *Sein* and the gerund *Seiendes*. The common convention is to translate *Sein* as Being (or being) and *Seiendes* as beings. Heidegger, however, sometimes uses the singular *Seiendes* where the plural *beings* would be inappropriate, for example, when he writes "das Ganze des Seienden," which is not the collection of all beings. I have modified all the translations I quote to accord with my usage.

6. M. Heidegger, *Pathmarks*, ed. William McNeill (Cambridge and New York: Cambridge University Press, 1998), p. 287; the original is in *Wegmarken* (Frankfurt am Main: Vittorio Klostermann, 1967), p. 207.

7. *Identität und Differenz* (Pfullingen: Verlag Günther Neske, 1957), pp. 54–58.

8. "Einleitung zu: 'Was ist Metaphysik?'" (1949) in *Wegmarken*, p. 208; Pathmarks, p. 288.

9. *Identität und Differenz*, p. 53.

10. When ideas like that of God as *causa sui* came to inform Christian theology, it became theo-logic. Both Heidegger's 1927 lecture, "Phenomenology and Theology," and the 1964 letter appended to it as "The Theological Discussion of 'The Problem of a Nonobjectifying Thinking and Speaking in Today's Theology'" imply a difference between such theo-logic and an original theology rooted in Christian faith and in concepts derived from faith. The letter describes theology as a mode of thinking and speaking that places in discussion the Christian faith, and what is believed, and mentions the danger of "projecting into faith ideas which are alien to it," though without naming such ideas. The idea of God as *causa sui* would seem to be an obvious example. See *The Piety of Thinking: Essays by Martin Heidegger*, trans. with notes and commentary by James G. Hart and John C. Maraldo (Bloomington: Indiana University Press, 1976), especially pp. 23 and 171–73, Note 2; reprinted without the translators' notes in *Pathmarks*, 39–62. The supposition of a Christian theology before the influence of Greek philosophy is reconfirmed in the 1949 "Introduction to 'What Is Metaphysics?'" in *Pathmarks*, pp. 287–88. Yet Heidegger's separation of faith and "later" Christian theology, that is, theo-logic, is questionable. Even if Christian faith originated prior to Greek-infected theology, it can be said that the development of this theology over the centuries acted as a source for faith. Today Christian faith, wherever it involves belief in

God as a being, is not readily distinguishable from the theology of *causa sui* and highest being. Heidegger also seems to forget that theology (or theo-logic) grew in interaction with other sources than Greek philosophy, and that the course of philosophy was affected by its non-Greek sources, Jewish and early Christian. I would suggest that the abiding philosophical notions of person, inherent dignity, due rights and expected duties, as well as the recognition that philosophy itself develops through historical traditions, are all unthinkable without the Jewish and early Christian thinking of a *personal* God involved in a *historical* relationship with human beings.

11. Heidegger speaks not of a new theology but rather of a "God-less thinking that must give up the God of philosophy, God as *causa sui*" and is thereby perhaps closer to the godly God. It is more open to him [God] than onto-theo-logic would like to have it." *Identität und Differenz*, p. 71.

12. This rejection, to be sure, regards first and foremost the possibility of rescue [*Rettung*] from the hold of technology. "It is my conviction that a reversal can be prepared only in the same place in the world in which the modern technical world originated, and that it cannot happen because of any takeover by Zen Buddhism or any other Eastern experiences of the world." "'Only a God Can Save Us': *Der Spiegel's* Interview with Martin Heidegger (1966)," in Richard Wolin, ed., *The Heidegger Controversy: A Critical Reader* (Cambridge, Mass., and London: MIT Press, 1993), p. 113.

13. This is Heidegger's famous characterization of the God of philosophy, the God that is *causa sui*. See *Identität und Differenz* (Pfullingen: Günther Neske, 1957), p. 70.

14. See the 1945 essay in NKZ XI, pp. 399 and 405; trans. Michiko Yusa, "The Logic of Topos and the Religious Worldview," *The Eastern Buddhist* 19, no. 2 (Autumn 1986) [hereafter English trans.], pp. 21 and 24. See also Nishida's comment on Nicolas of Cusa in his 1944 essay in NKZ XI, p. 139; trans. David Dilworth as "Towards a Philosophy of Religion with the Concept of Pre-established Harmony as Guide," in *The Eastern Buddhist* III, 1 (June 1970), p. 40. See also Nishida's comment distancing himself from Dionysius the Areopagite in the 1934 essay in NKZ VII, p. 432; trans. David Dilworth as "The Forms of Culture of the Classical Periods of East and West Seen from a Metaphysical Standpoint," op. cit., p. 23.

15. What prompted Nishida to use the terms of the West was most likely his concern to globalize philosophical thinking and to establish Japanese thought, his own included, in an international forum. Whether this adaptation distorts the contribution that the classical East can make to world philosophy remains an open question.

16. The earlier and perhaps first translation of *metaphysica* into Chinese, by Jesuits in the 17th century, carries the very same connotation of beyond form: 超形. This term was meant to convey the Aristotelian scheme where metaphysics follows after physics, the study of the physical, of nature: 形性学. See Nicolas Standaert, "The Classification of Sciences and the Jesuit Mission in Late Ming China," in *Linked Faiths: Essays on Chinese Religions and Traditional Culture in Honour of Kristofer Schipper*, ed. Jan A.M. De Meyer and Peter M. Engelfriet (Leiden: Brill, 2000), p. 291.

17. See for example Heidegger's usage of the terms *roots*, *bottom*, and *ground* to suggest the source of metaphysics, which is the tree as it were that has forgotten the ground in which its roots grow, in "The Way Back into the Ground of Metaphysics," the first section of the 1949 essay "Introduction to 'What Is Metaphysics?'" in *Pathmarks*, p. 277f.

18. The affinity here with Heidegger's frequent use of *erörtern* as an alternative to *begründen*, grounding or laying the foundation, deserves more attention. Heidegger

takes the common term *Erörterung*, meaning "discussion," in its more literal sense as "placing" (in context or in discussion; *Ort* means "place"). The question is whether there is any analog to Nishida's Nothing as ultimate place.

19. *Identität und Differenz*, p. 60.

20. Yusa's translation is generally accurate but misleadingly in that it often has "Absolute Being" for 絶対者, the Absolute, and has "the absolute transcends the relative" for 対と絶したこと, literally "that which breaks through opposition;" see English trans., p. 19. See also the more reliable German translation of Rolf Elberfeld, "Ortlogik und religöse Weltanschauung," in Kitarō Nishida, *Logik des Ortes* (Darmstadt: Wissenschaftliche Buchgesellschaft, 1999), pp. 204–84.

21. NKZ XI, pp. 396–97. The term I translate with hesitation as *oppose* is 対する, which commonly functions simply like the prepositions *to, toward, for, vis-à-vis*, and *against*, depending upon the idiom and context. Nishida's term and formulations do not imply that the Absolute has a first-person perspective, a consciousness of itself versus others. Thus the sense of 対する here is not captured by *facing* (Yusa's translation, p. 19), which does imply a first-person perspective; yet later we shall see how Nishida would negate the first-person perspective by speaking of the [human] self's death in "face" of the Absolute, as we could accurately say. Dilworth's translates the term 対する as "opposing" in Nishida Kitarō, *Last Writings: Nothingness and the Religious Worldview* (Honolulu: University of Hawaii Press, 1987), p. 68; and Elberfeld translates it as *gegenüberstehen* in Kitarō Nishida, *Logik des Ortes*, pp. 225–26.

22. Throughout his career, Nishida himself explicitly rejects pantheism as objectifying thinking or logic. The relevant text here is NKZ IX, p. 398; English trans., pp. 20–21.

23. Nishida writes of the "place within" おいてある場所 that contains everything as placed おいてある者. His thought contrasts with "the all-comprehensive" [*das Umgreifende*] of Karl Jaspers; with Wittgenstein's comparatively realist view, "The world is all that is the case"; and with Dieter Henrich's comparatively idealist view, "The world is at least as complex as the most complex thought of the world that we are capable of thinking" ("Self-Consciousness and Speculative Thinking," in *Figuring the Self: Subject, Absolute, and Others in Classical German Philosophy*, David E. Klemm and Günter Zöller, eds., [Albany: SUNY Press], p. 99). Nishida does, in fact, say that the world too can be called the Absolute 絶対者," and speaks of its creative activity. There is a two-fold tension in his thought here. The Absolute names both God and world, yet the latter two terms are not used synonymously, and Nishida disavows pantheism. The Absolute Nothing names not only a place or space but also the dynamic if discontinuous working of the historical world, "from the created to the creating." I do not attempt to relieve this tension here.

24. I use the term *Godself* to avoid gendered designations such as *God Himself*.

25. See NKZ IX, p. 394; English trans., p. 20.

26. *Religion and Nothingness*, trans. Jan van Bragt (Berkeley: University of California Press, 1982), pp. 116ff.

27. Heidegger sometimes takes *Sein* in this sense: "Sein, welches das Seiende *ist*": the To Be that is-es being. *Identität und Differenz*, p. 62

28. Think of the chiasm in Merleau-Ponty's *Visible and the Invisible*, or Heidegger's frequent use of the grammatical chiasm: "the truth of essence is the essence of truth," etc.

29. NKZ IX, p. 398; English trans., p. 20. Nishida says that pantheism is the result of objectifying thinking.

30. Nishida suggests this in his last essay: NKZ IX, p. 400; English trans., p. 21.

31. On the other hand, Nishida's thinking of the Nothing comes close to nominalizing and thus substantializing emptiness, a trap that was the bone of contention of many Indian Buddhist debates.

32. NKZ IX, p. 396; see the English trans., p. 19. This relation forms a forgotten alternative to the usual possibilities assumed in theism and idealism, as expressed, for example, in Jacobi's objection to Fichte in his letter of 1799: "God is, and is *outside me*, a living, self-subsisting being, or I am God. There is no third."

33. At least in one passage, it seems to work the same as 即非 *soku-hi*, namely where Nishida quotes the same passage from Daitō Kokushi to exemplify both.

34. NKZ XI, p. 399.

35. I have attempted to clarify it further in "Nishida and the Individualization of Religion," *Zen Buddhism Today: Annual Report of the Kyoto Zen Symposium* 6, November 1988, 70–87.

36. NKZ I, pp. 9ff. & 45. See *Inquiry Into the Good*, trans. Masao Abe and Christopher Ives (New Haven, Conn.: Yale University Press, 1990), pp. 3ff., 34.

37. Because of his own awareness of the psychologistic and subjectivistic overtones of the word, and perhaps because of his younger colleague Tanabe Hajime's criticism of his "intuitionism" and passive contemplationism, Nishida largely abandoned the talk of experience after the 1917 work *Intuition and Reflection in Self-Consciousness*, trans. Valdo H. Viglielmo with Takeuchi Yoshinori and Joseph S. O'Leary (Albany: SUNY Press, 1987).

38. The relevant passage about the two *nots* occurs in the preface to the third edition (1949) of the 1928 essay, "Zum Wesen des Grundes." See *Pathmarks*, p. 97. In the 1928 lecture, "What is Metaphysics?" Heidegger writes that the "nothing is encountered at one with beings as a whole" and that it "unveils itself as belonging to the To Be of beings." *Pathmarks*, pp. 90 and 94, translation modified.

39. This observation is not merely a lexical one, noting which texts thematize the Nothing and which do not. A central theme in the 1928 lecture "What Is Metaphysics?" the Nothing disappears in the added Introduction of 1949 until the very end where it is recalled as "the sole topic of the [1928] lecture." See *Pathmarks*, p. 290. The 1935 lectures "An Introduction to Metaphysics" and the published versions of 1953 do not include the To Be and Nothing among the various conjunctions listed: "the To Be and Becoming, the to Be and Appearance, the To Be and thinking, the To Be and the Ought." The theme of Nothing disappears entirely in the 1957 lecture on the Ontological Constitution of Metaphysics.

40. "Eine der Wesensstätten der Sprachlosigkeit ist die Angst im Sinne des Schreckens, in den der Abgrund des Nichts den Menschen stimmt." "Nachwort zu: 'Was ist Metaphysik?'" (1943) in *Wegmarken*, p. 107.

41. My translation of "Das Nichts als das Andere zum Seienden ist der Schleier des Seins." "Nachwort zu: 'Was ist Metaphysik?'" in *Wegmarken*, p. 107. See *Pathmarks*, p. 238, which also translates the version of 1949 as "The nothing: That which annuls, i.e., as difference, is as the veil of being, i.e., of beyng in the sense of the appropriative event of usage."

42. The 1938–1941 lectures on Hegel: "Die Negativität. Eine Auseinandersetzung mit Hegel aus dem Ansatz der Negativität" (1938/9, 1941) confirm this reading of a

Heideggerian tradition of the nothing bound to being/the To Be. For example: "Der Ab-Grund: *das Seyn. Seyn als Ab-grund*—das Nichts und der Grund zumal. Das Nichts ist *das ab-gründig Verschiedene vom Seyn als Nichtung und deshalb?—seines Wesens.*" Martin Heidegger, *Hegel* (Gesamtausgabe, vol. 68) (Frankfurt am Main: Vittorio Klostermann, 1993), p. 48; italics in the original.

43. "Einleitung zu: 'Was ist Metaphysik?'" (1949) in *Wegmarken*, p. 211. The first sentence reads, "Woher kommt es, daß Es mit dem Sein eigentlich nichts ist und das Nichts eigentlich nicht west?" The Kaufmann/McNeill translation of the passage has, "How does it come about that . . . that which is not a being—namely, the Nothing thus understood as Being itself—remains forgotten. How does it come about that with Being It is really nothing and that the Nothing does not properly prevail?" *Pathmarks*, p. 290.

44. For example, in Heidegger's discussion at the "Zurich Seminar," November 6, 1951; see the French translation of J. Greisch, *Heidegger et la question de Dieu* (Paris, 1980), p. 334. Compare also the discussion at the 1968 seminar in Le Thor, reported in Martin Heidegger, *Vier Seminare* (Frankfurt am Main: Vittorio Klostermann, 1977), p. 63, where "Das Sein ist Gott" is read as "das Sein «istet» God, das heißt das Sein läßt Gott Gott sein." [The To Be is God, i.e., the To Be "ises" God, lets God be God.]

45. Even here the question remains, as mentioned before, whether in Heidegger's thought such notions of God, the divine, and the holy are still governed by the word.

three

Light and Shadows from the Heideggerian Interpretation of the Sacred

Emilio Brito

The present exposition attempts to place in evidence both the considerable assets and the serious deficiencies of the Heideggerian interpretation of the sacred. This interpretation has the merit of overcoming approaches that tend to reduce the sacred either to an a priori category of reason (in the direction of Kant) or to an intuitive sentiment of the non-rational (in the line of Schleiermacher). In avoiding the double trap of a subjectivism of illusory transparent reason and an objectivism of obscure experience of the irrational ("subjective" at bottom, its depth notwithstanding), Heidegger attempts to think *das Heilige* beginning from the limpid disoccultation and impregnable concealment of Being. Attentive to difference strictly as difference, this "ontological" interpretation of the sacred is not confused with—despite the presence of real affinities—the Hegelian *Aufhebung* of the limits of subjective spirit and the opacities of objective spirit into the "re-ligious" identity of the Absolute.[1] The auroral play of dis-covery and retreat in Heidegger contrasts with the Hegelian night of transgression, for the latter is no longer the essential reserve of disclosure.

How does Heidegger understand the relation between the Sacred and

Being? The dimension of the Sacred, its openness, is to be thought in view of the truth of Being. The appearing of the Sacred is possible only in the clearing of Being. It is not the poet who speaks Being, but the thinker; conversely, it is not the thinker who names the sacred, but the poet. "The thinker speaks Being. The poet names the Sacred."[2] The more that thinking endeavors to speak the simple plenitude of Being, the more Being withdraws into its profound mystery. What Being preserves of itself does not allow itself to be encountered. It is present in its distance. The Most-High of Being allows itself to be named only in the hymn of the Sacred. In order to speak Being, Heidegger has need of a word such as that of Hölderlin. In dialoguing with the poet, the thought of Heidegger, always remaining what it is—thought and not poetry— grasps itself in a new manner. It says "the same thing" otherwise, recognizing in the words of the Sacred expressions by which to name Being, and show that *das Heile*—the originally intact that gives the well-being of dwelling to all things—is the heart of the truth of Being, the heart of the truth of time. Being appears henceforth as the Sacred. Supreme manifestation of the plenitude of Being—of Being of which the nothingness, nihilating and instilling anxiety, is the veil—the Sacred is discovered as the inviolable, beaming expanse that casts its rays over everything. The dimension of Being opens itself and preserves itself in divine sacrality.

Heidegger thematizes, in effect, not only the relation of the Sacred and Being, but also—and this is a second asset—that of the sacred and *divinity*. The sacred is designated as the trace of divinity, toward divinity (*die Spur zur Gottheit*).[3] It opens the space in which the divine that it delimits can appear. The sacred is the essential space of divinity, but divinity itself is not identified purely and simply with the sacred. Rather than being approached uniquely as the Clearing that is disclosed in the midst of the deployment of beings, divinity remains intimate with itself, drawing all radiance back toward the intimacy of its reserve. It comprehends every deployment in the inclusive unity of the same. Though it discovers its essence in the space of the sacred, it overcomes, by the depth of its simplicity, the dimension of the manifestation of Being in beings. It is also the plenitude and simplicity for god and the gods. Far from reducible to one among the regions comprising the Fourfold (*das Geviert*), it is "that which is not"—that which is neither the earth nor heaven nor humans nor god—that which is presupposed by all manifest harmony. It shows itself only in its unique retreat, and thus grants the diversity of appearing. It is in the sole dimension of Being as it opens itself and preserves itself in divine sacrality, that "god and the gods" can be approached as such. The "divines" can appear only in taking shelter in the originary time of the Sacred.

Heidegger also explains—and this is a third positive asset—the encounter between the *poet* and the Sacred. In the light of the Feast day, where the opening is clarified, the poet sees the coming of the Sacred, which is what the poet's word must say.[4] It is beginning from the Sacred that the poet is what he is. He is called to correspond to the power of the Sacred in awakening. But the poet never has the power to name the Sacred immediately by himself. A god—closer to the Sacred—is needed to bring a flash of lightning into the poet's soul. Thanks to the poet, the terror of the unapproachable Sacred is changed into the sweetness of mediate and mediating speech. Yet the poet is also exposed to supreme danger; for he must leave to the immediate its immediacy but still and at the same time assure mediation, grasping in his own hands the lightning that mediates. The poet remains thus between humans and gods. Demi-god, he must—in enduring his inequality to both gods and humans—hold open the gap, naming the Sacred for the gods and for humans. The poet loves exile in the aim of one day finding himself at home. The night of his peregrination is a nocturnal wakefulness, a vigil of waiting for destiny. The poet's heart wants essentially what comes, the unforeseeable Poem of the Sacred. The word of the poet is therefore also prophetic. The most essential distance makes possible pure proximity. When he shows the Distance that approaches in the coming of the Sacred, the poet lives close to the origin, founded firmly in the Sacred, which must come in his word. Thus founded, it founds what remains.

Finally and above all, not content with simply thematizing the relations of the Sacred—to Being, to divinity, to the poet—Heidegger also suggests what one could call the tautology of the Sacred: the Sacred is not sacred because it is (also somehow) divine;[5] in other words, the Sacred is sacred because it is sacred. It is thus that it resembles Being. The "Letter on Humanism" insists, in response to the question "what is being?," upon the necessary tautology: Being? "Es ist Es selbst."[6] So too on the subject of the *Ereignis*, could there only be tautology. What else to say about the *Ereignis*, asks the Protocol of the seminar on *Zeit und Sein*, than this: *das Ereignis ereignet*.[7] The Simple requires, in order to stand out as such, *reduplicatio*.[8] Essentially tautological, the sacred also resembles language: "In a general fashion," writes Heidegger, "language is not this or that, that is to say it is not something other and more than itself."[9] Language is language (*die Sprache ist Sprache*). *Die Sprache spricht*.[10] Likewise, the Sacred is not something other than itself: the Sacred is the Sacred. *Das Heilige heiligt*.

But how does it *heiligt*? This word elucidates itself. In *heilig* one hears *heil*: healthy, intact, unhurt, safe. The Sacred can appear only in the circle of the Unbroken, or Uninjured (*des Heilen*). Paradoxically, it is in experiencing *das Heillose* (the absence of the Uninjured) that the poets are on course toward the Sacred (*auf der Spur des Heiligen*); for it is misfortune (*Unheil*) insofar as misfortune that opens "the trace of salvation" (*spurt uns das Heile*), and salvation "evokes [*erwirkt rufend*] the sacred."[11] *Das Heile*—the dawning of the Uninjured, the salutary *Lichtung* of Being—conducts us toward *das Heilige*. But only Being grants to the Uninjured (*dem Heilen*) its rise into grace (*Huld*), as it grants to fury (*Dem Grimm*) its thrust toward ruin (*Unheil*).[12] The retreat of the Uninjured, one surmises, places humanity under an extreme menace.[13] Still, the retreat that subtends misfortune, or injury (*Unheil*), contains the salutary power of Being.[14]

In *heil*—as Hölderlin understood it and Heidegger meditates on it—there resonates the idea of vigor, vivacity, and ardor that characterize the Greek *hieros*.[15] It is with impetuosity that what is *heilig* accedes to manifestation. *Das Heilige* thus evokes the opening of a luminous epiphany. On the other hand, the expression also contrasts etymologically with the idea of a separate domain, as is characteristic of the Latin *sacer*.[16] In the wake of Hölderlin, Heidegger designates this powerful, omnipresent gushing by the word *chaos*. He does not understand this term according to the current sense that associates it with confusion (and also not simply in the line of Hölderlin's *heilige Wildnis*), but in the etymological sense of an initial gaping, eternal openness. This is the gulf hollowed out, the chasm opened and swallowing everything, the bottomless immemorial that grants every being its presence within limits, and that no being precedes. In this sense, Chaos is the Sacred itself.[17] In the face of the "chaotic" epiphany, the poet is the one who knows how to open himself to the Opening: he sings the Openness that gives place to things.

Might one not fear, however, that the irrepressible opening smothers the hymn in eradicating the reserve? In order to ward off this danger, Heidegger makes recourse to another term: that of the *Geheimnis*. "The nearness of the origin is a mystery."[18] *Heim* signifies the hearth of the home. To be sure, in relation to the inner chamber of the dwelling, we could never be profane (as if faced by the *sacer*); nevertheless, this *Heim* always remains mysterious. The *Geheimnis* always deepens *das Heilige* in preserving the *mustèrion*. In the Heideggerian optic, *das Heilige* is certainly an overflowing omnipresence (in the sense of *hieron*)—it must always be open—but it remains at the same time a mysterious reserve, bottomless abyss. By accentuating the secret of the Initial, Heidegger tries to free the Opening from having to show itself, and at the same time tries also to protect the abandon (*Gelassenheit*) from the danger of asphyxia from submersion in an irresistible epiphantic eruption.

Despite its radiance, the Heideggerian hermeneutic of the sacred is not devoid of shadows. In considering the Opening itself as the immediate,[19] does it not risk becoming absorbed by the Hegelian dialectic in which, it is true, every mediated presupposes the immediacy of the foundation, but also in which that immediacy is in turn posed through the mediation of the mediate? Is the immediately Open not—contrary to the Heideggerian accent on mystery—consigned by necessity to unfolding? Is not the Heideggerian Sacred thus suppressed—and definitively—in the mediating Word, in becoming exhaustively Hymn? Is not the hymnic safeguard of the Sacred a pure destiny, if one thinks it, according to Heidegger's suggestion, under the "Greek" form of chaotic Opening? Thus understood, thus opened to its uncoercible manifestation, is the Sacred not degraded into a simple theo-gonic power? Does it not become incapable of sustaining itself in a pure disclosure in which all *lèthè* is effaced? Lacking any insurmountable distinction between immediate depth and radiant mediation, the Sacred would be nothing other than source of-

phusis,[20] which would mean ending precisely with the result that Heidegger wished to avoid when accentuating the immediacy of the Opening.

In order to protect the Sacred from being swallowed in the inexorable relation of the immediate and mediation, in order to free the Opening from the necessity of pro-ducing itself, Heidegger turns for help to Christian mysticism, notably that of Eckhart. But does the impulse of *Gelassenheit* (at least in its Heideggerian transposition) toward mystery not reabsorb all transcendence into its own abyss? Does not the Heideggerian interpretation of the Sacred, despite all its precautions, thus arrive—and along a course no doubt less instructive than that of the dialectic—at the same result as Hegel: to an absolute identification between the nothingness of the manifest Sacred and the "nakedness" of the "poor" who abandons himself to it? Would not the Heideggerian union of *Gelassenheit* and Sacred—immanent correspondence between attunement and Opening—be only a pale version of the Hegelian absorption of nature and humanity in the luminous revelation of absolute Conciliation?[21] Whatever the convergence with Hegel, it would in any case be necessary to underline the distance between the terms that Heideggerian thought borrows from the Christian spiritual tradition and its own reduction of the Sacred to chaotic Openness. For the former belong to the New Testament's proclamation of grace, whereas the second does not succeed—in spite of its evocation of the *Huld*—in breaking the spell of necessity, "forever unscathed." Despite its effort to preserve the unfathomable latence, or inviolable secret of the *Geheimnis*, and the being-intimate-with-itself of the *Gottheit*, the Heideggerian approach to the Sacred remains closely menaced by the omnipresent effusion of the *hieron*.[22]

One may well object that certain "apophatic" themes in the later Heidegger resist precisely this danger. And one will no doubt evoke, above all, the Heideggerian strategy of tautology, which leads him to underline the contrast between the giving and the gift. As is related in the meditation on the *Es gibt* in *Zeit und Sein*, the *Geben*, as opposed to the *Gabe*, is that which does not in any way allow itself to be given.[23] Since there was givenness, it is necessary that the giving did not appear as gift—it is necessary that it is forgotten. The gift as gift is pure non-appearing; it gives itself only in the *epokhè* of the *Geben*. Through this suspension, it escapes disclosure and liberates the *Gabe* (the gift). As for the task of a "phenomenology of the non-appearing"—or aphano-logy—in the sense intended by the later Heidegger, it would be to leave the non-appearing in its non-appearing, of taking care rather than taking in view. But here is the difficulty: this saying or thinking could hardly define itself as phenomenology. Phenomenology and aphanology are two different things. Everything transpires as if Heidegger can avoid the Scylla of absolute disclosure only by foundering in the Charybdis of radical apophatism. Giving up appearance—and thus the domain of any authentic phenomenology of the Sacred—Heideggerian thought increasingly risks veering into *pure* tautology: of giving nothing to be seen, of no longer showing anything at all. To be sure, in attempting to articulate the singular monstration that lets appear what does not show itself, this tautology is still bound, in a certain measure, to the phenomenological attitude: fidelity to the thing itself, step back, *epokhè*. Yet in thus effacing itself before what calls, it runs the risk of acquiescing to that address only in an empty purity, of sacrificing the phenomenological deployment of the word of the Sacred to the "resonance of Silence" (*Geläut der Stille*).[24] This "sigetic"[25] would seek, finally, only the word to say a *Sage* that neither expresses nor exposes what is wholly impenetrable reserve. In this perspective, it is Being itself that would be, at bottom, reticence at saying itself, and thus ultimately Enigma. The "phenomenon" of this "tautological phenomenology" is no longer something that shows itself, but only what (does not) give itself to be heard. For the very possibility of phenomenology, and in particular for that of the Sacred, the Heideggerian tautology—the transmutation of phenomenology that it operates—could well be, in the final account, a "disaster."[26]

The thinking of Being that underlies the Heideggerian interpretation of the Sacred also elicits some reservations. Of course, Heidegger approaches Being as superconceptual *mysterium*. He underlines the "transcendence" (wholly-other character) of Being, as well as the difference between Being and beings. It is in order to progress toward the thinking of Being itself that Heidegger renounces the metaphysical tradition. However, this progression is also a regression in the measure that it revokes the distinction, hard-fought, between unlimited non-subsistent Being and unlimited subsistent Being. Through the Heideggerian difference, there is no true *analogia entis*. Should one not fear that what reigns in this thought—despite its manifest anti-idealism—is in fact nothing other than an identity that produces difference and at the same time englobes it? That Being has need of beings in order to be itself, Heidegger first denies but later affirms.[27] Regardless of what one makes of this (apparent?) contradiction,[28] Heidegger's final word does seem well and truly that of co-propriation. And from there, is not difference itself at risk of being built up, finally, into absolute identity? Were this the case, we could no longer be astonished before the "marvel of marvels," and would lose *ipso facto* the sense of the Sacred, for we would belong essentially to the necessary deployment of Being as such. From this angle, the Heideggerian thought of Being would not appear to escape the fatalist horizon of Greek thought. Although it attempts to think difference in its unfathomable mystery, it flirts with the danger of suppressing itself and transforming itself into a thought of identity. Would the famous *Kehre* thus do anything else than show the same from the other side? Admittedly, Heidegger declares that if we think Being properly "the question [of Being] itself places us in a certain manner at a distance from Being."[29] Yet this question does not conduct Heidegger himself to recognize that Being is truly free—because subsistent—with regard to all beings. Can a thought that, like that of Heidegger, does not overcome immanent transcendence toward the pure transcendence of subsistent Being conquer, as concerns its final depth, the forgetting of Being? How could it, since it suggests an irresolvable bond between Being and human being, and submits Being to the mode of beings, which is to say to temporality?[30]

It is true that Heidegger tries to avoid the impasse of identity especially by declaring that it is a matter of thinking Being in itself, which requires one to turn away from Being to the degree that it is, as is the case in every Metaphysics, thought only beginning from a being. To think Being in itself, to think Being as Being, requires one to abandon the thinking of Being as the foundation of beings, in favor of thinking Being as the giving that works by withdrawing in the liberation of the withdrawal—"that is to say in favor of the *Es gibt*."[31] But this concern to think Being in itself suggests once more that Being deploys itself without beings; Heidegger would thus veil the essential finitude of Being that he elsewhere so clearly proclaims.[32] From there, our thinker once again faces a Scylla and Charybdis: the thinker can elude the reef of identity only by sinking into the hypostasization of being-as-such. In effect, the thinker seems to succumb to a false dilemma: either, in order to think Being as such it is necessary to do so without a relation to beings, such that the latter disappear from the field of thought; or one takes beings into consideration, but then without reaching Being as such. Heidegger thus comes to hypostasize an indeterminate sense of Being, and this hypostasization of Being as such is translated by a growing indifferentiation in the domain of beings and being-there.[33]

Heidegger writes: "It is only beginning from the truth of Being that can be thought the essence of the sacred. It is only beginning from the essence of the sacred that can be thought the essence of divinity. It is only in light of the essence of divinity that can be thought and said what must be named with the word 'God.' "[34] If there is any truth in this famous series, the deficiencies of the Heideggerian thought of Being could only, one surmises, echo it, not only in an incapacity to furnish a sufficiently concrete presentation of the sacred, but also in the impossibility of elaborating a satisfactory philosophical theology. To be sure, Heidegger has seen very well that this type of questioning requires the most vigilant patience. And he was certainly not wrong to suggest that the decisive point is to free up the dimension of the Sacred through a clarification of the opening of Being, for it is only thus that we could discern the First, the Necessary that is gathered purely into itself—the Divinity—and finally name the High—God—in its effective deployment and real existence. Heidegger knows—as one sees most plainly in his elucidations of Hölderlin's poetry—that the more thinking engages itself in the simple plenitude of Being, the more Being withdraws into its unfathomable mystery. If he stumbles on the difficulty of saying "God," this is manifestly not due to some indifference or scepticism. And again, he is certainly not wrong to discard attempts to reduce God to a projection of our subjective evaluations or to the objectifications of an abstract ontology. But Heideggerian thought refuses to take the last step, to reach God along the line of being by exceeding immanent transcendence toward the pure transcendence of subsistent Being. Now, without this overcoming—toward God, across the parable of non-subsistent being—how could one maintain that being is more be-ing than all limited beings? It is impossible to stop at non-subsistent being, for though it is the light of all beings, it is without the power to produce beings from out of its own depths. It surely does bring beings to the truth, but beings, in turn, give Being the world where Being can be deployed. In view of its irreality (if one considers it outside of beings), non-subsistent being could not, in the final account, pretend to the title of Sacred. Being merits the name Sacred only if it has the power to gather itself fully into itself, across and against all finite beings. Its pure essence is to be in itself as itself—the pure being of the simplicity gathered into itself. One thus cannot say that it is deployed only as Being of beings. To the degree that Heidegger refuses to transcend toward subsistent Being—until God, Ocean of Being, living Spirit—he in fact, and in place of thinking being in itself, as he wished, succeeds only in masking the finitude of non-subsistent being.

This "ontological" weakness in Heideggerian thought is sure to come with an "epistemological" insufficiency. In what concerns the limits of thought, his position is utterly ambiguous. It tends either to transgress them in illegitimate fashion, or to close itself, no less illicitly, within its own boundaries. On the one hand, the radical dissociation of philosophy and theology that he puts into operation constitutes an inadmissible transgression of limits, for it is for God and God alone to decide whether his revealed Word also clarifies our grasp of being. On the other hand, Heidegger's thought also seems to situate itself under the rule of a disguised limitation such as will have come from the Kantian critical philosophy and its conception of "limits of thought." How else to understand his declaration that thought, out of respect for the proper limits of thought, can not be theist? Yet no such similar pretension to restrict or confine the light of Being would be allowed. Just as Hegel has criticized the "subjectivism" by which Kant anchored understanding in finitude, so now it is necessary to criticize the "subjectivism" of Heidegger (and despite his anti-subjectivist polemic) as concerns the problem of God. In effect, Heidegger approaches that problem according to the most arbitrary of presuppositions, when posing from the beginning the "free" thought of a subjectivity comporting itself from out of itself, and conferring on it the faculty of determining the modality of the "coming of God."[35] This conception, which contrasts by its anthropocentrism with the profound movement of the *Kehre*, seems wholly out of conformity with Heidegger's doctrine of the essence of philosophy as *Ereignis* of Being.[36]

It is by this double strategy, this equivocal exploitation of the limits of thought, that Heidegger attempts, on the one hand, to set aside the redeemer God of believers, and, on the other hand, to eliminate the God of the philosophers, which he misrepresents as simple *ens causa sui* without divinity. By insisting on the insurmountable opposition of these two figures of God, Heidegger—as opposed to Pascal—does not recognize that the God of the philoso-

Emilio Brito

phers, though overcome, is also conserved in the God of the Christians. In the confluence of the theology of philosophers and Christian theology, he sees only a confusion of registers that leads the second to lose sight of its most proper object. Hence the Heideggerian "destruction" of traditional Christian theology, parallel to that of classical ontology. Be that as it may, it is clear that Heidegger takes some distance from both the God of the Christians and the God of the philosophers, in order to turn toward the "sacred God" of the Poet. Neither the supreme being nor the God of faith, this other God would not be the object, says Heidegger, of either a rational theology whose source is Greek, or of a theology of Judeo-Christian revelation. The appearance of this God (which is neither *causa sui* nor creator and redeemer God) comes in the space of Being (which is no longer a foundation). It is the Clearing of Being that conditions both, and at the same time, the appearance of the sacred God and the experience of it that can occur in thought (in thought, and not in faith or metaphysical reason).[37]

It is clear that for Heidegger Being and this God are not identical, are not *das Gleiche*.[38] But, that said, it is necessary to bear in mind that "the similar, or semblant" (*das Gleiche*) and "the same" (*das Selbe*) do not coincide.[39] The Heideggerian thought of Being and what Hölderlin says in poetry concerning the God are indeed, in Heidegger's eyes, *das Selbe*. When Heidegger observes that Being is not God (though it is equally shortsighted to think of God as "not Being" as it is to think of God as "a being"),[40] he is simply challenging the metaphysical conception of God as supreme being. To this we add, however, that the difference between the Sacred and God (or the gods) does not merely repeat that of Being and beings, according to Heidegger's "ontological differ- ence." It seems rather to correspond above all with the difference of the "It" (*Es*) of the *Ereignis* (which places us "at a distance from Being")[41] and given being. Still, the ontological difference between Being and beings plays a role (as is suggested in Heidegger's use of the plural word *gods*): just as Being lets come beings and, in this way, addresses itself to humans, so the Sacred is decisive in what concerns the gods and "arrives" itself in theophanies.[42] It is along this line that emerges a correspondence between the gods and some beings (or to beings *überhaupt*). But *the* God, to the degree that it corresponds to the givenness of Being, is not, in the Heideggerian optic, a simple being. And for that matter, one also cannot consider the *gods* as simple beings pene- trating a horizon already open; for the theophany determines, from its side, the manner in which that horizon structures itself. It is, therefore, difficult to accuse Heidegger, as some commentators have done, of reducing God to a simple being.

Let us return to the Heideggerian relation between God and the Sacred, and to its relation to the distinction between Being and the "It" (*Es*) that gives Being. Even if the Sacred produces itself only when the God arrives (just as "It" does not find itself in some way over against the Being that it gives, this approach leads, despite all else, to submitting the God to the Sacred and, finally, to the *Ereignis*. The "It" of the *Ereignis*—a neutral "It"—would be more radical than God. The giving that is at work in the Heideggerian *Es gibt* does not admit a first instance that would take upon itself the enacting of the gift of a givenness.[43] Even if the dependence of the divine on Being can have a worthwhile sense (in the measure that the truth of Being is the space of the encounter with God), it would still be necessary, we believe, to think the givenness of Being beginning from God—a subsistent and eternal God, capable, in supreme freedom, of a truly gratuitous condescendence—in place of comprehending God through the anonymous *Ereignis*. Neither subsistent nor free, Heidegger's God—as opposed to Aquinas's God, and indeed Schelling's God—cannot be "Lord of Being." Heideggerian Being is not act of being, and it also could not be understood as act that makes being. In Heidegger, everything excludes the act of Being universally communicated by the will of the *Ipsum esse subsistens*, being as creative effect of the Creator God. Despite the developments in *Zeit und Sein* on the *Es gibt*, an economy of givenness, understood as dispensation by God of the being that God is absolutely, seems incompatible with the radical orientation of Heideggerian thought. This latter closes thinking from access to the being of the Absolute, as well as from access to the absoluteness of Spirit.[44]

The Heideggerian presentation of the poet also leaves something to be desired. While emphasizing the prophetic status of the poet, Heidegger tends to ignore everything that this status owes to biblical prophetism. Unilaterally, he situates the poet only in the provenance of the Greek experience of being. Besides, one has the impression that the task he gives to the poet asks too much. In Heidegger's approach, the effacement of the Christ and that *Überforderung* (overtaxing) of the poet go together. On this point, Heidegger could scarcely invoke the authority of Hölderlin himself. For Hölderlin, to attribute to the poet the role of mediator would be blasphemy. In contrast, Heidegger does not hesitate to consider the poet as a mediator between gods and humans. It is from this perspective that the mediation of Christ is eclipsed whereas the poets receive the mission of testifying to, from a mediating position, the being of gods and the being of humans. The passion of the poet thus replaces the Calvary of Christ. In place of the two Testaments, the works of the poet are deciphered by "the thinker" as a sort of holy Scripture, where the sacred is stated for our times. The Heideggerian thought of the sacred deploys itself in dialogue with poetic naming, while at the same time trying to strike out every bond between the poet and religion. Heidegger pretends that the experience that thought has in listening to the "poet of poets" is too originary to be called "religious." Against this, however, one must insist on the religious and not only "ontological" dimension of this poetry. More broadly, one will recall that the religious experience of the mystery *tremendum et fascinosum* is found at the root of the great "mythical" art of all peoples. While thus recognizing that the sacred also appears in poetry, one will also abstain from Heidegger's manner of

Emilio Brito

dissociating this manifestation from what takes place in the religious sphere. Rather than turning exclusively, with Heidegger, toward poetic access to the divine, one will attempt also to thematize the fashion in which the expressly religious attitude relates itself to the sacred.

Furthermore, one can critique not only the Heideggerian conception of the relation between poetry and religion, but also the conception of the relation between poetry and thought. For Heidegger, one will recall, not only is thought essentially poem, but poetry, in turn, is grasped as, in essence, thought. This position is exposed to a two-fold danger: comprised from an originary poetizing, thought risks exiling itself from reason; conversely, poetry grasped beginning from thought seems misunderstood in its aesthetic specificity. The Heideggerian tendency to consider the poet solely as the one who names the sacred seems overly narrow, for it applies only to certain *poetae vates* (visionary poets), and forgets precisely what is characteristic of the poet. Moreover, Heidegger's approach to the poetic text also risks emptying it of all content; not bearing within itself the light of its own speech, it is in danger of degrading into a mere "seeming." The poem does not truly "say" what it has to say; the word of the thinker, explicating the poem, pretends to articulate the non-said of what the poet serves only to suggest. This leaves the poem exposed, without defense, to the onslaught of thought. The Heideggerian *rapprochement* established between poetry and thought not only undermines the consistency proper to poetry but also, we emphasize, implies some danger for thought itself. The difference between the speculative and the poetic is at risk of being blurred. Hence, no doubt, the propensity of Heidegger's later texts to plunge thought into the void, to succumb to the seductions of the inarticulate and unexpressed.[45]

We now insist, finally, on four deficiencies that gravely affect the Heideggerian conception of the sacred: a misunderstanding of the personal dimension, an eclipse of the religious act, a forgetting of the communal aspect, and an exclusion of the ethical moment.

Even if one could admit that *numina*—that is to say, impersonal powers—are, from the perspective of the history of religions, "more ancient than the gods,"[46] one will abstain from reducing the sacred to an anonymous *Es*. For biblical monotheism, in any case, the personal character of religious experience is primary; the Sacred meets us as a Thou—a fact that invites deciphering the sacred as the phenomenon of the divine. Even if one must avoid, as Max Scheler rightly demanded, interpreting the personal love between God and people according to the model of personal love between finite beings in this world,[47] it is nonetheless evident that a phenomenological approach—notably, Scheler's own—that discovers in love the essence of the sacred, and understands holiness as the perfection of love, is much closer to biblical revelation than is the Heideggerian insistence on the enigma of chaotic Openness. For Heidegger, the sacred is ultimately impersonal. For us, the person belongs to the essence of the sacred. We estimate—with the *younger* Heidegger—that an "authentic philosophy of religion does not issue from preconceived notions of philosophy and religion, but that, beginning from a determinate religiosity—for us, Christian religiosity—there results the possibility of grasping it philosophically."[48] And it is the biblical experience of the sacred—or of the Holy—that we try before all else to reflect. For his part, the mature Heidegger has left the terrain of this "determinate religiosity" for the soil of pre-Socratic Greece, which is in sum that of an ahistorical and indeterminate experience of the relation between humans and Being (as well as the sacred): we are used by (*khreôn*) anonymous Being, which has need of us. These dull expressions contrast with the density of biblical terms such as fidelity, confidence, alliance, and promise—all of which express the living bond between us and the God who has deigned to reveal his Name.[49] For us, the sacred has a personal character. The act in which we apprehend it in its true depth can only address itself to people. To be sure, approached only as open Chaos, it seems impersonal; but if love is its fundamental determination then it could not fall into neutrality. In limiting himself to present the sacred as the anonymous force of the Opening, and in suppressing the personal dimension of both the manifestation of the Holy and the act by which we welcome it, Heidegger does not do justice to the sacred. In the religious path, it is a being that manifests itself first as personal that I discern as God. The real personhood of God can be recognized only thanks to a free divine communication. Now, the human correlate of the latter is not simply an act of thought, but the religious act (which implies, above all, an active love). Approaches displaying rather a gnostic tendency are always inclined to subordinate religion to thought, and to refuse to see in the divine a personal being that only a gratuitous revelation would make us plainly see. The notorious anti-personalism of Heidegger has something of this gnosticism in it, to the degree he confides only in *Denken* and ends up in a Neuter that does not have the power to communicate itself freely.

Incapable of acceding to a personal God, Heideggerian thought of the sacred is equally at a distance from the constitutive acts of religious experience, notably of faith and prayer. On this point, it is situated at the antipodes not only of Schleiermacher's *Glaubenslehre*—to say nothing of Pascal or Kierkegaard—but also, and more recently, the phenomenology of Scheler, as well as the philosophy of religion of an author as deeply marked by Heidegger as Bernhard Welte.[50] Aside from some youthful sketches,[51] Heidegger has not elaborated anything approaching a true phenomenology of religion; he neither studied the religious act in its formal structure and material content nor examined the multiplicity of its manifestations, nor applied himself to reflection on the criteria permitting one to distinguish religious acts from other cognitive acts. These lacunae are not unrelated to the increasing lack of differentiation of *Dasein* in Heideggerian thought. The more radical the *Kehre* turns, the more our relation to Being becomes an anonymous event where the concrete consistency of the self disappears. Under these conditions, it is impossible to recognize, with Scheler, that a divine spirituality awaits the religious person in the intuition of his or her own spirituality, immediately grasped as an image; it is also impossible to perceive, still with Scheler, that the *summum bonum* can be truly known as such only in and by an active love. In failing to recognize himself, Heideggerian man becomes incapable of relating himself to the divine Spirit. Authentically religious acts can be excluded, and the whole domain of their manifestation abolished, *only* when the relation to our existential self is neutralized to the profit of a pure "being-the-there" (*être-le-là*), that is to say the place of the impersonal event of Being. This permits Heidegger to avoid the pit of subjectivism (such as one can indeed impute to other conceptions of the sacred—including, for instance, that of Rudolf Otto); yet this comes at an exorbitant price, for the species of ontological structuralism that it proposes renders impossible all true religiosity. Inversely, the religious person can remain religious only if he or she refuses to acquiesce to the domination of the Neutral. At this juncture, the contrast between Eckhart and Heidegger is striking. Heidegger, as is well known, reproaches the Eckhartian *Gelassenheit* for a failure to have freed itself from the will. But without willing, how could the mystic turn himself toward the God of love? Eckhart wished to act in loving union with God. Heideggerian *Dasein*, in comparison, can neither truly love nor—Heidegger's insistence on *Danken* notwithstanding—truly thank. The unfathomable enigma of the *Ereignis* could never grant with free goodwill anything at all; there is likewise no true gratitude in the openness of *Dasein*, for its part. Detached from the religious context, Heideggerian *Gelassenheit* expresses nothing more than resignation to the inscrutable abyss of Being.

In spite of these limits, however, at least some Heideggerian notions—including most notably those that describe the movement by which *Dasein*, tending by interest, deploys itself in time[52]—can be put to the service of a philosophical interpretation of faith, as Welte has been able to show.[53] In other words, some of Heidegger's notions can be employed to elucidate general forms of faith that are themselves not specifically Christian, but that Christian faith presupposes.

Heidegger overlooks, in addition, the communal dimension (or sociological condition) of the encounter with the sacred. He does not do justice to the fact that religious acts refer necessarily to a "church." Wherever one observes a religious life, one also finds that it has a defined group as its substrate. The actual encounter with the sacred is not a private affair, but one that is eminently collective and essentially communal. It is the religious community to which one belongs that teaches one what the sacred is and what the gods are. The sacred is always the sacred for a specific collectivity. In the absence of recognizing a religious community, the sacred is at risk of vanishing. In the final account, the sacred is essentially bound to the cult of a "church": the cult is the hearth of the sacred, such that it is impossible to understand the sacred adequately if one forgets the cultic sphere. Detached from the ensemble of beliefs and practices that unite those who adhere to them into a single religious community, the experience of the sacred could hardly be fulfilled.[54] Of course, during the 1930s Heidegger did indeed underline this "communal" aspect, but then in the most ambiguous manner possible—that is to say, in relating the "Fatherland" to the Hölderlinian experience of the sacred, promoting the *Führer* to the rank of a demi-god, evoking the "gods of the people" and the "new gods of the Germans."[55] The later work—after the collapse of Nazism—no longer proposes this political pseudo-theology of the worst species, yet at the same time the Heideggerian approach to the sacred also seems to lose all collective roots. Taking some distance from the "patriotic" sacred while at the same time avoiding all concrete religious community, Heideggerian *Dasein* perhaps does have a "disposition" for the sacred—and is no doubt immediately "open" to its call—but it does not have religion. From the religious point of view, this is only an insipid abstraction. On this point, the contrast between the Heideggerian perspective and the sort of philosophy of religion defended by Franz Rosenzweig is most revealing: Rosenzweig emphasizes the social and ritual roots of the sacred. In his view, each of the two great religious cultures of the West—Judaism and Christianity—represents an attempt to bring us to the order of the sacred, an order defined by a time, space, and specific ritual always lived in and experienced through belonging to a society (the Jewish people or the Christian church). There are, of course, differences between how each of these communal dimensions are lived and experienced; Christian revelation, observes Rosenzweig, must institute the community itself since, unlike the Revelation at Sinai, it has not existed from the origin. This implies a dissemblance in the very experience of sacred time (experienced by the Jewish people as a quasi-natural collective experience, whereas the Christian must conquer his or her faith against an original paganism). However, in both cases, accession to the sacred involves a social and ritual dimension—a dimension cruelly lacking in the Heideggerian conception of the sacred. As opposed to the solemnities of Judaism and Christianity, the "feast day" evoked by Heidegger[56] is not inscribed in any "liturgical year." In Roman Catholicism, one will naturally think of a figure like Maurice Blondel. In the first version of his *Action*, Blondel argues that the religious life is not a simple function of the individual but rather of the wider social body. For religion to unfold itself, there must be cooperation and edification, and one must render oneself part of the overall work, committing oneself to its edifice. It is only thus that each person finds in the other the secret of their common aspirations. It is thanks to this practical union that people attach themselves to one another "in a bond so powerful and so gentle that they form only one spirit and one body."[57] Fashioning that by which people bind themselves to one another, religious action alone exercises the wonder of forming the diversity of spirits into a single ecclesial body. And there can be no question of a true re-ligion except in the course of a common discipline and a life of conformity with it. No religion, thus, without communion; no effective communion without the organic determination of rites, practices, and traditions that permit the constant interpretation of thought by acts, and that offer to

each a social verification of the truth. One sees immediately that the Blon-
delian philosophy of communal practice is diametrically opposed to the Heideggerian theory of an "asocial" sacred.

To all of this we add the observation that Heidegger scarcely addresses the
relation of the sacred to the ethical dimension. According to his perspective,
the sacred would seem in essence ethically indifferent. Now, it is not necessary
to transform religion into a narrow moralism[58] to recognize that a sacred that
does not obligate us in any way is not truly sacred. Religions everywhere
associate the veneration of the sacred and the idea of ethical obligation. The
domain of law is sacred in origin; in the beginning the law belonged to religion. Together with myths and rites, it constituted the objective religion of the
community of the cult. From this point of view, religion is *nomos*, law. Without
the observance of this law in which it finds its support, the community itself
could not subsist. One might well object that Heidegger, too, considered the
Sacred as Law (*das Gesetz*),[59] but one must also take into account the fact that
this Heideggerian law is confused with the mediateness of *Phusis*, which mediates everything: "ontologized," de-ethicized, it no longer expresses anything
more than submission to chaotic Openness. One is plainly to seek a better
account of the originary bond between the sacred and ethics-justice than
Heidegger has indicated. The emancipation of justice and ethics from religion
is a relatively recent phenomenon. Originally, the law was grasped as the
foundation of the justice instituted by the Divinity itself. In the *nomos* of the
people is revealed at the same time the law of the divine, which confers on
norms the character of sacred commandments, the transgression of which
constitutes a profanation (we specify that the domain of the sacred is not
confined to the cultic sphere, but extends to the prescriptions of communal
life). So, the sacred includes, essentially and originally, the moment of having-
to-be, of obligation, of ethical norms; it is of the essence of the sacred to imply
an unconditional demand. One recognizes the authentic religion in the sacred duty that it proclaims and that the faithful must obey. It is only there,
where such a law is in vigor, that the sacred, in the full sense of the word, can
be recognized. All religion is law.[60] An author like Emmanuel Levinas has
placed in evidence—not without excess, to be sure, for he tends to exclude *all*
sacrality in the name of an extreme experience of alterity and transcendence—
the ethical deficiency in Heidegger's conception of the sacred. To this latter,
Levinas opposes the Hebraic accent on the Other: the Other recognized as
face, assigns me to my responsibility and reveals to me the Infinite. Against the
immanence of the sacred filtering through the world, the Jewish thinker insists on the transcendence that opens toward exteriority in the appeal of the
Stranger. Turning away from a naturalist ontology, he elaborates a metaphysics
centered on ethical assignment. Instead of remaining riveted—with Heidegger—by a fascination with the Soil, he tries to let himself be addressed by the
other person. In Levinas, the relation to the other person appears more revela-

tory than the unfolding openness to gaping Chaos; the "numinous" obscurity of the impersonal Sacred cannot rival the light that shines from the face of the Other. According to Levinas, it is therefore necessary to leave sedentary meditation of the sacral universe for the restless nomadism of ethical relations— relations that are not merely preliminary to religious life, but are that life itself.

The movement toward transcendence, Levinas has well understood, could not pass over the ethical encounter with one's neighbor. In this sense, metaphysics is played out in ethical relations. The transcendence that our hearts seek is not at all that of an anonymous Opening that ultimately assures the power of the Neuter, but that of an Other who awakens the freedom turning toward Him. Only the movement of openness to the other can permit the true encounter with the Wholly Other. Nevertheless, one can, in our view, transmit a greater appreciation of Heidegger's thinking on the sacred and the divine than one finds in the severe assessment by Levinas. In reminding us that God can lose to representation all that God has of holiness, or all that God's distance has of the mysterious, the meditative thought of Heidegger can—no less so than the metaphysics of Levinas—signify to the theologian an opportunity for greater vigilance. At the same time, and above all, Heidegger's thinking can also serve to convey or dispatch further reflection: in the measure that it instills in us an admiring expectation before the "gift" of Being, the decentering enacted by the Heideggerian attunement to the hymn of the sacred remains beneficial. It orients us to the vertiginous *Ungrund*, to the abyss without "why," of the origin where everything returns. Against every immediate theism—and, it is true, not without ambiguity—Heidegger follows the course of a thinking according to the mystery of difference. Its inadequacies notwithstanding, it can therefore also prepare the reception of the extraordinary Word of Revelation. Reciprocally, the Face of the One and Only, by revealing itself to be recapitulating as much as it is irreducible, dis-closes the sacrality of powerful Nature—"marvelously everpresent"—as its "unsuspected" parable.

NOTES

1. Cf. G. W. F. Hegel, *Encyclopedia of the Philosophical Sciences* (1830), §554.
2. M. Heidegger, *"Was ist Metaphysik?"* in Gesamtausgabe (GA) 9 (Frankfurt: Klostermann, 1955), p. 51 [Professor Brito's essay works so closely with Heidegger's German texts, and indeed with nuances not always clearly reflected in the various English translations, that reference to the German has been retained throughout—*Translator*].
3. M. Heidegger, *Holzwege*, GA 5 (Frankfurt: Klostermann, 1972), pp. 251, 253.
4. M. Heidegger, *Erläuterungen zu Hölderlins Dichtung* (Frankfurt: Klostermann, 1981), p. 103.
5. Ibid., 59.
6. M. Heidegger, *Wegmarken*, GA 9 (Frankfurt: Klostermann, 1976), p. 331.

Emilio Brito

7. M. Heidegger, *Zur Sache des Denkens* (Tübingen: Niemeyer, 1969), p. 45.

8. Cf. J.-F. Courtine, *Heidegger et la phénoménologie* (Paris: Vrin, 1990), pp. 393–94.

9. M. Heidegger, *Was heisst Denken?* (Tübingen: Niemeyer, 1971), p. 99.

10. M. Heidegger, *Unterwegs zur Sprache* (Pfullingen: Neske, 1990), p. 12. Other Heideggerian tautologies include "die Welt weltet," "die Zeit zeitet," "der Raum räumt" (*Unterwegs zur Sprache*, p. 23), and "das Ding dingt" (*Vorträge und Aufsätze*, II [Pfullingen: Neske, 1967], p. 50).

11. M. Heidegger, *Holzwege*, GA 5, p. 294.

12. M. Heidegger, *Wegmarken*, GA 9, p. 191.

13. M. Heidegger, *Unterwegs zur Sprache*, p. 76.

14. M. Heidegger, *Die Technik und die Kehre* (Pfullingen: Neske, 1976), p. 41.

15. On this term, cf. C. Colpe, ed., *Die Diskussion um das "Heilige"* (Darmstadt: Wissenschaftlichen Buchgesellschaft, 1977), pp. 180–97 and 237–43.

16. Ibid., 243. On the word *sacer*, cf. ibid., 232–37.

17. M. Heidegger, *Erläuterungen zu Hölderlins Dichtung*, p. 63.

18. Ibid., 24.

19. Ibid., 61.

20. Ibid., 56f.

21. It is true that this absolute Conciliation, as opposed to that of Hegel, would not be sealed by Spirit—not, in any case, in the Hegelian sense of *Geist*. To be sure, Heidegger does use the word *Geist* to speak of the Sacred, but the Heideggerian Sacred, as opposed to the Hegelian Absolute, does not entail a "concept" of freedom: it is not "intelligence free in itself" (cf. Hegel, *Encyclopedia of the Philosophical Sciences* [1830], §553). Its deployment is thus closer to the Schellingian *Natur* than to the Hegelian *Geist*.

22. Cf. M. Cacciari, "Il problema del sacro in Heidegger," in M. M. Olivetti, ed., *La recezione italiana di Heidegger* (Padova: CEDAM, 1989), pp. 203–17.

23. M. Heidegger, *Zur Sache des Denkens*, pp. 8, 23f., and 46f.

24. M. Heidegger, *Unterwegs zur Sprache*, p. 30.

25. Cf. M. Heidegger, *Beiträge zur Philosophie: Vom Ereignis*, GA 65 (Frankfurt: Klostermann, 1989).

26. Cf. Courtine, *Heidegger et la phénoménologie*, pp. 392–405.

27. M. Heidegger, *"Was ist Metaphysik?,"* GA 9, p. 46.

28. Cf. W. Franzen, *Martin Heidegger* (Stuttgart: Metzler, 1976), p. 61; L. B. Puntel, *Analogie und Geschichtlichkeit* (Freiburg: Herder, 1969), pp. 505f.

29. M. Heidegger, *Zur Sache des Denkens*, p. 10.

30. Cf. S. Bohlen, *Die Übermacht des Seins. Heideggers Auslegung des Bezuges von Mensch und Natur und Hölderlins Dichtung des Heiligen* (Berlin: de Gruyter, 1993), pp. 9–19.

31. M. Heidegger, *Zur Sache des Denkens*, p. 6.

32. On the finitude of Being, see for example M. Heidegger, *Kant und das Problem der Metaphysik* (Frankfurt: Klostermann, 1973), p. 222; *Beiträge zur Philosophie*, p. 410.

33. Cf. L. B. Puntel, *Analogie und Geschichtlichkeit*, pp. 504–505.

34. M. Heidegger, *Wegmarken*, GA 9, pp. 181–82.

35. M. Heidegger, *Identität und Differenz* (Pfullingen: Neske, 1957), pp. 46–47.

36. Cf. G. Siewerth, *Gott in der Geschichte* (Düsseldorf: Patmos, 1971), pp. 264–93.

37. Cf. M. Zarader, *La dette impensée. Heidegger et l'héritage hébraïque* (Paris: Seuil, 1990), pp. 134f.

38. Cf. Heidegger, *Beiträge zur Philosophie*, p. 263.

39. M. Heidegger, *Vorträge und Aufsätze*, II, p. 67.

40. M. Heidegger, *Wegmarken*, GA 9, p. 162.

41. M. Heidegger, *Zur Sache des Denkens*, p. 10.

42. Cf. R. Schaeffler, *Die Wechselbeziehungen zwischen Philosophie und katholischer Theologie* (Darmstadt: Wissenschaftliche Buchgesellschaft, 1980), pp. 254f.

43. Cf. J.-L. Marion, *The Idol and the Distance*, trans. T. A. Carlson (New York: Fordham University Press, 2001), pp. 200f.

44. Cf. C. Bruaire, *L'être et l'esprit* (Paris: P.U.F., 1983), pp. 103–106.

45. Cf. P. Ricoeur, *La métaphore vive* (Paris: Seuil, 1975), pp. 397–98.

46. The question is controversial. Cf. Colpe, *Die Diskussion um das "Heilige,"* pp. 346, 350, 411, and 424–25.

47. H. U. von Balthasar, *Herrlichkeit*, I (Einsiedeln: Johannes, 1961), p. 187, also rejects this "vulgar Christian interpretation."

48. M. Heidegger, *Phänomenologie des religiösen Lebens*, GA 60 (Frankfurt: Klostermann, 1995), p. 124.

49. Cf. L. B. Puntel, *Analogie und Geschichtlichkeit*, p. 520.

50. Cf. B. Welte, *Religionsphilosophie* (Freiburg: Herder, 1985), pp. 167f. and 182f.

51. M. Heidegger, *Phänomenologie des religiösen Lebens*, pp. 1–156.

52. Cf., for example, the notion of *Vorsicht* ("pre-vision") at M. Heidegger, *Sein und Zeit* (Tübingen: Niemeyer, 1972[12]), p. 150.

53. Cf. B. Welte, *Was ist Glauben?* (Freiburg: Herder, 1982).

54. Cf. C. Colpe, *Die Diskussion um das "Heilige,"* pp. 364–70 and 422–23.

55. During the period of the *Beiträge*, Heideggerian meditation, "far from confronting the individual before the singular experience of the divine, as apart from the faith solidified in constituted Churches or fixed communities, is oriented to a resolutely historical or 'historial' determination of being-there, and opens itself again to the plurality of a people assembled into a new alliance or charged with a mission. Postmetaphysical 'theology' is thus made resolutely theologico-political. It is to the people—the people to come, the people 'truly popular'—people of Being, that it belongs to await the god." (J.-F. Courtine, "Les traces et le passage du dieu dans les *Beiträge zur Philosophie* de M. Heidegger," in M. M. Olivetti, ed., *Filosofia della rivelazione* [Padova: CEDAM, 1994], pp. 519–38, reference from pp. 535–36).

56. Cf. J. Greisch, *La parole heureuse. M. Heidegger entre les choses et les mots* (Paris: Beauchesne, 1987), p. 349.

57. M. Blondel, *L'Action* (1893), trans. O. Blanchette (Notre Dame: University of Notre Dame Press, 1984), p. 379.

58. Cf. C. Colpe, *Die Diskussion um das "Heilige,"* pp. 423–24.

59. Cf. M. Heidegger, *Erläuterungen zu Hölderlins Dichtung*, p. 62.

60. Cf. C. Colpe, *Die Diskussion um das "Heilige,"* pp. 373–77.

The Work and Complement of Appearing

Jean-Yves Lacoste

I

At the heart of phenomenology, a paradox: the real is always already there for those who have "eyes" to "see," an opening that permits it to appear—yet thought is always defined as a quest for the real. We do not inhabit a world of appearance from which it would be necessary to take leave in order to reach the essential; we inhabit the field of appearing where being is given to us without disguise; "so much appearing, so much being." Things exist in as much as they invite themselves to us. Were we but able to render account of this invitation, were we only to perceive that it is not in disguise that things appear to us, and were we, finally, to know the conditions under which consciousness is open, all the work of philosophy would be, by right, achievable. Constituted as "rigorous science," it would thenceforth have only to describe what we all see or understand—which is to say, to describe it better than non-philosophy, but to do so in presupposing that philosophy and non-philosophy speak of the "same thing," and that the experience of the non-philosopher does not maintain its relation to things in the deceiving mode of opinion.

It is no minor achievement to come down to this, and to do it philosophically. The real is what appears, and not a *Hinterwelt* to be dwelt in only by "ideas" or "things-in-themselves." There is no "saving appearances" by founding them in a non-appearing. And what in Nietzsche was still only a cry would actually be accomplished in Husserl who, to be sure, loses all the pathos but gains in the probing force of conceptual articulation. Human life is not lived in the cave, but fully in the element of the real. These are crucial affirmations for which it is not enough to merely assert as so many primary evidences, and which must be discussed in order to know their violence. However, one cannot stop there. And when it is accepted that naïve commerce with things is right, and that its reasons are manifested in a second and "institutionalized" naïveté, namely philosophy, it is not the case that in the field open before the naïve gaze, wherever that gaze opens itself and whenever it opens itself, there is necessarily opened up everything that must be thought, insofar as one takes the risk of thinking. Now, it is indeed for this, if not only for this, that the work of art makes its intrusion into Heidegger's thinking as a philosophical object. This is not—and it is almost to do injury to the reader to make this specification—because the real has many hues and shades, and not because one must pay philosophical attention to all things to which we pay pre-philosophical attention: for this would amount to saying only that the task of description is always to recover, which is to say that one must describe each phenomenon with scrupulous respect for the proper style of its appearing, and so forth—remarks that are quite right but also quite obvious. The philosophical interest of the work of art is due to the fact that, following the lines of force in Heidegger's argument, it makes the clear and distinct appearance of what it is not depend on its own appearance, its "setting to work (*met en œuvre*)."[1] This then is the problem, or the ob-jection (pro-blem). We are told that "in the midst of what is, art breaks open an open place, in whose openness everything is otherwise than usual."[2] But just what is this "otherwise" and this "usual"? There is no mystery in the proposed answer. We see things, and their appearing does not misrepresent their being. In a being is thus confided to us, if we know how to see it, that which philosophy professes to seek, "being." And it is perfectly possible to adopt the approach that considers every being, in fact, to reveal to us all the riches of ontology: a common flint (*humble silex*), for example, suffices for Gilson to discover all that "being" means.[3] . . . Now it is precisely this sufficiency that we are invited to doubt. And this doubt could take the form of a thesis: in order to perceive exactly what being means, it is necessary to pass from a thought of letting-appear to a thought of making-appear. If it is good method to philosophize on the work of art, and if philosophy tells us that it is necessary to look upon or read works of art, this is because art makes appear that which—"elsewhere"—does not appear in plenitude.

A task thus imposes itself: to specify the phenomenological status of the non-appearing. The task exercises a strange allure. Phenomenology wishes to find being in appearing, and the idea of a phenomenological investigation of non-appearing superficially resembles that of a square circle. Would the "true," the "essential," the "originary," the "meaning of being," and so forth be in withdrawal from the phenomena? Would it then be necessary to admit and think this withdrawal in order to weigh the phenomenality of phenomena— would the thought of non-appearing (or "malappearing") be phenomeno-logically indispensable? And, finally, would it be possible to make the non-appearing appear? In this ledger of charges, three demands must be met. One would first have to state the effects upon phenomenology of a thought that wishes to strike a path toward "being." Next, it would be necessary to state how this thought obliges itself to a hermeneutical practice of description. And, third, it would also be necessary to attempt to say that the work of art fulfills itself in the order of its hermeneutical function. On the present occasion, we will pass immediately to this third demand, moving toward its opening to a philosophy of liturgy.

II

The work of art is among the things that make the "meaning" of being appear in greatest clarity. The work of art would be a thing that makes the "meaning" of being appear in greatest clarity. And this would be for a good reason: because the work of producing, of rendering in images and design (*le travail de la mise en œuvre*), also possesses the capacity to make appear, such as is required by the hermeneutical work of thinking. Earth, world, relation of human being to earth and world, etc.—all of this does not await the work of art in order to come into being; none of this would be "created" by art. If one thing is certain, it is that the language of "creation" is absent from the Heideggerian commentary. It is by "producing" that art works, just as it is by "producing" that a tool is fabricated, and the secret of production is not in the faculty of making or letting be one more being,[4] but in the faculty of rendering patent. To the question "what evidence is won for us by the magic of the work?", the answer is simple: at bottom, what belongs properly to great art is that it shows *everything*, or almost everything. Thus, art most assuredly does not "represent" any more than it creates. Heidegger's *Introduction to Metaphysics* dedicates some lines to the painting by van Gogh that also furnishes the primary example of the essay on "The Origin of the Work of Art," and affirms this point in plain language: "actually," the painting "represents (*darstellt*) nothing."[5] This is not strictly precise, for there is indeed an image. But it becomes precise when the text specifies that in seeing the work "you are immediately alone with it as though you yourself were making your way wearily homeward with your hoe on an evening in late fall after the last potato fires have died down"—it is the being of the "earth" that is imposed here, and the earth is not a being but an a priori condition of experience and manifestation. This condition was known to us, for the painting re-actualizes an experience. The essential that it gives to be seen was not hidden from us. The work nonetheless constrains us to see it. And if we do not see it, then will see only a pair of shoes; the being will conceal being, and being will conceal itself in the being more than it will light up for us there.

Perception—and let there be no doubt either that the work of art is first of all perceptible, or that it opens itself first to the constitutive powers of perception—thus furnishes only the preliminary. In the strict sense, we see only the being. And what the work makes appear remains in fact imperceptible and unperceived—the idea of an "image of the earth" would be a monstrosity engendered by an objectifying thought. That being the case, how to speak of an appearing of what does not fall under the influence of sensible understanding? The essay on the work of art does not pose this question, but it certainly does permit a response to it. Its thesis is that the "work" is disclosure, and that this is the "event of truth" insofar as one admits (and this is no longer a thesis, but an axiom) that truth is defined as "manifestedness of the being." Disclosure, on the other hand, is defined in hyperbolic manner as the transformation into "non-being" of all preliminary, "ordinary," *gewöhnlich* commerce with what the work shows us.[6] "Everydayness" is absent from the essay, but the concept is nonetheless present in other terms: the annihilation spoken of is indeed that of everyday relations. In disclosing what things are, the work shows us that we were in error or superficiality. One must insist, because the text is insistent. One uncovers what was covered. And the favor of the "work" does not grant us a greater truth that would come to enrich a lesser truth that would be truth all the same, but gives us the truth pure and simple. We were thus not "in the truth." We might have argued, quite legitimately, from the presence of things, such as they are given to us, in flesh and blood, in the phenomena. But the things were present—and-veiled, present-as-veiled (to which, besides, it is necessary to add that nothing in the text accuses us of responsibility for this; on one hand, we are next to nothing in what occurs in the work and which tears the fabric of "habitual" understanding, and on the other hand, the domain of the habitual does not appear as that of an impoverished experience, but only as that of a poor experience). We might perhaps have been content with a Husserlian concept of truth,[7] and neglected the deeper stakes of appearing. Understood as manifestation, the work "illumines" a being and implicitly denounces the obscurity in which it first appears to us. In providing us with the means to put an end to the "theory of two worlds," Husserl bathed all appearing in the same light. But when the truth is seen to be assigned a place, and when it is necessary for us to win that place in order for things to be manifest to us, then a conclusion is imposed: light is not always already made for the simple reason that phenomena do not deceive. Phenomena do give us the thing itself—but they give it to us obscurely.

It is therefore necessary to admit a disjunction or at least a distension, the weight of which is all the greater because it is (a) necessary for the intelligence of the essay of the work of art, but (b) absent from the letter of the essay. And what is disjoined or distended is nothing other than the bond that seems to unite the theory of perception and the theory of truth. The text thus tells us that the work of art makes the truth of things appear, and what appears is earth and world (accepting the proposed deciphering of van Gogh's painting). Now, if the text does not tell us what is *our* power of understanding earth and world, it is at least certain to us that this power is not conceded to perception. And inasmuch as the lessons of *Being and Time* remain present in our memory, this negation will be accompanied by a position: we will have to say that this power of understanding boils down to affect (to *affection*), to say, in other words, that we "find ourselves" in the element of affection when we come before the work of art. In reality, the world is not seen but felt. We exist in the mode of being-in-the-world without necessarily having clear and distinct knowledge of it; but when we learn that we are in the world, it is in learning this that we "find ourselves" in the world. And this "finding" is perceptible precisely when referred to *Befindlichkeit*, which is the Heideggerian name for the primitive structures of the affect.

There is a paradox in this. The essay on the work of art not only says that it wishes to put an end to the reign of *aisthèsis* (or rather it wishes to put an end to "aesthetics" in order to render *aisthèsis* itself), but also tells us again that this reign is that of *Erlebnis*. And all the descriptions and analyses incontestably practice a "reduction," hitherto extraordinary in phenomenology, that consists in bracketing the addressee of the work of art. By saying that the truth of the work appears in affective life, do we not re-establish the sort of "subject" that Heidegger has certainly not intended? The paradox, however, permits itself to be resolved. From the fact that a phenomenon is given only in affectivity, it would be strange to conclude that affectivity is its measure and, in the final instance, perhaps its author. After all, the world that the analyses in *Being and Time* turn around and return to is revealed to us only in the life of affects. "Existence" cannot be reduced to affect alone, but it is in affect, in the profound region of affective life peopled by the experiences defining the being of Dasein, that it manifests what it is. When Dasein reaches an understanding of its "uncanniness," it is in anxiety that it does so (and when anxiety ceases to be the master-experience, it is other affective experiences—boredom and serenity—that occupy the initiative of Heidegger's texts). One must also *know* what one is, and one would have to say with Alquié that the relation to one's own death cannot be founded solely in the aspect of affect, because death is unknown in the sphere of the immanence of affective life.[8] But once one has agreed with this evidence, a second evidence will still remain—that of a power to integrate to affective understanding the knowledge that affect can not grasp by itself. This power is an essential mark of existence. In truth, Heidegger's polemic against objective understanding wishes to say nothing else than this. Objective understanding is proposed as an achieved figure of understanding. There can be no doubt that a true process of understanding is at work in everything that is modeled on the ideals of "science." Things are more than objects, but they are not less (the conference in 1953 would say this clearly:

technology is not the fruit of a misinterpretation of the nature of things, for the things are essentially in "danger"). And when we want objectivity, control and prediction, it is not a chimera that we pursue: this must be said, if we wish to prevent the phenomenological quest for the primitive or the originary from seeming to entertain troubling collusion with irrationality (*déraison*). However, what is most important lies elsewhere, in the affirmation of a richness of appearing that overflows its reception in objective understanding, and in such a manner that objective understanding is truly intelligible only if we perceive that it rests in fact on a foundation that it does not recognize—that of affective understanding.

At the beginning is not the opening of the entire perceptual field, but the opening of the affective field. We are defined by being-open, just as we are by the fact of having always already decided in some manner what it means to be. And if one asks about the essence of this openness, the response comes without ambiguity: the reception that we reserve for phenomena is governed by the logic of affection. Feeling is thus more profound than perception. This greater depth therefore permits justifying the work to which Heidegger submits the Husserlian concept of phenomenon. Husserl wants to see trees and hear sounds, and to prove that he is occupied with trees or sounds and not "mental processes"—and this is no small thing to have proven. Heidegger, in contrast, is preoccupied with the meaning of all of this, with its "being," with the non-being that contains the secrets of the being, with the transcendent, and so on. Yet he is thus preoccupied without forgetting the axiomatics of phenomenology—and this implies that, for Heidegger, the essential cannot be conceived in terms of a substantiality that would be necessarily non-appearing, or in terms of a transcendence that can only support a conceptual anagogy. The essential, the foundation, if one agrees to speak of such a thing—all of this is invisible and inaudible to us; it cannot be the object of a sense-perception. And unless one simply refuses the entire phenomenological project, a supplementary axiom must be posed: if it is necessary to have all of this appear (having already dismissed the hypothesis of an appearing in the element of the concept, for a conceptual calculus makes nothing at all "appear," unless in a metaphorical sense), this can only be an appearing for affectivity.

It is necessary to specify, and to resolve the difficulty that has been underlined. The essential is given to the affect. But in order to maintain this thesis to the end, one must still interpret the affect, and thus still show that it is in fact not the emotive chaos that it seems to be—a chaos made of experiences that are always unrepeatable, of which one would sooner say that they may all apprehend a meaning but never more than a fragment of meaning, so that "the" meaning would have to be destined once and for all to fragmentation. What are we to respond to someone observing the affective polysemy of the essential? We know the joy of those for whom "all is good," the anxiety of those for whom everything collapses under the menaces of nothingness, the boredom of those for whom nothing merits lingering over it, and so forth. How does one move from this contradictory abundance to the unity of a meaning? And how thus to accede to a possible affirmation of the true? Two elements of a response are available to us. (1) On the one hand, the supreme law of appearing is that of time. Not only are phenomena given temporally, but they also reveal time itself—and the reality of time, whatever the abundance of experiences in which it is attested, escapes all ambiguity. Heidegger's final word in 1927 disentangles all the affective complications of appearing and confirms what the affect certifies in a diffracted way, though without governing it. (2) The affect must, however, submit to an interpretation put on the trail of the originary. The originary is certainly time itself, and *Being and Time* is interrupted just when it would have come to the most urgent thematization—that of the "temporality of being itself." But temporality must be thought of as beginning from the phenomenon of time—and there are phenomena only for us, that is to say for Dasein. Thus, one must give/restore coherence to the plurality of phenomena in which time appears to us. One need not go so far as to claim that this gift or this restoration is accomplished by Heidegger in a manner immune to critique. The rigor of a project is one thing; the success of its analyses is another. In any case, one point can provisionally suffice for us: if one admits this rigor, and the possibility of success, then the language adopted in the essay on the work of art must cease to surprise us. This language in fact imposes itself.

III

To speak of the truth is nothing else than to speak of the unity of meaning, or to speak of the appearance in which this meaning is knotted and given. One can speak of this only in banking on the success of interpretation, in believing in the possibility of a hermeneutical victory. Light can thus be shed on the bond between the work and truth. It is a banality to say that the phenomenality of the work of art puts pressure on affective life, yet there is truth in this. Pleasure, enjoyment, savor, joy—these words do not refer back to the work of perception or to that of rationality, but to the life of affects. However, this is not the affectivity of a "pure ego," but of an ego caught up in the world (or caught up in the more complex play of earth, world, etc.), and to whom the meaning of its being-in-the-world can be the object of an affective disclosure. It is to such a disclosure that art proceeds. It is well known that Heidegger is interested only in great art, and he says so explicitly. Yet his choice of examples reveals a partiality that must not pass unnoticed—would the gothic cathedral "say" what the Greek temple says? And would a portrait by Titian "say" quite the same thing as a pair of shoes? In any case, there is a coherence between Heidegger's interest and his choice. Art brings things into clear view, which is to say that it gives us things as they *are*, placing the full weight of interrogation on this latter word. This question has not been resolved, and Heidegger never says that he has managed to resolve it. However, it is posed with sufficient scruple for one at least to know which manifestation one can expect from things, and from which things. Since we know that we do not have perpetual pure experience of the world and the earth, and since we also know that experiences that do not show in a cogent manner that the existence of the world and of the earth are not pseudo-experiences, there can be no doubt that the work of art has the power to show us a little more than world and earth—and what it would thus show would also warrant being called true insofar as joy, love, and so on, may be called true because they manifest an inalienable dimension of existence. Still, we are told that no manifestation could dream of a greater character of urgency than that of the world, and the earth calls for the same judgment. To make patent the reality of either of them would thus comprise, quite legitimately, the highest service that art could render us.

If the work of art impels philosophy to pronounce the most important words, it must be possible to say that it exercises enough pressure on the affect to stimulate the experiences that these words describe or designate. The end of the work of art is not to give birth to philosophical treatises on the work of art. Art is the working of truth, and the interpretation of this truth is carried out by prudently eliminating every measure that a "subject" could impose on an "aesthetic object" (the only measure is that of being).[9] Still, this healthy prudence does have its imprudent side, where it risks leading one to believe that in refusing the aesthetical and its order of constitution one substitutes for it a philosophical object that itself appears only in order to be interpreted—which, in other words, appears in its truth only through the good offices of interpretation. Now this is certainly not the purpose of the essay, if one is willing to read it while bearing in mind the *Daseinsanalytik* that Heidegger without doubt has not given up at the time of its composition (and it would be rash to think he ever gave this up, at least if one reads the Zollikon seminars). What the philosopher perceives, or what the philosopher pretends to perceive, is the work of art as such, which is to say as it appears to everyone. And if the philosopher's analyses are exact, it is for everyone that the work of art opens this space where everything is different than otherwise—or, more precisely, where there appears in complete clarity what otherwise appears only in the muddle where "originary" phenomena are mixed with less originary phenomena. One must therefore say that the work exercises a constraint on us, or at least that we will not see it such as it is if we evade this constraint. World and earth are not seen, but felt. Nor is the evidence conferred on them by the work of art only something to see: it is also something addressed to the affect. In the final account, and by simple definition, we are not masters of affective life: affective life is an undergoing and *only* an undergoing (*un pâtir*). Can life nonetheless be bound necessarily to the things that affect us—can things always impose a unique affective response? It is on this point that the questioning continues to be necessary.

There can be no doubt that the truth may pass unperceived—and this goes not only for truths the knowledge of which has no existential or ontological weight (the roundness of the earth has been unknown, and this unknowing did not strain the labor of philosophical thought), but also for the truths that unmask what it means to exist (after all, it is only since 1927 that the existence of the "world" has been truly known in concepts!). It would therefore be inexcusably naïve to believe that the earth and world, such as our everyday commerce with things conceals them beneath a certain non-understanding, are imposed on us in the work of art with an evidence prohibiting evasion with the same necessity, for instance, by which pain is imposed on someone who burns himself. It is said that the worldhood of the world is imposed on us in anxiety, or non-habitation, or stress. But, to be sure, it is also said that this goes for the worldhood of the world as well as for being (the two are inseparably related): what is most important is also what we feel least often. It is already obvious that the appearance of things rarely compels an affective response— everyone who plays with fire suffers, but what excites fear or joy in one person may not excite fear or joy in another. A *fortiori*, the affect responds to the non-being that is the a priori condition of appearing only by showing itself clear of all determinism. And *a fortiori*, one causes more problems than one solves when one attributes to certain beings an ontophantic power that we do not perceive clearly how it impels affectivity to ratify without qualification the existence of the world and the earth, as well as to everything that gravitates around them.

How and in what measure do we ratify, in the element of feeling, that which the philosopher affirms is the truth of the work of art? Heidegger's text does not respond, and it would be easy to say that the true, even when it is thought as "process" or "event," is independent of the reception that we reserve for it. The earth is round even when believed to be flat (for example, by all children who have not yet received the rudiments of geography . . .). Care is more originary than uncaring, even if mundane existence testifies to the success of diversion. And van Gogh's painting reveals the earthly reality of our being, even if we see only a pair of shoes painted with talent. The undeceitful presence of the real is thus not enough for us to see or feel the real as such. (Is there any other reason for attending to philosophy?) The Heideggerian response, however, is quite clear, and reads like an answer to this last objection: philosophy interprets; the work makes appear. We can refuse the claims of philosophy, and we can remain "insensible"—the adjective is perfectly adequate here—to what the work renders patent. But just as the first refusal, in cases where the claims of philosophy are strong, can only exhibit the resistance of our prejudices or our lack of intellectual agility, so the second refusal (of the work) would exhibit a certain inaptitude for grasping what appears to us. Hence when Heidegger speaks of the light projected on things by the work, and of the mode in which the work makes them "ring out," *klingen*,[10] it is understood that when the things appear to us outside of the work, they shine and resound rather less. And it is also understood, via elementary logic, that our response to this lesser resounding must not be treated as a case of the response that we bring to phenomena bathed in a reduced light. Heidegger is not the first to have related the true to what he is reluctant to call the beautiful, but he does describe it in terms that classically serve to speak of the beautiful. It is not Heidegger but Thomas Aquinas who has defined beauty as "splendor of the truth." And it is certainly not an idiosyncrasy of Scholasticism or of Heideggerian phenomenology, but a trait generally common to all thought examining the work of art, to have believed to discern in the work a givenness in which there arrives a complement of being and a complement of appearing. And if this complement happens not to be perceived, there is reason to doubt our aptitudes for perception and feeling.

Now, in a certain sense it is necessary to doubt them. The Heideggerian interpretation of the work of art places all the hazards of subjectivity between parentheses, and suggests that this placing between parentheses is called up by the work. Yet this same instance that imposes a reduction at the beginning also permits the reintroduction of a subject at the end, perhaps to the misfortune of the interpretation. For the interpreter knows, in effect, what one must perceive and feel, but in saying "one must" comes up against the unmasterable reality of affective responses. The correct response is the one that the interpreter alone furnishes, but this response is not affective, and it is presented in a formulation remaining within the strict limits of a description. This description is of course offered as the guide for perception and feeling, and its offer of service may be accepted, since after all it is never in a situation of absolute naïveté that we deal with works of art, and it puts into play a number of codes without which we could not learn to see. However, description cannot impose its law to the very end, and indeed it would be strange were this possible. It appears in an essay dedicated to the "origin" of the work of art and takes us into the language of the originary, of what has a meaning that we cannot go beyond. The description does also tell us that in the work the originary is given to us as such, that it occupies the foreground, and is endowed with evidence—and were we to acknowledge this evidence, we could thus make an economy of all the labor of discernment necessary to accept in order to reach significations that are at once most profound and most deeply buried. Has it been said enough that the tone of the descriptions appearing in the essay on the work of art is always that of remarks claiming to be banal? In *Being and Time*, the originary is recognized as that which comes to experience only rarely: this is why its hermeneutics are also heuristics that bring to conceptual evidence what concrete existence maintains in the confused non-evidence of affective life. The work of art, on the other hand, fascinates the philosopher because its work is interpretation and decision of meaning, and because this decision coincides with the philosopher's own. What phenomenology sorts out, art too will have sorted out. And it remains for the philosopher only to articulate the (miraculous) coincidence of the two. If the philosopher can tell us so quickly which truth is manifest in the work, and if he can tell us that the work manifests it in all evidence, this is because the philosopher is himself in the know about the essential. And all of this must be shown before claiming its clear expression in the work. At least, it is from giving himself up so quickly to the evidences that the philosopher discerns in the work that he can next affirm that they are indeed evident and perceptible by all. All of this trips over the uncontrollable reality of the affect.

The first principle of the affect is certainly not the absence of principle. The logic of affection does not unfold in the absence of things but in response to things, or in any case in response to the primordial fact that there are things and that we live among them. Even if this logic must concede a major place to the phenomenon of auto-affection, this latter is never to be conceived as the expression of a worldless ego: even if nothing that is present here and now serves to render account of the affective tonality of my present, it is always a form of living by being-in-the-world that this tonality will express, and being-in-the-world is a being with things to which feeling is related. One thus does not pose a pseudo-question when asking about the affective responses stimulated by the appearance of the work of art.

To pose this question with more precision, we must appeal here to something that Heidegger's text does not discuss: the elementary structure of captivation (*ravissement*).[11] The word itself says a great deal, but requires further specification. We speak of captivation in order to signal a rupture that Heidegger himself indicates, and in plain language: when this remarkable being that is the work appears to us, all other beings become non-being for us; the world (under the traits of "everyday" experience) disappears when it appears. In short, the disappearance of the everyday world has as its correlate the appearing of the essential, and the concept of captivation serves to designate at once a power exercised by the work and our own power to consent to the disappearance of the "habitual" order of things. And this "captivation" cannot be thought through to the end without also having named the power of making-appear that the work exercises, as well as our own power to consent to this appearance. These two powers can be registered in the concepts of, respectively, "obsession" and "enjoyment" (*jouissance*).

(a) If this or that appears to me, it cannot be inferred that only this or that appears to me, nor can it thus be inferred that a phenomenon annuls all the other phenomena in the present where it is given to us. Appearing is, in fact, co-appearing, and existence is constantly able to let more than one "thing" at a time appear. Not only is possible for me to let the same thing appear in several sensory fields (one can simultaneously see and touch the same cube), but I can also touch one thing and see another (let us say, stroke my cat and see a bouquet of flowers). Against this primitive fact, it is possible to perceive an objection: the equally primitive power of attention. Attention may be defined as power to exclude, and to let only one thing appear. In the act in which I pay attention to only this thing here, that thing there must disappear, or no longer appear except in the background. The latter does not cease to be, but is no longer for-me, or is so only in a more attenuated mode. By *obsession*, one will thus understand the quality proper to an appearing that does not only solicit attention (for many things merit our attention to them, and in a certain sense all things merit it), but which, in the proper sense, requires it. It is with regard to other phenomena that we currently employ the vocabulary of obsession (we say, for instance, that a pain or a memory obsesses us), and our utilization of the same lexicon signifies the surprising affinities that unite phenomena as diverse as pain and captivation. Incontestable differences also exist. I might refuse the work of art the urgent attention that it demands, but I could never make pain disappear, and I undergo the experience of pain without paying any "attention." But in the latter, as in the former, we are dealing with an imperious reality: that is, with a phenomenon to which it is essential, at the risk of not perceiving it for what it manifests, to completely occupy the entire field of consciousness. (Of the work of art, I would certainly like to believe that this is only a first word, though one that it was absolutely necessary to have pronounced). The military metaphor says it well: to obsess is to lay siege, and not to occupy. In any case, it strongly expresses what is in question here: a presence that does not boil down to co-appearing, but exists alone for us—a presence that puts pressure on consciousness by requiring that we suspend everything that is not it.

(b) Obsession serves to designate a mode of appearing and not an affective tonality. The affective field that opens to the appearance of the work of art would thus be that of enjoyment, or pleasure. The work of art "pleases" us. However minimal it is, this formulation elicits interest in what it is necessary to call a "fundamental tonality." Pleasure, enjoyment, joy—these experiences and their entire retinue are nearly absent from *Being and Time*, though we must not infer too quickly from this that they would not be at the measure of Dasein. One should rather conclude, backed by the text, that they do not truly express what it is to "find oneself" in the world, that they are not revelatory of the more originary element of affective life. Now, if the reality of the world shows itself as such to us when the world weighs on us, the work of art cannot be received as such without suggesting a new (or another) topic of affect.[12] Short of leaving the exact contours that the work of art offers us in a provisional state of indeterminacy, its description supposes that one accepts at first sight its distances from all the worldly "logic" of existence. A painting by van Gogh does not please us like one of Mozart's sonatas pleases us, or like a poem by Hölderlin does, and so on. But it is no small thing, even if it is also not everything, to see here and there at work a same sort of affective ratification that one can express in the same lexicon, a bit roughly, but exactly. It is also no small thing to observe that in its rush, this ratification neither has any meaning in terms of the world nor makes any statement about our being-in-the-world. As for what concretely the work diverts us from (and this can be our "concern" or "care," but it can also be a theoretical labor on which the fact of the world does not weigh in clear and distinct manner), this is, ultimately, the economy of appearing where *Being and Time* would like to discern the fundamental and the originary. The appearance of the work of art is hailed (*saluée*) as God himself hails the work of his hands in finding it beautiful and good. And the first language that we would find here to give voice to this emotion is that of praise or benediction. In the depths of being-in-the-world, there is "malaise." The field of experience opened by the work of art is that of what may be called (on first analysis) "being-well-there" (*bien-être-là*). Only on the condition of saying this could one say that "a work is actually a work only when we remove ourselves from our *Gewöhnlichkeit* [commonplace routine] and install (*einrücken*) ourselves in what is disclosed by the work."[13]

Obsession and enjoyment: naming these two experiences does not open us to more than the beginning of an interpretation, and the beginning remains notably on the hither side of what Heidegger's text tells us. The work of art is not solely to obsess us, and it is not solely to lighten the weight of the world on us. And it would be entirely licit to suspect the play of captivation and enjoyment of being no more than a moment of the existential economy of diversion. It is, nonetheless, the language of truth that is presented to us in the essay on the work of art, and the truth knows not how to divert. The work is aletheiophany and ontophany, and aletheiophany because ontophany. It thus invites us to an ontological labor of the affect (to a labor of the affect grasping in its element what thought grasps in its element). Now, how is it that affective reasons coincide with philosophical reasons? In Heidegger's text, everything plainly happens as if a pre-established harmony were uniting the two. Everything also happens as if the philosopher had needed to pay attention to the work of art (or to *works* of art, in any case) to discover what he denied in 1927, the existence of a possible birthplace (*patrie*)—what he calls the "earth"; everything happens thus as if it was through the mediation of works of art that the existence of the earth is imposed on him, commanding him to reorganize his questions. But it will be agreed: none of this tells us how the affect will appropriate the true; none of this tells us how two languages will meet (and meet without error): the vague language by which affective life expresses what it lives through the work of art, and the language, in principle rigorous, in which philosophy tells us which truth comes through the work.

Frankly, Heidegger evades this discussion. When we ask ourselves what to say about a painting, we assume that the work of art shows but does not say, because it faces us in silence. Now if the truth in question here is not something that is the propriety of languages, it is nonetheless under the concept of diction (of poetic diction, *Dichtung*) that philosophy thinks the secrets of the work. To show and to say: it seems that convertibility reigns here. The theory of poetic language appearing in the essay on the work of art is without doubt only a sketch, and it would be necessary to read the commentaries on Hölderlin, Rilke, Trakl, and Georg to know more. Still, the essay does confess everything that we need to know for present purposes. It first of all takes up a negation, denying the "current representation" according to which language is to communicate and express everything that must be communicated. It next adopts a position: language serves to *name* a being, and the act of bringing to speech is identical with making appear; it does not testify to appearing, but gives appearing to things. And speaking, language uncovers and *founds*.[14] It is in this measure that it is—"originarily"—poetic diction. From there, the eventual aporiae of the affective response do not merit the least attention (and do not receive it!). If the work is simultaneously ostension and act of speech, it suffices to see and to read . . .

The discussion is nonetheless well and good evaded, and for a reason already set forth: the proposed descriptions, even if they do not say much, nonetheless do seem to say a little too much, attributing evidence—or an excess of evidence—to what perhaps does not possess it. The achievement of the work of art would be its disclosing something essential that is otherwise in danger of passing unnoticed. One would have to conclude that any perception that does not seize on this essential is at bottom non-perception. One would also have to conclude, on the other hand, that the philosophical commentary does not itself have the mission of making appear, but of sanctioning an appearance. And one would thus have to conclude that it has the authority only of the correct regard, or of the correct affect. Still, things are not so simple as that. For it is high time to relate that, on a precise work—the pair of shoes painted by van Gogh—Heidegger has been accused of being purely and simply mistaken.

IV

It is already long ago that Jacques Derrida drew our attention to the research dedicated to that painting by the historian Shapiro, and to Shapiro's conclusion: it is a pair of city shoes and not those of a country peasant that van Gogh will have represented.[15] The interest of this conclusion is anything but anecdotal, first because it forces us to concede the arbitrary character of an interpretation, and second because it also forces us to turn still more closely to the source of affects.

The pre-established harmony of which we have spoken was thus only an artifice. Around the pair of shoes, the philosopher saw appear in complete evidence the plot of land that they had trod, the labor of the people, and the native soil given to them to inhabit. But nothing of all of this could appear, since the thing that the painting makes us see comes in fact from another region of experience. Because there was an error about the thing, there was also an error about its "meaning." It would thus be quite possible to attempt a new description of the painting with the laudable aim of showing that the "meaning" is ultimately given to us when the thing gains a new identity. Such an attempt would not be immune from some ridicule. We would be free to say that these shoes were made to pace the cobblestones of the city, but that these cobblestones were not the asphalt of our cities, and that the people there almost felt themselves to be peasants. We would be free to propose that the experience of the "rooted sedentary" and that of the "uprooted emigrant"[16] are only superficially opposed. We would be free to observe that in Heidegger the concept of "earth" functions to render us an autochthony that, if it exists, defines us in the city just as it defines us in the country. We would be free to do so, but we would do nothing more, if we use this freedom, than develop a strategy of immunization aiming to prohibit all falsification. There will indeed have been an error, but it assuredly would not concern anything but the individual description of an individual work, and would have no bearing on the other descriptions proposed in Heidegger's essay. What is more, the error would be somewhat excusable, since we have had to wait for Shapiro to know that we were all misled, perhaps in accepting Heidegger's commentary too quickly. But is it totally excusable? Truthfully, no. For a detail in the history of art forces us here to admit that the Heideggerian description is not only inter-pretive, but well and good over-interpretive—and by over-interpretation one must understand a constraint that makes things say more than they say in themselves. One can speak truly without saying everything. At the same time, certain things can say more than other things, and they can possess a function of symbolic convocation of the real that other things do not possess. In any case, this thing here does not say apodictically what the interpreter presents us as being the full secret of its appearing. And this is because he knows too well, it seems, that the interpreter forces the thing to say too much.

Still, it might well be that the manoeuvre (or in any case the mistake) has a more profound significance. Superficially, there is nothing here for us to criticize beyond a certain impatience. One of the ends of the essay on the work of art is to introduce a new concept: the "earth." There can be scarcely any doubt that this word has acquired its right of passage in Heidegger's lexicon only after being imposed as a candidate for the dignity of a concept in the course of reading Hölderlin's work—and so there is some justice in Heidegger granting it full philosophical status when discussing the work of art. One might thus conclude that it is out of undue haste to make a new dimension appear that Heidegger would have taken as evidence for this new dimension a paint-ing by van Gogh where it is not in fact given. The pleasure of catching the philosopher in a flagrantly precipitous moment (and in Derrida, this pleasure is anything but innocent . . .) would, however, blind us to the remarkable problem before us: that of the plasticity of affective responses excited by the work of art. For if Heidegger has made a mistake in interpretation, if the painting does not purely and simply represent what he thinks it does, if it is simply illicit to introduce by this bias the process of manifestation that culmi-nates in his description of the Greek temple, one must still grant that nothing in the work—such as it appeared to the philosopher, and such as it still appears to anyone who does not know precisely what it represents—formally prohibits apprehending in it what Heidegger apprehends there. The interpretive ar-bitrariness of philosophers is one thing (which one must not encourage . . .), but the interpretive arbitrariness of feeling is another, and it is of longer range. This latter must be drawn into the open. Regarding the van Gogh, Heidegger wishes to say too much. But in his haste, would he not have been guilty, in the end, of not having said enough? There is no lack of reasons suggesting that this question is the right one.

V

Feeling is not only interpretation (the experience of physical pain leaves no room for interpretation). However, to feel (*ressentir*) the effects of an experience is frequently to interpret. Anxiety says that the world is distressing; joy says that it is beautiful and good. If one agrees that the affect exercises a power of understanding, one must thus agree that these affirmations do not proceed from a naïve projection of the "interior" on the "exterior," but from a true impression of the world on us. The impression is plural and shows the plural character of the phenomena of the world: it is a property of the world to make us anxious, but it must also be a property of the world to excite joy, and it is the whole work of the hermeneutics of facticity to coordinate these properties. The analysis can still be refined in a manner justifying Heidegger's own reinterpretation in a manner introducing the "earth" into the play of manifestation. And if one refuses to see only a hiatus between descriptions where the "more originary" phenomenon is non-inhabitation and descriptions where it is a matter above all of tasting the presence of a mother earth, it may be necessary to submit that the reinterpretation proposes that we conceive a doubling of the originary. At the beginning is, in fact, the play of the world and the earth. The two are co-given: to have an earth is to be open to the world, and we can be open to the world only in founding ourselves on an earth. Nevertheless, one cannot think this co-givenness, and moreover one cannot think the modes in which this "differend" is lived in affective experience, without accepting an ambiguity. On the one hand, no one (not even Heidegger) can disqualify the experiences that, in *Being and Time*, show the weight of the world on us. On the other hand, no one can disqualify the experiences that give ulterior expression to restituting a dwelling to us. This gives rise to a hypothesis: would not the primitive situation of feeling be upstream from both the world and the earth—not the pure appearing of one or the other but the very appearing of their contention (*débat*), an appearing that thus does not summon the affect to receive things as pure manifestation of the world or as pure manifestation of the earth? There is only determined affective life (and this would go for acute determinations like anxiety or joy, but also for the more fluid determinations of "everyday" experience). Must it be the case that things in general (and the work of art in particular) have the power to impose this determination on us? This is not obvious.

The work of art is a presence that imposes itself, and the van Gogh furnishes a pure example of this. What it gives us to see—the thing that it represents—is what we in fact never take note of; in other words, it constrains us to look upon what we mundanely content ourselves with seeing. This means not only the most banal things but, more so, things—shoes—that we expect above all to pass unperceived, since only the shoes that poorly serve us impose themselves on our everyday attention: shoes that make us suffer because they do not fit our feet, shoes unsuited for the terrain we walk, and so on. Through the mediation of art, what was only an "instrument," that which had as its mode of appearing "everyday availability," appears in the foreground, first of all, and moreover appears there in losing all relation with everyday experience. The shoes are, commonly speaking, only shoes, but no restriction weighs on what this painting asks us to regard. It thus turns out that the least of things, insofar as it effectively appears to us, merits occupying us forthwith. If such demands are not addressed to us only by works of art, it is at least certain that every work of art does address them to us. (And if we perceive it in a "subsidiary" mode, in the first analysis, at least, the work of art purely and simply ceases to be perceived at all). These petitions are received only in the element of affect: in the terms of a phenomenology of perception, nothing renders the pair of shoes I now lace more "interesting" than the pair of shoes whose representation is offered in a painting. That being said, nothing in the appearance of this work *dictates* our affective response. The logic of the affect is not anarchical. Sufficiently free with respect to the logics of perception because the same thing could be apperceived today with boredom and tomorrow with happiness, it is nonetheless closely related to it and the idea of affective responses is not without foundation. But when the work of art impresses itself on, together, our power to perceive and our power to feel, no law bears down on the constitution of the affective field with the rigor of laws that bear down on the constitution of perceptual fields. Rather, a single law comes to bear here: that of "attraction." Yet *where* does the work attract us? The question must not be posed without prudence. To the rush of affective responses, in reality, it is only (and perhaps by definition) the moving outline of a field that confronts us. This field is instituted only by the phenomena of attraction, or of captivation, and these phenomena are nevertheless only liminary. The field will be truly constituted only when the work will have convoked for me, whether wholly or in part, the non-apparent that it can make appear. It will constitute itself most frequently by partial convocation, by determination and diminishment of the possible. If the work manifests our relation to our native earth, it will not manifest what else it could manifest—for example, the pathetic fate of the mortal of whom there remains for us only a pair of shoes. In any case, evidence is not primary. The work of art is certainly allotted a mode of presence that is a mode of evidence, and this is said well enough by the emphatic formulation of Heidegger: the work of art renders as non-being every other being than itself. To consent to this evidence still does not suffice to decide affectively the ultimate meaning that this appearance reveals, or reveals for me. One does not need to tell Heidegger that the possible overflows the real.

But in the interpretation on trial here, the real—under the species of the highly determined affective field of "earthly" experience—certainly does violence to the possible.

The perpetual threat of error is not enigmatic: beyond error about the thing, there is error about the logic of feeling. The life of affects is cognitive. Still, one must, in order to support a thesis at once both healthy and violent, avert the objection that necessarily proceeds from the complex relations of affection and perception. There is neither affection without perception, nor perception without affection. There is no perception without affection, because the notion of it is abstract and because description is valid only if this abstraction is recognized and mastered. And there is no affection without perception because feeling may not be dissociated from the life of meaning, and because here too the abstraction must be known. *Being and Time* proposes, incontestably, a phenomenology of affect indifferent to every phenomenology of perception, where everything can excite the phenomena of anxiety, non-inhabitation, and so on, because these phenomena reveal the pure fact of being-in-the-world, of which the affect can be grasped always and everywhere. Now, in redistributing the existential topic of manifestation, Heidegger's essay on the work of art forces one to recognize that there was indeed abstraction there (it is certainly the world as such that gives rise to anxiety, but there are anguishing situations, etc.), and thus to render to feeling its rootedness in a flesh that it is not certain can perceive the world or the earth, but which in any case perceives things that command or permit the affect to recognize the existence of the world and the earth. Again, one must not ignore the suppleness of the relation, and the relative independence of affective understanding with respect to sensible understanding. The true problem is not that Heidegger wished to hasten the appearance of the earth, but that the affective field of earthly experience constitute itself perfectly well on the basis of a failure of perception, or more modestly upon that of an uncertain perception of what it "truly" perceives, and that entrusts itself to two heterogeneous facts: the phenomenon and a factual error about what the painting is supposed to furnish the image of. Concerning the complement of appearing born of the work, one can provisionally understand that in the work, it falls to a thing to bring out the meaning of its beingness, the horizon in which it is what it is. The work is perceived in order to be felt, perceived-and-felt. The horizon, in contrast, is not perceived; and, if it is only felt, this could thus always be because the affect is misled by the enrootedness of its own field in the perceptual field. The philosophical lesson of Heidegger's imprudence is thus of primary importance. If a vital relation to the "earth" defines each of us, and not only the Black Forest peasant, no one can be surprised that the life of affects lets this relation appear without reason, in the same manner that anxiety shows without reason the existence of the world: in order for the world and earth to appear, it suffices that they "exist." And yet, if, as *Being and Time* tells us, the world must appear to us, and if, as the essay on the work of art tells us, the earth must appear to us, they could not co-appear: the appearance of the world will blur that of the earth, and the appearance of the earth will prohibit that of the world, or will in any case limit it to the appearing of an "opening" without present affective charge. Of the "least of things," however little it obsesses us, we can thus expect that it lets what is most important show itself—the relations that unite us to everything, to "the being [*étant*] in its totality." Nonetheless, we cannot expect that it works at the simultaneous manifestation of all these relations. When the earth is manifest, the world slips into the background; when the world is manifest, the earthly dimension of experience becomes inapparent. And if the least of things and *a fortiori* the work of art, which is the thing truer than any other, is given to an ability to feel that is affected by a fundamental duality, no pressure of things on affective life could put an end to this duality or this duplicity. The primary phenomenological meaning of the affect is to make the world or the earth appear. On this account, every making-appear is inseparably true and partial.

Heidegger's hermeneutical mistake would thus consist in failing to perceive the strange relation between manifestation and ambiguity, or let us say in not having perceived that ambiguity can be the truth. When this ambiguity is recognized, his error about the thing (i.e., the van Gogh) ceases to burden the analysis. It is always possible to adopt the defensive strategy that would think to annul the error by saying that the earth certainly can appear as such through the mediation of a work that brings to presence a thing that is essentially "urban." But to this, it would be necessary to oppose a description that neutralizes the affective resonances. Van Gogh's painting is neither an "image of the earth" nor an "image of the world" because it can make either of the two appear. The few phrases with which the philosopher describes the phenomena that show through by the grace of the work are, in the final account, too brief. Identified as a "pair of peasant shoes," the work stimulates the affective appearance of the country path, the toil that makes it yield its earthly fruits, the nearby farmhouse, where rest will be given, and so on. Now this appearance is not more than inchoate, and remains far from permitting one to think that the presence of all of that has already decided the sense of being. If it is necessary to provide man with a dwelling place, if being-in must be qualified as inhabiting, then the familiar representations that flow spontaneously from the pen of the thinker from Fribourg can serve as a symbolic thread leading into philosophical work. For familiar that they are, and whatever might be their spontaneous power of evocation, it would still be naïve to think that the phenomena of the earth, the dwelling place, and so on, are essentially bound to them. The earth is everywhere and the world is everywhere. Heidegger knows this. But he forgets it during the time he writes a few lines, and even if he has good reason to forget it, this is what gives one cause to think.

What must be thought can be said quite simply, first in conceptual terms and next in experiential terms. (1) World and earth are co-given (their differend is the a priori according to which being is given), and the thought that is preoccupied with the earth risks forgetting the world, just as the thought preoccupied with the world leaves the earth unseen. In effect, the earth—when the word becomes a concept, thus when it designates a phenomenon that must be made to appear in order to bring to light what we are—does not impose itself as a unique horizon. It does not impose itself as a horizon at all, for that matter, since it is a soil that is always present, since the language in which to greet its appearance is that of rootedness. A world has only the being that has an earth, and only the being who exists on the earth is in the world. The evident refinement of the analysis is thus not without risk, and the risk is of making only the earth appear, forgetting the world. Are we witness to such a forgetting when the hasty reading of van Gogh is proposed to us? It is tempting to think so. It is not phenomenologically illicit, but phenomenologically banal and fruitful, to make only this or only that appear, to let only a single "thing" appear at one time. Still, it is necessary that the description concentrating itself on a single thing not persuade itself unduly that only this thing exists. And it remains necessary, above all, that this thing be able to appear alone while appearing in its truth. What, then, would be the exactness of an appearance of the earth that does not sanction the co-appearing of the world? (2) The description would be inexact because it gives figure to an essential play of return (*renvoi*). The painting speaks to us of the human condition, and with all the more authority because man himself is visibly absent; its logic is not that of *mimèsis* but of the index. A full reading of the index would thus sanction the ambiguity of the beginning. Rootedness in the earth or "fallenness" (*Verfallenheit*) in the world? The alternative is in fact erroneous, because it would have us believe in the existence of two regions of experience when it is really a matter of two faces of the same experience. Feeling can certainly not be grasped simultaneously from one and the other. Is it, for all of that, too simple or naïve to suppose that it lives from an oscillation as much as it lives from the determination of affective fields? Here and now, we cannot make the double experience of anxiety *and* of joy, or of boredom *and* serenity, for example. The peaceful and laborious belonging to the earth (or any analogous experience) still does not safeguard against the menaces of anxiety or mal-aise. Anxiety and mal-aise (and with them all the experiences that reveal the phenomenon of the world), if the "earth" is as originary as the "world," are for their part equally menaced by the ineffacable presence of the earth. In principle, nothing prevents us from admitting (though it would still be necessary to prove it to some degree) that the pressures of the work of art on affective life solicit the constitution of one affective field rather than another: the fascination exercised by one of Piranese's engravings cannot certainly convoke an experience of the earth . . . The true objection emerging against the Heideggerian reading of the van Gogh is in any case quire precise: no other truth is in fact disclosed there than that of an ambivalence. Before the pathetic spectacle of a man of whom only two shoes appear, we are not mistaken if we feel only the vanity of life lived in the world. But we are no more mistaken if we allow the work to evoke everything that permits to also have, on the earth, a dwelling place. Through the magic of the work, both of these are present to us. The hermeneutical sin would thus be of rendering one inattentive to this double presence.[17]

VI

The secret of all art would be "poetic diction," and it is thus advisable to note that such a diction contrasts with any common economy of saying, for the good reason that it perpetually critiques every understanding that responds to it. Insofar as it participates in a logic of representation, the work of art certainly binds us to a univocal language: it is the latter that the painting represents, and not the former; and, if one refuses to agree with what it represents, one thus sanctions, at one and the same time, hermeneutical anarchy and anarchy of the affect. Yet, because the interpretation must, to avoid the risk of partiality, return to the primordial possibilities of affective life, it must therefore also recognize that the univocity of representation does not in any case guarantee the constitution of a unique affective field. Perception gives itself to feeling, but feeling is ambivalent. If the work must be more than the occasional cause of a manifestation of our pure power of feeling (and if it is not that, then it would be better not to read Heidegger . . .), then its "truth" must have the force of constraint. The work does not only make things appear in their truth, but also makes them "over-appear" (*surapparaître*). However, it would be a mistake to attribute to this over-appearing—to the bare fact of over-appearing, whichever work makes it—the power of constituting our active response. In order to end with the conceptual apparatus of the aesthetic (that is, with the conceptual apparatus in which a "subject" measures its "object"), the essay on the work of art thinks the work beginning from itself. A single word, *overflow*, must thus be pronounced (and indeed, it is pronounced: *Überfluss*). 18 There is no mystery in this word. In the final account, it names the critique, by the work of art, of the restriction that it exercises on the experience it stimulates. The language chosen is that of truth, but must also be that of overflowing. The work of art gives, and gives first of all to feeling (even if it finally appears necessary to say that it gives as essentially to thinking as to feeling). At the same time, the givenness—and this is, to be sure, the *articulus stantis et cadentis* of the Heideggerian interpretation, and of any interpretation that takes its point of departure there—exceeds what receives it in the perceiving and feeling ego that we must undoubtedly place between parentheses for the good health of our analyses, even if it does not evidently cease to be the addressee of the work. This work is this *or* that, not this *and* that. Either the life of affects is consistent with the work of perception (as well as with the pure work of knowledge), or it becomes futile to bind its working and truth. The true difficulty remains, and in a certain sense Heidegger responds to a problem that he has posed only obliquely. The work is not an event of the truth in re-presenting what was already present, but in conferring a presence. That to which it confers presence is the thing itself, but the "itself" of things includes everything that is symbolically and affectively knotted around them. Ultimately, none of this is measured by the present of a perception and the aim of a subject.

If we so loosen, in preliminary fashion, the presence of the work from the perceptive/affective reception that we reserve for it, we do nothing else than bind presence and surplus. The being of the work announces itself in its appearing, but it thwarts the idea—or the dream—of total comprehension. At any rate, we know, having learned it from Husserl, that "adequate perception" does not exist: we will never perceive something under all its aspects in the synchrony of a single gaze (and this could also be said of what appears to us in a non-visible mode). It is necessary to add that there is likewise no adequate affective comprehension. There are good affective responses (in the face of the odious, horror imposes itself; in the face of honesty, respect imposes itself). But just as everything is always given to be perceived from a perspective, so no affect can respond to everything that gives itself to feeling (the odious can also submit to an affective neutralization—which is still a mode of affective comprehension—and be viewed with detachment; honesty can be suspected of being only a tactic; etc.), and so *a fortiori* the work of art cannot be apprehended in a comprehensive (all-encompassing) manner. The whole—the patent truth—does not open itself without remainder. Affection is partial, and this is not by deficit: its powerlessness to feel everything actually honors the superabundance of what appears to it.

Over-appearance: the term is thus permissible, and it ceases to be the pre-conceptual index of the wonderment excited in us by a masterpiece, only if it serves *first of all* to think the limits of comprehension. We cannot accept the language of truth without also accepting the language of verification. Because the work of art is also an object, we cannot disqualify the understanding that deals with it objectively, and whose fruits will never be negligible: we cannot refuse to know what the painting represents exactly, or refuse to know the instruments for which a musical score has been written, and so on. Yet, because it is a matter here of the "splendor" of the true, verification happens in the element of affect; and, if it is possible for us to determine the conditions by which the affect "deceives" us (the painting might stimulate malaise because it awakens disagreeable memories in us, even though those memories say nothing of the painting itself) or "tells the truth" (the phenomenological leitmotiv of a grasp of things in themselves and in the manner of their appearing certainly imposes a *task* on us, but the task is not truly unrealizable), all verification is thus dedicated to a certain partiality—and if we refuse to acknowledge this, and above all think it, we are mistaken about the truth that we are to verify here. There is cognitive force in the affect, for the simple reason that the phenomenon of the work of art is a phenomenon-for-affect, because the work is perceived only in order to be felt. The truth debated here is debated in the mode of theory, but its advent is not for the sake of *theôria*. However, the affect can exercise its power of knowing (of verification) only restrictively, maintaining as unknown (leaving unverified) some regions of the knowable to which its aim presents the closure, or leaves sealed.

There is thus a problem that, as the present juncture, it is possible only to indicate. Nothing appears without possessing evidence, but what appears is marked with the seal of the habitual (and by "habitual" one must undoubtedly understand more than the "everydayness" that *Being and Time* describes: the world of habit is the world where the work of art is absent, and habitual experience is the experience that has already seized a thousand truths, but it also does not know the truth that is put in play by the work of art). At the heart of the book from 1927 there figured the idea of a person "in" the truth; at the heart of the essay on the work of art is that of a person who "faces" a process of contingent manifestation, and what this process offers such a person is more than the non-illusory presence of things. The working of the real imposes a detour: it is the case not only that "the work belongs, as work, only to the realm that is opened up by itself,"[19] but also that it is through access to this domain that we see the appearing of the true. The truth of things is not outside them; but their most proper appearance is, in a certain manner, outside them. One does not go from the thing present in the world of habit to the thing put to work, as if one from truth to another, or as if from "appearance" to the phenomenological reality of appearing—and it is for this reason that it is necessary to speak of "over-appearance." But which gaze, or which feeling, could do justice to the over-appearing? The philosopher is himself capable, but must not be taken at his word, because it is he who *thinks* the experience of the gaze and of the affect, and especially because his interpretive work always risks saying more than it does not say about a gaze and a feeling for which the work of art is a figure of the incomprehensible. When we deal experientially with the complement of appearing, it is indeed an excess that we strike up against. Not only is the work "more present" than the rest of the things, but it is even in some sense too present. It is the phenomenological object par excellence, the object to which there could be no possibility of attributing a being that would not also be an appearing. But it is also the object whose appearance informs us, in exemplary fashion, of our incapacity to grasp the totality of what appears. The work of art is that being whose appearance "nihilates" (*néantise*) every other being. When it appears, it appears alone, and it is the only being there: over-appearing makes everything else dis-appear. We can respond to its appearance, it seems, only with the authority of perception and feeling that also underwrite our response to every other appearance. The surplus of appearing satisfies, in principle, the desire to see everything and feel everything. And yet, the question arises: under what conditions could we think the presence of a person to the work that would correspond to the surplus of the presence of the work? In the face of this question, one might see that the texts do not leave us without an answer. Instead of sorting it out, or perhaps in order to better manage that task one day, we now propose a perspective: that of a phenomenology interested in *liturgy*.

VII

To the paradoxes of the affect, liturgical experience—the logic of being-before-God—first opposes its own paradoxes: the paradox of an experience suspicious of feeling to the point of constituting itself as non-experience, as night of feeling; the paradox of a critique of being-in in the name of a being-toward that blurs every topology; the paradox of an ipseity that refuses to constitute itself on the basis of a metaphysics of subjectivity and wishes to leave the way clear to a passivity more originary than any intentionality. As for the paradoxes analyzed in interpreting the work, it seems that the paradoxes of liturgy throw no light on them whatsoever. Undoubtedly, there are parallels to be found here and there. Just as the work of art gives itself in an *aisthèsis* resistant to any recruitment by aesthetics, so the Absolute is perceived, on the hither side of death, only in spiritual gestures resistant to any recruitment by theories of religious experience, whether the latter is associated with the posterity of pietism and of Schleiermacher or of James. Just as the work of art crystallizes the real in giving itself as still more real, and just as poetic speech "renders the being more being," so liturgy (at once as *esse coram Deo* and as cultic practice) summons beings—bread, wine, water, fire, human body, etc.—in endowing them with a complement of appearing, or if one wishes, a complement of presence. But what would this be? A little bread and wine, two worn shoes: would these be similar cases, caught in a same logic of over-appearance or over-manifestation? This is not certain, and for a reason that would merit prudent consideration, though perhaps it can be mentioned schematically.

We would thus say that the nocturnal (non-experiential) face of liturgy permits taking leave of a certain type of appearance (or pseudo-appearance) in feeling, but that liturgy can also anticipate a great light. In the time of the world, it teaches us that its profound logic is not first of all one of an affect perpetually certain of what affects it, but that of a death of feeling: that of faith, understood in its strictest sanjuanist sense. But in the time of the world, liturgy also holds us to a second language, which is that of a resurrection of feeling. Resurrection of the flesh—one cannot manage such a concept (or such "news") without confessing that the affect, too, can be resuscitated and, who knows, participate henceforth in its own resurrection. In the essay on the work of art, and in other texts, it is an eschatology of beingness that Heidegger proposes; and if one is to perceive the coherence of this proposition, the only practicable course returns to the play (transcendental, "initial") of the world, the earth, and their appearance in the life of affects (thus, their appearance in all the forms of *Befindlichkeit*). Now this play is not the only one in which we are capable of participating. Here and now, we can also taste a well-being-there, a comfort (*aise*), which leads to the margins of the world and the earth and recalls our creation. Here and now, we can also taste a joy that shatters the

Jean-Yves Lacoste

limits of the world, the earth, and all of the "initial" life of affects. This joy, in order to be pre-*eschatological*, is not, therefore, any less *pre*-eschatological. It does not institute the definitive, and it does not live from a present realization of the *eschaton*. But, in gestures that implicate our body, and that also implicate some things chosen among all the things of the earth—bread, wine, water, fire, and still more—it is indeed a matter of perceiving and even tasting the definitive. Art renders a being more a being, but it does not make the world less a world, and it does not make time lead elsewhere than death. Liturgy, in contrast, tells us that world and earth can be placed between parentheses. It says that the liturgical use of certain things (and here one must give the term *things* the strong sense given to it by Heidegger, in his later texts) contributes to this placing between parentheses. And it says that this placing between parentheses does not imply a certain death of feeling without also giving it the anticipated space of a resurrection—without giving it the "deposits" (*arrhes*) of the life that will not pass.

NOTES

1. [A crucial stake in the present essay, as indeed in the essay by Heidegger which it takes up, is to be found in the relation between the more substantive sense commonly assigned to the word *work* as it appears in *work of art* (*œuvre d'art*) and a more verbal sense in which the work of art *works* (*œuvre*), intervening in the manifestation of being as beings, or in the appearing of appearances. Lacoste's original title for this essay, *Mis en œuvre et complément d'apparaître*, makes it plain that this latter sense will be highlighted here. This has been difficult to render consistently in smooth English, but the reader is advised that, with few exceptions, familiar expressions like *set to work* or *put in play*, have been set aside in favor of the simpler "work." It has been thought that this decision in favor of simplicity is licensed by the manner in which the context generally makes plain the author's specific intention.—*Translator*]

2. M. Heidegger, "The Origin of the Work of Art," trans. A. Hofstadter, in M. Heidegger, *Poetry, Language, Thought* (New York: Harper and Row, 1971), p. 72. The original German text is "Der Ursprung des Kunstwerkes," in M. Heidegger, *Holzwege*, *Gesamtausgabe*, vol. V (Frankfurt: Klostermann, 1977), p. 59. [This text is henceforth cited as *Origin*, with the English reference followed by reference to Heidegger's original German. This order of citation will be followed with all of Heidegger's texts, and the latter will always be to the pagination appearing in the margins of the *Gesmatausgabe* editions. The translations have sometimes been slightly modified to preserve the flow of Lacoste's text.—*Translator*].

3. "To the degree (. . .) that one descends in the hierarchy of being, to the common flint which thinks nothing, says nothing, does nothing save be something that is, one comes to the point where, because there is nothing else to see, it is impossible to remain blind to this evidence that all beings are, without exception, even if they are nothing else, at least this—that they are" (*Constantes philosophiques de l'être*, Paris: Vrin, 1983, p. 146). To be sure, Heidegger himself affirms the fundamental equality of all beings with respect to being: "An elephant in an Indian jungle 'is' just as much as some chemical combustion process at work on the planet Mars, and so on." M. Heidegger, *An Introduction to Metaphysics*, trans. R. Mannheim (New Haven: Yale University

Press, 1959), p. 3; *Einfuhrung in die Metaphysik, Gesamtausgabe,* vol. 40 (Frankfurt: Klostermann, 1983), p. 3. But not all furnish the same elements of response, and we speak here only of diversity of responses. For a critique of the ontological presuppositions in the analyses furnished by Gilson in *Peinture et réalité* (Paris: Vrin, 1972[2]), see E. Martineau, *Malévitch et la philosophie* (Lausanne: L'âge d'homme, 1953), p. 38.

4. Cf. *a contrario* Gilson, for a vision of art as capacity to "increase the number of [real] things" (*Peinture et réalité,* p. 330). Space "offers itself to the painter as absence of the being which he has, to speak thus, the vocation of producing, in order to not let pass an occasion to increase the real without taking advantage of it" (Ibid., 199).

5. Heidegger, *An Introduction to Metaphysics* 35/27.

6. *Origin* 71/59.

7. On the Husserl/Heidegger differend concerning truth, see always the classic thesis of E. Tugendhat, *Der Wahrheitsbegriffe bei Husserl und Heidegger* (Berlin: W. de Gruyter, 1970[2]).

8. F. Alquié, *La conscience affective* (Paris: P.U.F., 1979), p. 132.

9. *Origin* 72/59.

10. Ibid, 72/60.

11. On this, see J.-Y. Lacoste, *Le monde et l'absence d'œuvre* (Paris: P.U.F., 2000), pp. 67–77.

12. On such a topic, cf. the analyses of O. Becker, *Dasein und Dawesen, Gesammelte philosophische Aufsätze* (Pfullingen: G. Neske, 1963), especially pp. 11–40 and 67–102; and O.F. Bollnow, *Das Wesen der Stimmungen* (Frankfurt: Klostermann, 1956).

13. *Origin* 74–75/62.

14. *Origin* 75/62.

15. J. Derrida, "Restitutions. On the Truth in Painting," in *The Truth in Painting,* trans. G. Bennington and I. McLeod (Chicago: The University of Chicago Press, 1987), pp. 255f.

16. Ibid., 260.

17. In his interpretation of Kandinsky (*Voir l'invisible,* Paris: F. Bourin, 1988), Michel Henry furnishes a good means to avoid this sin: to conceive that "art [. . .] does not represent anything: neither world, nor force, nor affect, nor life" (p. 208), and that its proper power is of giving feeling to "life," "invisible life spread everywhere under the envelop of things and sustaining them in being" (p. 229). "To make felt everything that can be felt, to make experienced everything that can be experienced, all the forces of our being which one will see are also all the forces of the cosmos, such is the ambition of abstract painting" (pp. 98–99). To express life, understood as "the Night of this abyssal subjectivity where no ray of light could ever filter down, which no dawn could ever dissipate" (p. 24), such would be the true power of the work. For a reading very close to the "original chaos" of affective life, see what we have said about these constitutions, de-constitutions, and reconstitutions of the world in *Le monde et l'absence d'œuvre,* pp. 85–101.

18. *Origin* 75/62.

19. *Origin* 41/30.

Affective Theology, Theological Affectivity

Adriaan T. Peperzak

Complaints about "the God of the philosophers" have become commonplace. But why should we care? Have we not agreed that philosophy is secular through and through?[1] What about theology, however? Is its God better? Is its God more desirable, admirable, lovable, adorable? In order to be true, the God of theology should be as inspiring as the God of meditation, prayer, and devotion. Do we experience such an inspiring God while reading theological works? If so, does this mean that they are written in a spirit akin to the classics of contemplation? If not, what causes their deficiency?

Theological classics—and all theologians who continue the premodern tradition of Christian *theologia*—express a double allegiance: while instructing the community to which they belong, they meditate on the God who brought them together with other Christians. Theology is a kerygmatic charisma within their church and, as apologetics, it is a public enterprise in the culture of their surroundings. Within their community of faith, their speaking is directed to the assembly, but as a response to God's revealing deeds and words, it is also directed to God. Responsivity *coram Deo* and responsibility for the faithful community mark their language. Both orientations have a dialogical structure; however, is this structure not frequently obfuscated by an overwhelming *speaking about* without end?

I. Theology

Following the development of western theory and logic, theology has become systematic and objective, instead of remaining contemplative, anagogic, and mystical. Many Christians regret this development; but are they capable of returning to the contemplative forms of thinking and teaching practiced in pre-modern times? Can they overcome the objectifying character of theology without losing the benefits of universally valid and anti-subjectivistic thought? The following reflections focus on the dialogical and responsive character of authentic contemplation. In particular, they emphasize some affective moments of any attempt to honor God as a "living God."

II. Speaking

Science, literature, philosophy, and theology are modes of speaking (or writing) about things, persons, events, or other issues. Speaking can be done in many ways: by allusion or suggestion, narratively or evocatively, in a meditative or instructive manner, in letters, treatises, or prayers. Science and modern philosophy have insisted on the objectivity of their observation and thought. They study objects and try to capture data in the empirical and conceptual nets of their objectifying approach. A specific attitude is required for such an approach: instead of being biased by "subjective" preferences or presuppositions, one should be neutral and interested only in those truths that can be recognized as universally valid by all other unprejudiced intellectuals. The overall perspective is panoramic: the universe is given to an Archimedean point of view; its truth demands a freestanding location from which the universe can be observed. If involvement is unavoidable, one should, as much as possible, try to bracket one's own interests to concentrate on the "objective" (i.e., un- or universally interesting) reality alone.

"Objectivity" is the result of a *particular*—and thus unilateral—attitude. To proclaim that the "objective" attitude is the only one worthy of truth would thus be the greatest bias. Once caught in the objectifying attitude, one does not see or hear or taste or smell or feel any other aspects than those that characterize ob-jects: things that can be posited, displayed, collected, numbered, dis-assembled, reconstructed, and so on. It is, however, obvious that many phenomena do not fit into the framework of objectivity: for example, expression, smiling, speaking, thinking, confidence, friendship, engagement, concentration, actions, motivations, persons, and least of all, God.

Amazingly, the specialists of objective thought seldom notice that their own speaking and writing show a different structure than their subject–object model tries to make us believe. In talking *about* certain phenomena, they adjust them to certain parameters of the objectifying game, but in doing so, they cannot prevent themselves from *speaking to* others. Their interest in objects is caught in another kind of interest: what they have discovered *about* their topic must be told, offered, handed over, *communicated to* and *shared with* other interested people.

There is no way to reduce speaking—or, in general, communication—to some form of the relation between a subject and an object. As *addressed* to another person, speaking is similar to giving, facing, greeting, turning toward, devotion, service, and other manners of addressing, all of which approach someone not as a "direct object" or "accusative," but instead as a "dative." An addressee is not an object. The addressee, the act of addressing, and the "addresser" disappear from our awareness as soon as we, in the science of philosophy, concentrate exclusively on the objective features of the person in front of us. We then no longer face this person; if we speak, we speak *about* her *to* someone else; we are no longer involved in a personal relationship with her, although we might know many truths about her body and mind.[2]

Modern phenomenology has made us aware of several intentionalities other than the objectifying ones, but I am not aware of any exhaustive descriptions of the intentionalities that are suggested to us by *all* kinds of phenomenality. The descriptions of such phenomena as facing and being faced, greeting, addressing, giving, honoring, thanking, forgiving, and so on, especially remain quite underdeveloped, even though worthwhile beginnings toward remedying that situation have been made.[3] And yet, are such phenomena not more revealing of human existence—in that they include religion, devotion, and faith—than all the objective, useful, and aesthetic phenomena that have been described and analyzed at length? Philosophy will have hardly begun so long as we do not know what, for example, greeting, praising, and thanking are. Does theology already know what these things are?

Speaking can be understood as a metaphor for all kinds of addressing, even those that originate in non-human phenomena. Dogs and birds, flowers and trees, even things and machines can speak to us, as many fables, myths, and poets have demonstrated. *All* the phenomena of the universe can be perceived as addressing us, each in its own characteristic way. The analysis of speaking may, therefore, offer us a universal paradigm to clarify the essence of phenomenality as such. If everything "speaks" to us, we are invited to "respond" to such "speech." Which kind of openness and perception, and which attitudes and reactions are suggested by the various instances and dimensions of this amazing universe?[4]

When I hear someone speak to me, I am forced to react: even silence is an answer, though such a reaction might express my contempt or anger or indifference. Speaking thus necessarily generates a response. If the response is spoken, the roles are reversed, marking the beginning of a dialogue. To speak is to be engaged in an exchange of questioning and responding. Appropriate responses try to honor (i.e., try to do justice) to a preceding address, and each response is a new provocation to new exchanges.

Several often neglected features of speaking are remarkable. First, no language as system, structure, or text clarifies its mobilization through the speaking or writing of its author or interpreter. No text says anything unless a speaker brings the text to life. Second, no one can speak unless other speakers have spoken to him or her. How, otherwise, would we have learned to speak? The history of speaking does not seem to have a beginning; when speaking, we vary an ongoing tradition thanks to which we can communicate with other participants of the same tradition and, at least to some extent, with people of other traditions.

An ethics of speaking could begin by reflecting on the correspondence inaugurated and demanded by any address. How do I respond appropriately to your turning to me in saying "Hello" or some other word(s)? Appropriateness is a form of doing justice to that which confronts and provokes us. My response should be fitting, befitting, adequate, decent, appropriate. The address suggests—albeit vaguely—the contours of a fitting response, even if it leaves much to the addresser's trial and error. It excludes certain attitudes (for example, the objectification of both the speaker and the addressee) and indicates some properies of a respectful answer. Most often, however, it leaves several answers open. *Correspondence* could be a name for the perfect relationship between a phenomenon and the way it is accepted, perceived, and allowed to exist and manifest itself.

The preceding remarks are much too sketchy to provide a phenomenology and ethics of speaking, but presumably they are sufficient as introduction to an analysis of the dialogical and communicative structure that, somewhat similar to the structure just indicated, characterizes human affectivity.

III. Affective Correspondence

To be exhaustive, phenomenology would have to pay attention to all phenomena that compose the universe. But do all phenomena deserve attention? If a phenomenon draws our attention, it must be interesting, at least to some extent. A complete description of its being would therefore include a characterization of the mode in which it has awakened our interest. The fact that it is perceived as interesting shows that it has some (real or putative) worth or value for us. *Value* is therefore an aspect of all phenomena that succeed in drawing our attention.

Every phenomenon has its own characteristic appearance and interesting worth. It is the task of phenomenology to describe accurately and distinguish the entire variety of manners in which all types and instances of things and persons, situations, and occurrences draw our attention by being worthwhile. If such a reconnaissance of the universe is to succeed, we will have acquired an overview of "the many ways in which a being is."[5]

The most immediate dimension of our contact with the phenomena is affective experience. Phenomena affect us: in confronting them or being involved in phenomenal constellations, we are "touched." To be touched or impressed or affected is not a mere sensation, however; it is a challenge—e.g., in the form of a shock or a temptation: the phenomenon invites me to welcome its appearance through an appropriate affect and already suggests the manner of such a reaction. To perceive what and how something *is*, I must be open to it: it wants to be taken for what it shows itself to be. Whether a thing or person will be allowed to display its own being or, rather, will be distorted or mistaken for something else depends on our attitude. Not all phenomena are beautiful or welcome, but even the monstrous invite an appropriate (albeit negative) response. Affection is our basic form of response. The mixture of splendor and horror that fills the universe provokes the mixtures of our affectivity: admiration and horror, enthusiasm and anxiety, sympathy and avoidance, hope and fear, desire and hatred, in many shades and degrees correspond to the phenomena's many modes of impressing on us.

When myth and fables and poems evoke the "speaking" of birds and trees or the ocean and the sky, they emphasize the "dialogic" that structures our dealing with the phenomena. Even on the level of immediate moods and emotions, we are summoned to respond to the provocation of beings that emerge. Correspondence seems to be the law for all levels of our dealing with the universe.

The appropriateness of our responses to the phenomena that "speak" to us includes not only openness and sensitivity, but also adjustment and attunement. Some appearances suggest joy; others call for anger or fear; still others make us fall in love. Emotional perfection presupposes accuracy and proportion; it heeds and respects, without understatement or exaggeration, all that comes to the fore. It does justice to the various forms and values that characterize each being's manifestation or concealment. It admires or abhors the *aisthetically* revealed *ousia* or *idea* of all occurrences.[6] Each thing, person, or event demands an emotional response that fits and befits its challenge.

The fact that each phenomenon contains a demand becomes clear when we realize that our affections are accompanied by a self-critical feeling that tests their degree of authenticity. On all levels of our awareness, experience *evaluates itself* as soon as it takes shape. Emotions are a good example: while being angry or enthusiastic about something, I am already beginning to feel whether my reaction is genuine or feigned, justified, proportionate or exaggerated, or otherwise failing in "justice."

With regard to our surroundings (our home and workplace, and the universe insofar as it concerns us), our affective response, rather than being a constellation of particular emotions, consists in a general and diffuse attunement or *Stimmung*, or mood, that is so deep and permeating that we are most often not aware of it. We are in touch with the world by feeling ourselves involved in it, by being tuned and attuned to its rhythms and colors. In its difference from particular emotions, a basic mood is the way in which we let the universe attune us.

If perfect appropriation does justice to the phenomena, while many emotions in fact miss, mute, or exaggerate their appeal, an ethics of emotions and moods is necessary. How do we learn to be affectionately accurate, mature, and just? What is a well-attuned mood if we have to live in this world that is neither hell nor paradise?

Appropriation is not a one-sided task. Neither the human subject nor the phenomena are sovereign in producing a determinate adjustment. Phenomena, too, can be primitive, underdeveloped, deficient, evil, or horrible. What affects us, moves us. For example, a block of marble may suggest that this material should be reshaped into a more harmonious form. Or the sight of a limping dog might move me to take care of its healing. Or the physical atmosphere of a house might be so depressing that we want to change its windows and furniture. Or someone who shows a mixture of talent and lack of skill might make us wish to provide him or her with a higher level of education.

When a thing or situation suggests that I change it, my motion and motivation should follow the orientation that seems indicated by that situation or thing. My intervention is normal and "natural" if it allows the challenging phenomenon to unfold in a "natural," "normal," or even "ideal" way. Such a response would at the same time realize my dealing with the world in a proportionate manner. Correspondence can thus lead to peace and harmony. However, harmony and peace in the face of horrible actions or events are impossible without an appropriate degree of enmity and counterviolence. An ethics of our dealing with evil would prescribe appropriate expressions of anger and hatred. Justice includes the courage of an honest fight.

IV. Desire

Nothing could move me if were I not sensitive to its motivating force. What makes me obey its challenge? Of all phenomena that interest us, it can be said that they, at least to some extent, motivate us to an active involvement with them. But how could we be motivated toward such activity without moving ourselves, and how could we move ourselves without desire? Of each and every phenomenon that touches us, it can be said that it "moves by being desired" (*kinei hōs erōmenon*).[7]

Desire (*erōs*) is the motor of all we do, but it would not move us were it not awakened by a call from elsewhere. We are not even aware of many desires until some desirable phenomenon reveals to us that we have "always already" wanted it. Do we know—can we ever know—what we ultimately and originarily Desire? The fact that the ultimate Desideratum differs from the desiderata that correspond to the multiplicity of our desires, needs, wants, and inclinations becomes obvious through the endless repetition of disappointments that accompany our most satisfactory experiences. Though we find pleasure, joy, delight, and even bliss in the happy moments of our lives, all these findings at the same time testify that we have not yet found the ultimately Sought. The Desideratum does not show up among the phenomena of the universe, and the universe is not desirable enough for the insatiable passion that devours us. What we thus desire "in the end" and originarily reveals its desirability through the many desirable ends and "objects" that seem to promise it but then, in full experience, disappoint that passion. The Desirable is what we continually seek, but it is never found. The fact that it hides and withdraws before our seeking does not disprove its reality—on the contrary, it shows how infinitely open and *erotic* we are—but it teaches us that seeking itself, if done correctly, is the way of coming closer to the Sought.[8]

What, then, is the correct method of the quest? Since we want to focus here on human affectivity, our first question regards the role of moods, affections, and emotions in the approach of God.

If it is true that all phenomena of the universe show themselves to us as somehow desirable or undesirable, what then makes them so? A tree, a girl, the sun, the light, a friend, the beloved, beauty, love itself, justice, and so on, impress us as admirable and attractive, tempting, worthy of love—enjoyable. On the contrary, war, violence, and greed confront us with the destructive presence of evil, and awaken our scorn and wrath. Why do we enjoy or abhor certain phenomena? Let us concentrate first on the enjoyable ones. If we welcome them in the right way, they content us and make us feel at home, capable, growing in knowledge and strength, confident, reconciled, and at peace. The universe is composed of innumerable levels of forms of enjoyability. The Greek word *hēdonē* covers many primarily *qualitative* (and not only *quantitative*) differences in desirability and enjoyment. To be affected (i.e., to be touched and moved) differentiates into attraction, inspiration, enlightenment, shelter, warming, being appreciated, honored, loved, and so on. Each kind of phenomenality has its characteristic appeal; all kinds together reveal the manifold possibilities of *being* to interest and "please" us. The worthwhile features of the universe respond to the multiplicity of our desires. Do they also respond to that Desire that seems to be disappointed each time it attempts to grasp the Desirable *par excellence*—to the Orient that has no precise name because it seems to be always "more" and different than anything that can be had?

V. Analogy and Denial

Being impressed by a particular phenomenon, I experience that it does fulfill one or some of my desires, but not completely. Its desirability is not a final answer to the question that lies in my desire: while offering itself, it stresses its limitation to "only this," but "no more than this." Repeated enjoyment does not solve the question, but rather intensifies our nostalgia for a better answer. If I try to be as welcoming as possible, the enjoyable phenomenon "tries what it can," but never wholly succeeds. It thus refers to another fulfillment that is really full: fully Desirable without any disappointment. However, this referral does not reveal the essence of the Desired itself.

The reference signified by the sun, the heavens, the ocean, the mountains, the landscape, the flower, the friend, the judge, the upright, the truth, goodness, and all beauty not only refers, but also designs and expresses. As Bonaventure wrote, the phenomenal universe is a mirror (*speculum*) through which we catch glimpses of the utterly Beloved.[9] God is radiant, great, just, benevolent, powerful, and so on; nothing greater and better than God can be thought; God is the greatest, the best, the highest . . .

However, the similarity between the *highest* Good and other goods, as suggested by the phenomenal signposts of Desire, is so dissimilar—it is crossed by an abyss so "great" and deep—that no analogy survives unless it is *also*, and with even more intensity, *denied*. While embracing some being as a reflection or image or trace of the Desired *kat'exochēn*, we must experience the infinite difference that separates the Incomparable from all ("other") beings, including ourselves. This experience is the pain of never being able to grasp, see, touch, embrace, or feel the Sought itself. Such an experience is the highest or deepest form of suffering and utter disappointment. What apophatic theology does in words, affectivity experiences as an overwhelming emptiness, night, and desert. Any enjoyment of heaven and earth is then destroyed by a general disgust that hollows the phenomena. Though they continue to satisfy our needs and desires, they reveal a void, and even a horror, more profound than all splendor, a nothingness that terrifies us so long as we have not learned to risk the loss of all satisfaction. The test of Desire lies in living without, or despite or even against, all desires, i.e., in the tolerance of not being radically touched and moved by anything else than the One who makes the ultimate and original Difference. An element of extreme dissatisfaction (which cannot be chosen, but only consented to), agony, and ongoing death belongs to the emotional verification of the ultimate quest. Without any shade of it, apophatism is vainglorious, a lie.

The fact that apophatic theology and the confrontation with emptiness do not paralyze a "man or woman of desires"[10] is due to their loyalty with regard to the dynamism that defines the human way of being. A human being is an erotic animal. Only idols can stop us from searching further than the limits of the phenomenal universe, or deeper, or differently; in any case, *beyond*.

Since *beyond* is neither a spatial or temporal, nor an imaginative or conceptual determination, the dynamics of Desire keep us oriented despite our inability to represent the principle that moves us. Blindly we follow the orientation of our most original Affection. *Trahit sua quemque voluptas. Kineitai hōs erōmenos.*[11]

Beyond does not entail separation. God cannot be set off against the totality of phenomena (i.e., the finite universe), as if God were only greater, better, more *beingly* than the universe. Hegel's argument against any conception that understands the difference between the finite and the infinite as one of separation is solid: a separated infinite would be finite because it leaves something out—an other, albeit "smaller" substance: the totality of finite beings.

If the Infinitely Desirable is not opposed to the universe, it does not compete with any part of whole of it. Therefore, the affective, imaginative, conceptual, or ideal negation of the universe (which, as universe, is necessarily composed and therefore finite) cannot by itself provide the answer to the question of how we may find God. Apophatism and affective nights can only be half-truths, parasitic moments of truthful discovery. If God cannot simply coincide with the totality (which, as composed, is finite), while God's difference transcends all opposition, God is neither separate, elsewhere, absent, far from, above, or before; nor a part or element of the whole of our universe. In a very exceptional, obscure, and incomprehensible sense, God is present *in* and *as* the phenomena, whose dissimilarity hints to and darkly signifies that *presence*. The phenomena form a mirror *in* which we dimly descry God's pres-absence. Somehow, God is not outside or absent, but rather—though in an utterly uncommon sense, wholly different from any temporal or spatial presence—inside, present, and close. Neither here nor there, neither far nor close, neither separated nor identical, God determines that in us which precedes and predetermines us—our Desire—while at the same time affecting us *through* and *in* the universe. It is God's Desire in us that moves us to God's Desirability *in* and *beyond* all desirables.

In and *beyond* together define the finite infinity of the human universe. Analogy and negation, universal enjoyment and suffering, radiance and deepest obscurity together compose the mixture of "pleasure and pain" that marks the best kind of life. As mortals, we cannot escape this mixture. But who cares for "happiness," if such a mixture makes us good?

VI. Appropriate Affection

A mixture is not a synthesis. If we pursued an analysis of the *conceptual* structures involved in the mixture of analogy and apophatism, we would have to discuss Hegel's dialectical synthesis of affirmations and negations as complementary moments of the one and total Idea that originates, encompasses, and *is* the totality of the finite. As "identity of identity and non-identity,"[12] the Idea doubly unifies all differences in a contradictory attempt to think the coincidence of infinity and totality, thereby missing the incomparability of the only true Infinite.

The paradox of God's pres-absence "in" the universe does not allow for a third, higher, all-encompassing concept (a totality that would enclose God and the universe) in which the similarity and dissimilarity of the Incomparable are fully integrated. However, if it is true that both the *via affirmativa* and the *via negativa* are held together by the reference of human Desire to God's beyond, would this not indicate an *affective* answer to the question that arises from their mixture? Is a *via eminentiae* opened by the erotic dynamism itself that refers the analogical totality of the comparable to the incomparable otherness of the infinite beyond that escapes all names?

A long tradition of spiritual theology has explored the experiential quest for God as a transformative dialogue between "God and the soul."[13] This framework has not erased the natural, social, and historical world in which all "souls" are involved, but strong concentration on the adventures of the "inner" life has sometimes led to an exaggerated spiritualism. Where this danger was avoided, the world was evoked in the form of ambivalent desiderata whose God-oriented references had to be freed from their seductive potentialities by *askesis* and mortification. Among these desiderata, the most revealing was and is the human person, especially in the figure of the neighbor. Loyal to the most fundamental conviction of Christianity that love of God, love for God, love of Jesus Christ, and care for the neighbor imply one another, the "masters of spirituality" have insisted on the coincidence of their deepening union with God and their growing charity toward all human beings. However, the theological explanation of this faith and the experiences in which it unfolds have not been as elaborate as their descriptions of the moods and emotions that characterize the various stages of the affective approach to God. One of the reasons for this disproportion might lie in the underdevelopment of a philosophy that could do justice to the personality of persons by showing that encounter, respect, compassion, friendship, love, and so on, differ essentially from all our modes of dealing with impersonal realities. The aforementioned *objectifying* perspective of western philosophy, and the lack of concentration on the *dative* character of interpersonal (and other) relationships can be detected in many classical texts of theology, but a scholarly proof of the proposed diagnosis would demand several books.

VII. A Proposal

The foregoing considerations have led to a multiplicity of questions and suppositions rather than to a conclusive theory. In order to summarize the perspective from which they were formulated, I can only briefly indicate some (hypo)theses that together would constitute a sort of research program for further investigation.

(1) To find the ultimately Sought, God would have to be given, but such givenness can be granted only by God (him-, her-, it-)self. God-self must address, touch, affect, impress, and thus provoke us to an appropriate

response. In order to be touched by God's address, we should allow it to impress us—in the first place on the most immediate, affective level of our moods, passions, emotions, likings, and dispositions.

(2) God is never given in a face-to-face relationship. Divine invisibility includes our inability to hear, smell, taste, feel, intuit, or comprehend God's own presence. God's self-givenness is a hidden one, beyond senses, affects, and concepts. Does this mean that this givenness always remains foreign and absent, never close or present? No: God's "presence" is neither opposed to, nor suppressed by an immemorable past or an always-delayed future. God's "time" is different: its presence is simultaneously past and future, and therefore none of them.

(3) God-self is hiddenly given "in" and "as" our historically experienced universe (which includes the secular and religious interpretations of its meaning that constitute our heritage). Responding to God's givenness coincides with our responses to the actual situation of our universe, insofar as this profoundly hides and reveals God's creative and redeeming "presence," "past," and "future." Appropriate correspondence enables us to feel, perceive, hear, welcome, and handle all phenomenal givenness in gratitude and hope—not merely as a constellation of symbols, but as the enigma of data that call us to integrate their lovability into the infinite Desire that orients human lives. Such an integration coincides with the overall recognition of God's always-and-never-being-past, always already having come, and still coming to "presence."

(4) The givenness of the phenomena and their challenge remain ambiguous so long as our affectedness hesitates at the crossroad indicated by their enigmatic character. When the "book of nature" (with an emphasis on the personal and communal adventures of humanity) is read in light of the Scriptures and the hermeneutical illuminations of their mysterious sides, this may result in valid commentaries; but all testimonies remain empty so long as they are not authenticated by an appropriation that adjusts the speaker's moods and passions to the double presence of the immediately given but enigmatic world.

(5) Among the phenomena, you and all other persons constitute the most emphatic and enigmatic presence of the hidden *Presence* that challenges me *in* and *as* the (visible and invisible) universe. Your facing me and speaking to me is the most impressive way in which God's blinding obscurity and thundering silence calls for an appropriate response. Amazingly, the most accurate revelation of that Presence occurs in the humiliation of innocent persons who accept their passion as the sacrament of God's compassion. The human history of this compassion is the phenomenon in which God's givenness crosses the boundary between phenomenal self-sufficiency and the dimension of a very para-doxical attunement. This attunement is, first of all, a pathos. The Christian tradition of "spiritual" life has described it through a constellation of words like *acceptance, con-*

fidence, patience, kenosis, humility, sacrifice, and *mortification.* Though overuse has worn them, these words may still be resurrected, on the condition that we think their content as inseparably united with gratitude, loyalty toward the earth, enjoyment of life, and hopeful reaching out to the always already present and still desired proximity of the hidden Speech.

NOTES

1. In my essay "Philosophy-Religion-Theology" (*International Journal for Philosophy of Religion* 25 [2001]: 1–11), I try to show that, on the contrary, philosophy cannot separate itself from the religious dimension.

2. I base the foregoing on previous developments in my book *Platonic Transformations: With and After Hegel, Heidegger, and Levinas* (New York: Rowman and Littlefield, 1997), pp. 189–204, and my essay "L'addresse de la lettre," in M. M. Olivetti, ed., *Religione, Parola, Scrittura* (Padova: CEDAM, 1992), pp. 145–56.

3. My debts to Emmanuel Levinas and Martin Buber are obvious in the following pages.

4. See my "Provocation: Can God Speak Within the Limits of Philosophy? Should Philosophers Speak to God," in M. M. Olivetti, ed., *Intersubjectivity and Philosophical Theology* (Padova: CEDAM, 2001).

5. Though Aristotle, in *Meta* Γ (1003a33) focuses on the plurality of manners in which being appears for our *legein* (saying), the various ways in which it surprises our feeling and hearing should not be neglected. Being is also differently felt, heard, smelled (etc.), to be.

6. Cf. Peperzak, *Platonic Transformations,* pp. 11–14, 88–93, 104–106, 133–45.

7. Aristotle, *Meta* Λ (XII, 7, 1072b3).

8. Cf. Gregory of Nyssa, *Life of Moses* II, 163.

9. Bonaventure, *Itinerarium mentis in Deum* I, 5.

10. Ibid., Prologus, 3 end.

11. Are we still permitted to understand Virgil's desire of delight and Aristotle's moving absolute as hints in the right direction?

12. G. W. F. Hegel, *Gesammelte Werke,* vol. 4 (Hamburg: F. Meiner, 1968), p. 64.

13. E.g., St. Augustine, *Soliloquia* I, 7.

Immanent Transcendence as Way to "God"

Between Heidegger and Marion

Ignace Verhack

After Nietzsche and Heidegger, philosophy seems to have written off the metaphysical theme of an ascending desire (*eros*) for God or the divine. There are no more worlds "beyond" or "above" this one for that desire to aim at. Through the collapse of the classical responses, the human capacity for transcendence has become a riddle. And with this, so too has our human being-in-motion also become a riddle. In *Being and Time*, Heidegger takes the view that Dasein is "invested" with transcendence through its inner relation to death. The superiority of freedom is achieved at the moment when Dasein gains admission, through death, over this Dasein. And it is from here that the movement of Dasein must be understood. What Heidegger takes over from Nietzsche is the will to self-overcoming that in the Nietzschean man becomes both an undergoing and a transition. Heidegger, however, lets the perspective of newness found in Nietzsche fall away. What motivates us to move toward self-fulfillment in the free space of the "nothingness" of our transcendence? The "nothingness" of transcendence cannot be absolute emptiness. Later, Heidegger came to think of it as the "veil of being." It is a not-something that is, yes, trusted by our understanding so long as we understand the meaning of our own freedom. What must we have already understood in order to understand our own freedom and movement?

It strikes me that the classical theistic worldview such as it has been elaborated above all by the modern "natural religion of reason" has, at this moment, become one of the greatest obstacles to coming to a *sense* of the deeper, motivating source of human *movement*. This worldview tries (using reason) to present us with a "final," "supernatural," but also and above all moral explanation of the "meaning of life"—before the question could ever be posed in *hermeneutic* terms. Modern theism is really, in turn, the historical offspring of western "onto-theology." It is "onto-theology" that has become religion. The contemporary implausibility of modern theism is in this sense an exponent of the crisis of "onto-theology" as such. Does this mean that "after the death of God," ultimately, one can think and talk about God only in a "dogmatic" and/or fideistic manner? The following investigation wishes to trace a few lines in this comprehensive field of problems. I will begin with a few marginal remarks on the contemporary critique of metaphysics as "onto-theology."

I. The Critique of Onto-theology

Statement of the Problem

Is it still possible, in the wake of the Heideggerian deconstruction of metaphysics as onto-theology, to make "God" a theme for philosophical thought? After Heidegger, a critique of "[the] western metaphysics" as onto-theology is not seldom conceived and understood as a fundamental ban of the god-question from the ontological thinking of philosophy, as a radical division of property between the theme of being such as Heidegger has taken to be the central theme of philosophical thinking, and the thinking of God that would then be remanded as a theological theme to the particular sphere of faith and religion. Furthermore, this latter proposal would mean as a consequence that thinking about God could no longer be correlated with a legitimate intellectual *question* of thought, since "after Heidegger" it would be an established insight that philosophical thought about God *can* be nothing other than one of the "manners" of forgetting being and of misunderstanding the epochal character of the comprehension of being by which this thinking of God has come into existence. Every re-introduction of the metaphysical thought of God into the thinking of being could thus be reduced to a non-recognition of the *Differenz* between being and beings.

Still, all of this leads one to easily forget that Heidegger's critique of metaphysics as onto-theology remains, in the final account, marked by a search for a more divine god. For, so it goes, to the god of the *causa sui* that is found in metaphysics, "One can neither pray nor sacrifice . . . Before the *causa sui* one can neither fall to one's knees in awe, nor can one play music and dance before this god. This godless thinking which must abandon the god of philosophy, god as *causa sui*, is thus perhaps closer to the divine God. Here this means only: god-less thinking is more open to Him than onto-theo-logic would like to admit."[1] The whimsical character of this passage notwithstanding, one must take seriously the question of precisely how Heidegger has characterized the essence of "metaphysics" and its "god." Does this "more divine god" fall wholly and completely outside of the domain of thinking? Has Heidegger, with this approach to the (predominantly modern) idea of *causa sui* (leaving aside the fact that it is a contradictory expression), really set forth on a "right" (*sachgerechte*)[2] way to the essence of "the" metaphysical concept of God from "the" metaphysics of Plato to the present? In what sense and to what degree would a new awareness of what is said to be the "onto-theological" structure of "the" whole of western metaphysics lead to discrediting the thinking of God such as has developed within ("the") metaphysics?

The Argument of the Critic

The marginal remarks that we have wished here to place alongside the idea of onto-theology are indebted above all to the way in which Heidegger has defined metaphysics as onto-theology in *Identity and Difference*, but also to the commentary by Jean-Luc Marion has given in *The Idol and the Distance*. Even more than Heidegger, Marion emphasizes the functional character of the "metaphysical" conception of God. According to Marion, not only is a grounded being the highest, but the highest, by virtue of its *function* as final ground, is itself grounded by the being—or, more specifically, by and from the being in its need of a ground.[3] This *logical-functional* character[4] of the metaphysical conception of God would be the reason why the metaphysical conception of God must be "abandoned,"[5] in order to prepare the way for "a more divine god." Marion has developed a particular approach to understanding the ontological "origin" of onto-theology: "Metaphysics thinks being, but in its own way (*La métaphysique pense l'être, mais à son guise*)[6]." This means that it thinks of what being does (= being in its *verbal* sense, a sense that metaphysics does not recognize—a verbal sense of "being" that Marion clarifies as "enterprise of being" [*entreprise d'être*]) immediately in a *substantial* sense, which is to say in terms of or from out of beings. By locating the center of gravity of onto-theology historically in modern thought, Marion moves somewhat quickly over the fact that, at least according to Heidegger, being has established *itself* as ground. Marion's problematic is in fact another one than that of Heidegger. Marion wishes to show that the metaphysical conception of God is "idolatrous." In metaphysics, being (in the verbal sense) is thought in such a way that even it requires a grounding in beings. Hence is being thought as an absent being (conversion into "being" in the substantial sense), and then finally as the highest being that represents in itself the highest figure of the fullness of being.[7] Marion speaks here of a reciprocity between the being in its "being" and the highest (or "supreme") being, and this according to a "relation of mutual grounding."[8] The highest being "gives the reason [*rend raison*] for beings in their Being," but in fact is called up only *in order to* guarantee the foundation of this being (functional interpretation), "to give the reason (*rendre raison*) for it" (Leibniz).[9] In this way, the God of metaphysics shows its dependence on that which thinking *itself* expects from it, wants from it, or presumes for it. Onto-theological thinking "gives rise to and finds in it [God] the *ultima ratio* which it needs in order to give the reason for [. . .] other beings."[10] The being of the being, in the sense of ground, can therefore be thought, in the final account, only as "*causa sui*," which would thus immediately be the metaphysical conception of god. According to Marion, this *function* of the concept of god, which must at the same time also be understood as a "making available of the divine," can be further specified by reflecting on the onto-theological structure of metaphysics in Heidegger (though the two standpoints do not say the same thing along this line).

Heidegger makes a distinction between the manner in which being "lights up," appears, and is understood, as it were, in advance in a particular period (that of metaphysics), and the manner in which beings appear *as* beings within this "clearing." One could say that through the "clearing" of being, beings are "approached" in a particular manner. For Heidegger, this means that, in this period, beings "fulfill" and thus found the clearing of being in a characteristic way. It is on this distinction that Marion speculates when he makes a distinction between "being" in its verbal and substantial senses. In the period of metaphysics, it is thus the case that being appears as "ground" or "logos," and this in a manner that makes beings appear as something somewhat predictable for and by thinking. Here, the metaphysical identification of being with the logos-origin *in and of beings* must consequently be understood as the manner in which beings (in their own way)[11] ground (support, fulfill) being.

In metaphysics there is thus at work, according to Heidegger, a well-specified "clearing" of being: being appears there as ground that presents itself. As onto-theology, metaphysics gives expression to the comprehension and thought of beings (as beings and as the whole of beings) corresponding to the clearing of being as "ground." This is a comprehension and a thought in which being-as-"logos"[12] is "forgotten" to the degree that it is reconciled with the principle of logical intelligibility in and of beings. In this way, being appears as a "logos" *by which thinking can account for itself as "Logic."*[13] The "being" that is the "matter" or "topic" (*Sache*) of thinking shows itself here "in the essence of reason (*in der Wesenart des Grundes*)."[14] Metaphysics is therefore, in its main characteristic, "above all logic. . . which thinks the being of beings" (*überall Logik . . . die das Sein des Seienden denkt*).[15]

II. Marion versus Heidegger

Let us leave aside the precise manner in which Heidegger fills in the onto-theological schema, and focus attention instead on the way that Marion attempts to escape from it. In *God without Being,* Marion speaks of a giving or a gift of distance by which this distance (*écart, distance*) appears to him as the formal distinguishing feature of this gift *as gift.* This is a giving that can no longer be thought of in terms of being, a gift from distance that is itself also a gift *of* distance.[16] On closer inspection, this seems to involve a giving or a gift that would, on one hand, deliver the play of being and beings, but at the same time, on the other hand, undo or free beings from being. Marion is playing here on two senses of the French word *délivrer,* which can mean both bringing something and freeing something. "Le don délivre l'Etre/étant"[17]—the gift delivers being/beings. The gift first brings being/beings: "It delivers it in the sense first that the gift gives being/beings, puts it into play, opens it to its sending, as in order to launch it into its destiny." This is followed immediately by something like a raising-up or elevating of the sense of the "first gift": "The gift delivers also in that it liberates [the] being from being [. . .] rendering [the] being free from being . . ."[18] The gift also frees the being "of" being. From its "distance," the giver disposes freely of *what* it gives; it is not itself affected by its own gift (i.e., being), and does not enter into the play of being and beings. God "strictly does not have to be (*n'a justement pas à être*)."[19] There are thus two moments in the gift: it gives being as that in which a being *is appropriated to itself* (Marion systematically connects this thought with the Heideggerian *es gibt*). But the gift also liberates. As gift it also works, despite appropriation (what Heidegger called *Ereignis*), as a disappropriation (*désappropriation*).[20] This would be the reason why the being, in spite of being as "envoi," can still be (immediately?) given back to God (*renvoi*). The gift at the same time makes the being loose from that to which—being—it was appropriated (in the *es gibt*). The gift, says Marion, liberates by its indifference with respect to being/beings.[21] Ultimately, the gift also liberates *itself* from being; it liberates itself as it were from its own engagement in the delivery of being. How can it do this? By exercising itself as gift in the name of what *comes after it* and is greater than it. According to Marion, this is "charity itself."[22] Here, charity stands as the symbol for the whole Christian-theological thematic of God's self-gift in being human and in dying on the cross. This means that the "first gift" (the ambiguous gift of being that in fact knows two moments, binding and unbinding, appropriating and disappropriating) is followed in turn *by*, but at the same time also *stands in the sign of* God's "supernatural" self-gift. The first gift stands in the sign of the second, the Greater. What we take from Marion is that the first gift (the gift of being) stands in the sign of and is a trace of a second gift that must itself make the first gift understandable. "Being/[the] being . . . can, if it is viewed as a giving, give therein the trace of another gift to be divined."[23] We can follow Marion to this point.

This does not take away the fact that Marion's thinking is strongly contestable on a few other points. To begin with, there is his abrupt proposal of the external, distant character of the gift, as *gift of distance.* Consequently, there is the difficulty, not be underestimated, with his thought that the gift (as gift of being) remains *indifferent* to what it gives. This is another way of saying that the second (greater) gift overflows and drowns the first. This entire thought of and from distance can only be philosophically arbitrary and even inaccessible when, in any case, the first moment of the first gift (delivery) cannot be brought into the context of a purely philosophical reflection and in a properly ontological way. And Marion refuses this. For him, the gift can be discovered only at the moment when the being gives itself back to the giver.[24] Only belief in caritas knows the gift, even where it would be a matter of the gift of being. This implies that the ontological, according to our rational conception of it, cannot in fact be understood as "gift" (at most as "*es gibt*" as "*Ereignis*"), and also that being-oneself (as way of *being*) cannot, from the ontological perspective, be understood or assumed to be a response to this gift. Being-oneself is not understood as responding to any gratuity. Being does not prepare us in any way for what Marion calls *renvoi*, "disappropriation" or "return gift." Self-appropriation seems for Marion to be nothing other than the self-affirmation of the being in its own process of self-appropriation, or "*conatus essendi*" (our interpretation of "[the] being remains in its appropriation to Being"[25]). With respect to such an appropriation, the distant giver remains indifferent (*indifférence*). Still more, it is this indifference that frees the being from being (*délivrer*). Through the gift, the being is *exempt* from being (from *avoir à être*) and can even (in an arbitrary way?) become established by God in the sign of a "greater gift." In this way, what Marion has called the first gift becomes completely incomprehensible.

Why this first gift (that of being/beings), if it would be given by God only so that we may decide for it ourselves: "but the gift may decide being/[the] being (*que le don puisse décider [de] l'Etre/étant*)"[26]? In a certain sense, Marion is right: were it the case that being is given with a view to something else, then God has freely and from his own will given it a higher, meta-ontological destiny. Being (or our comprehension of being) cannot give us, strictly from itself, a decisive answer about our ultimate destiny. What remains problematic about this has to do with the fact that, ultimately, *charité* would thus play itself out wholly "outside" being, which is to say *in distance*, or again, in and as *renvoi*, or "inner" return-gift from the being to God. Here, the danger of a new disincarnated "supernaturalism" that as such has nothing to do with the "world" and that in the meantime reduces the world to the "place" of a "leap into distance," is certainly not conceptual. "The giving traverses distance by not ceasing to send the given back to a giver, who, the first, dispenses [*dispense*[27]] the given as such—a sending destined to a sending back."[28] It seems to us that this would completely reduce religious faith to a "cry" (to a blind and fideistic faith), unless *being* is in the first place understood, *itself* and *inwardly*, as an enigma, as something through and through questionable in the sense of what can never lead a being to definitive appropriation and thus can never come to a definitive answer to its own question; this reduction of faith will be the result, furthermore, unless the enigma of being can be brought in connection with the possibility of *letting go of oneself*.

Faith is not a cry. Grace does not work alongside or apart from nature: *"Gratia non tollit naturam, sed perficit"*—grace does not take away nature, but perfects it.[29] What in our judgment escapes Marion in *God without Being* is an independent hermeneutic of being that would have freed itself from what the later Heidegger[30] (and in the background, also Levinas)[31] have said about it. In other words: what Marion overlooks is that his Christian position can have a philosophically accessible meaning only on the condition that *being itself* (as "Ereignis") "is" an essentially ambiguous play of appropriation and disappropriation. The other gift, says Marion, "can, precisely, distort being/(the) being by disappropriating in it what the *Ereignis* appropriates."[32] It occurs to us that it already belongs to being to give by taking away, and to take away—to disappropriate—in order to be able to give an end (to appropriate). It is on the ground of this paradox, which can only strike us with perplexity, that we can know ourselves to be ultimately powerless and adrift.[33] "[We] must at least preserve this impotence as the trace of a possibility"[34]—as a trace that refers to the Greater.

III. Immanent Transcendence

In order to escape from Marion's fideism, it will be necessary to make *being* a subject of questioning once again. In taking this course, the ontological conceptions of *being* and god can no longer be our guide. The fact that the metaphysical foundational thinking of the Greeks initially supported a religiously oriented conception of being does not exclude the possibility that it might have later penetrated the theme of the divine with its own "logical" conceptuality—just as it is also not unthinkable that the "logical" conception of being that is at work in onto-theological rationality could have, from a historical point of view, *imposed* its own schema on each further articulation of our human conception of being. In the work of someone like Derrida, this has led to the reproach of logocentrism. If this is indeed true, then Heidegger's critique of metaphysics as onto-theology can contribute to freeing what has been suppressed and giving it back to history. The first question to address to metaphysics *as*, or *insofar as* onto-theology thus asks not so much whether its manner of founding thinking is epistemologically legitimate,[35] but rather whether the understanding of being-as-ground that lies at its basis may be conceived, *hermeneutically*, as an exhaustive and exclusive opening of the very *meaning* of being and possibility-to-be. The following considerations are intended as initial steps toward exploring another understanding of being.

Real goodness does not reveal itself to a gaze that seeks justification in a calculating-controlling sense of beings. This is a gaze that sees only lack and scarcity, and tries to master this lack in an "economic" manner defined by will to self-preservation. Goodness speaks to our hearts. It shows its splendor only in and for an attitude that takes joy in being and that in this higher light also *loves* the being without calculation. This joy is possible thanks to signs and traces that point to the inner fullness of being. This is given to us; we succeed to it *partly*. Thus our being, as act (as activity, work, creativity, becoming, real life), bears its own fullness *in itself*. This does not mean that we are full and complete from the beginning, but that all our seeking and striving is a journey toward the fullness that lies hidden *in* being itself, and is partly given to us as possibility. The fact that we bear the fullness of being in ourselves means, in addition and above all, that the fullness of being is not "something" (not a being, no ontical definition, no determinate subsisting good that must be reached in order to be fulfilled and happy), but lies in being itself insofar as this is for us the taking of a share that at the time *invites sharing*. The truth of being appears on the way itself. "Life is like a text that bears the key to its own riddle, but gives it up only after repeated readings."[36] Then fullness of being lies *in* the deepest meaning of participating in and for *this* world. And truth is then a way that must be taken, rather than the object of a clarifying knowledge or a gnosis that we could possess.

How do we in our lived existence come upon the trace of the fullness of being? The following questions may help put us on the way. Why do we care about "something" or "someone" (such that "giving" must be taken literally as giving something up, as offering)? What is it about us that, in the midst of multiplicity and becoming, and in spite of so much brokenness and misery, we are concerned with things and people? What do we stand or lean on here? What is the connection, but also the difference, between "caring about someone" and "having an interest in something"? I can care for someone because he or she can put me in fuller possession of myself. In that case, do I really care about him or her? Must all willingness to "concern oneself with something or someone" be understood in the final analysis as an enlightened utilitarian, eudaimonistic, or even metaphysical self-interest aiming at more complete *self*-realization? Would that not be to accept all too quickly the path set before us by the thinking formed in Ancient Greece? What is the meaning of gratuity? Why do we continue to cherish it, and why do we continue in all silence to hope for it? How is it that we can be graciously disposed to someone or something? How is it that we are able, in times of common need, to transcend ourselves and put previous enmity behind us? Ultimately, what is it in us that is concerned with plurality, becoming, change, multiplicity, and entering and remaining in relation? What is it that is concerned? What is it for us to leap into the breach for someone (to stand up for them, in their place)? Why do some people risk their lives for such things? These questions must not be reduced immediately to the question of what this sort of behavior promises to give me or contribute to human collectivity. To refuse this reduction is to preempt a prejudiced and even exclusively utilitarian answer to the question of meaning, the origin and the motive of our *very being-on-the-way*, and to admit the possibility of being concerned with something, of something or someone "meaning something" to us.

True goodness is not possible without giving oneself away to something or someone in a real-concrete, oblative sense. This risky gift occurs in an ex-centric movement without return to oneself. It is a movement to "something" or "someone": to "something" or "someone" by which the "self" as such *is transcended*. Here, the "other" is not purely an exterior limit of the "self" and which as such would then have to be respected in a rational-ethical sense. Here, the other itself is the source of the actions[37] of the I. Being-good is thus a stepping-beyond-oneself that can come about only in entrusting oneself to a dimension that holds one in a position of ex-centricity from one's "self." Being-good may be taken up into knowledge, but *without* this admitting any rational claim on the *meaning* or the *future* of this being-good itself. The giving of a ground shows itself here as what by definition remains withdrawn from the knowledge and power of the "subject." It lets every being rest on its own ground, but this now is no longer a ground that establishes the being in its possibility in order to "gather" the fullness of being, in a substantial, "identical" or self-related sense, "back into itself." To the contrary, it is precisely the ground that must make it possible for the being to *participate* in a specific and irreducible way in the circling movement of the current by which being spreads and expands as being-good. There is a form of change—namely, being-good, blessing—that is higher than the immutable being-as-essence.

In order for the self-forgetting sense of blessing and giving to occur, there must come to light something that is itself the inner *ground* of all surrender. This ground is not itself a being, but being; more specifically, being has a goodness insofar as being is itself in the first place a *self-overflowing* "is." Sharing in and caring about something thus points to "something" (being) that has itself flowed into us, or is given to us, as gift. At the same moment, this given also comes into us as something stands *over against* us and appeals to us. Giving, it calls us into itself. Giving, being opens up a "middle" (milieu) in which we "can" be. It does this as a universally binding "middle-among-us" that is itself no longer a being. Moreover, being is here the bearer of a specific fullness of which everything has a share and in which everything is rooted in a teleological sense. Hence this fullness expresses itself in that milieu as something like a center that remains excentric with respect to the being and that in that sense remains withdrawn from the being. Being as "middle" is something that cannot be "known" by re-presentational thinking, and whose "middle-point" can be thought only as the *unnoticeable* site of a no-thing. Because, viewed ontically, this middle is not "something," its center (middle-point) can be considered "empty." It is therefore nothing less than the ungraspable middle of fullness by which and around which everything is kept in motion. It is that around which everything is gathered and in which everything is bound together with everything.

No one can grasp this middle by his or her own reach, for it is itself not "something" (it is not itself one or another being within our own reach). Still, it is in an intimate way immanent to the striving movement of the being: it is that which *brings* a being into movement, but without itself being something by which that movement could be satisfied and fall still. It is immanent to the movement as that which attracts: this means that it is what motivates and enlivens the circulating essence of ontological movement. Since to that degree it is not itself "something," it never passes unnoticed when it emerges into our intentional acts and aspirations. It attracts and sets in motion, without possibility of what moves absorbing it as object of satisfaction or final condition. It sets in motion as the awakening ground of what we, looking back at ourselves, can in more than one respect and more than one direction call our *dynamic of transcendence*. It thus attracts as the meta-ontical sense of unity and aim ("Über-Sinn") that is inherent in the fullness of being-itself (*esse*) that comes over us. Being is not only expansion of itself in an unsurveyable multiplicity (*proodos;* to move outward). It is at the same time also internalization and unification of that same multiplicity (*epistrophè*, return),[38] and this toward an inner center the "sense" of which always escapes the grasp of our objectifying thinking. We would like to understand this "Über-Sinn," as sense of unity and aim, as an immanent transcendence. As *immanent transcendence*, this immanent "ground," which according to our understanding can also be thought as "middle," "center," "aim," or "point," is equally that by which everything is decentered from itself and withdrawn from its own substantial center of gravity.

According to our understanding, this "middle" is *religious*. It is religious because it binds. However, it is not transcendent in the classical metaphysical sense of the word, for it possesses no subsistence of its own, as would be the case for the "highest" being in the whole of what is.[39] As such, it is something unintegratable that differs from every being (*Differenz*) and that, moreover, cannot become the object of a re-presenting, justifying thinking. It "is" the point from which there flows every claim to found and justify and where everything that can empower the being as a being and bestow goodness. That it flows forth means that what is in this sense unintegratable as source and origin of all blessing must in the first place be understood as *blessing* in the most proper sense of the word. *Being-as-ground announces itself to us as blessing*. It is a "no-thing" that evokes in us a specific form of non-representational—adjoining and receptive understanding and thinking, in the light of which everything that "means something to us" can become something to love and something to be there for.

Far from contending that this "thinking of the middle" such as we have evoked it here would be irreconcilable with the metaphysical "way of transcendence" conceived and defended by the great metaphysicians of the past, it nonetheless seems to me salutary and for our times necessary to ask whether we will not have to first discover the way of immanent transcendence that can eventually return our finitude from inside out to that metaphysical transcendence. This would be the question of whether we must first think through that middle-point that is not possessed by any being; that middle-point through which all of our favors and blessings pass at the moment when "we care about something"; that incomprehensible "middle" in which we are anchored to our most proper Possibility and to its fullness that always lies ahead of us and comes toward us as future. If the metaphysical conception of transcendence is still to have a future, then we must first rediscover that "middle" that binds everything together, in order to then suppose that it is *there* that the visible and invisible, the infinite and finite, and the eternal and the temporal (understanding each of these pairs in the metaphysical sense) are bound together in their enduring difference.

All of this leads away from thinking the essence of the good in terms of complete self-possession, and toward identifying it with a giving that is self-abandon. Goodness is then to be thought of as the mutual accomplishment of being in the being, by which being itself is understood first as self-expansion. This opens a way to thinking of God as gratuitous self-gift par excellence. This was also the standpoint of Marion in his early works, but then he never gave it a truly *ontological* significance. In any case, it would mean that God cannot be known or found by wishing to "possess" God as highest good, with eros; to the contrary, God can be known or found precisely in our mutual accomplishment of the self-denying gift-character of being. Then the place that we have called "the middle" can make it possible to bind God infinitely more "intimately" with our "horizontal" loves *in time and space* and with every act of abandon to the other people than we might ever have dared to suppose from a more "vertically" oriented and traditionally onto-theological perspective. And then it would be so not only that this given goodness is the world-immanent way along which a person can come to God, but it could also be the case, ultimately, that God who, as the first, has prepared and given his own perfection for us. This permits us to foresee a moment of original encounter in which, "after secularization," "after the death of God," and "after the critique of onto-theology," the trace of and to a living God could be *found* in this world once again.

NOTES

1. "[k]ann der Mensch weder beten, noch kann er ihm opfern. Vor der Causa sui kann der Mensch weder aus Scheu ins Knie fallen, noch kann er vor diesem Gott musizieren und tanzen. Demgemäß ist das gott-lose Denken, das den Gott der Philosophie, den Gott als Causa sui preisgeben muß, dem göttlichen Gott vielleicht näher. Dies sagt hier nur: Es ist freier für ihn, als es die Onto-Theo-Logik wahrhaben möchte." M. Heidegger, "Die onto-theo-logische Verfassung der Metaphysik," in *Identity and Difference*, bilingual edition with translation by J. Stambaugh (New York: Harper and Row, 1969), p. 140; English translation, p. 72. This text is henceforth cited as ID, with reference to the English followed by reference to the German. It is in this essay,

particularly beginning at p. 58/125 and following, that Heidegger defines the essence of metaphysics, in a manner that becomes definitive for him, as onto-theology.

2. ID 72/140 (Stambaugh translates *right*).

3. In J.-L. Marion, *The Idol and the Distance*, trans. T.A. Carlson (New York: Fordham University Press, 2001), p. 16; original French, *L'idole et la distance* (Paris: Fayard, 1977), p. 35 (this text henceforth sited as *Idol*, with reference to the English followed by reference to the French). Marion speaks of a "divine function" (cf. 10/28: "role of a foundation") that is valid only within onto-theology and that Descartes and Leibniz call *causa sui*. It is a matter there of a god "who serves as foundation but who receives a foundation himself." Moreover, by founding, this god receives back from the (founded) beings a faithful image of that *by* which they are and *of* which they are.

4. In Heidegger, this involves, above all, the thought that philosophy itself "requires and determines that and how the deity enters into it (*verlangt und bestimmt, daß und wie der Gott in sie komme*)" (ID 57/123), and this from out of a still unseen/not yet recognized "need for grounds." Now, god comes into philosophy as that which accords with the "ultima ratio," that is to say with the ultimate, calling for meaning (60/127). The entire question is thus, as Heidegger himself proposes, through which or by which sort of *founding correlation* god is called into thinking. "Metaphysics must think in the direction of the deity because the matter of thinking is being, but being is in being[s] as ground in diverse ways" (60/127).

5. ID 72/141.

6. *Idol* 13/30–31.

7. *Idol* 14–15/32–33.

8. *Idol* 15/33.

9. *Idol* 15/33.

10. *Idol* 15/33.

11. See ID 69/137 ("not only does being ground beings as their ground, but beings in their turn ground, cause being in their way") and 72/140, where the latter grounding function is attributed to "the supremely original matter (*die Ursache*)," which is to say god as *causa sui*. This reciprocity between being and beings is understood here by Heidegger from out of the "perdurance" (*Austrag*) of being and beings in their mutual and underlying difference. The literal meaning of the German *Austrag* is settling or fighting out of a battle. With this, Heidegger aims at the event in which the difference between being and beings is "settled," as if it were a matter of fighting out that difference. Metaphysics thus represents a single, well-defined manner of settling this conflict (and moreover of making it forgotten). A distinction is also "settled" and "fought out" in the aforementioned "grounds," where not only does being ground beings, but beings in their turn also ground being. Ultimately, this function of settling can be fulfilled only by the highest being: ultimately, "god" grounds being (the grounds). "Grounding itself appears within the clearing of perdurance [*der Lichtung des Austrags*] as something that *is*, thus itself as a being that requires the corresponding accounting [*entsprechende Begründung*] through beings, that is, causation, and indeed causation by the highest cause" (70/138). In the end, this thinking of "perdurance" (*Austrag*) appears as an attempt to couple the mutual difference and inner belonging-together of being and thinking into a more original ontological event that would precede the intention of that thinking.

12. Recall Marion's verbal sense of being.

13. ID 57/124.

14. ID 58/125.

15. ID 70/138. See also 57/124: In all *Logien* it is a matter of a *Begründungszusammenhang* whose ground is given accountability by thinking, by which they "dem Logos Rede stehen"—address and call to account.

16. J.-L. Marion, *God without Being: Hors-Texte*, trans. T. A. Carlson (Chicago: University of Chicago Press, 1991), pp. 101–103; original French, *Dieu sans l'être. Hors-texte* (Paris: Fayard, 1984), pp. 147, 151. This text is henceforth cited as GwB, with reference to the English followed by reference to the French.

17. GwB, p. 147.

18. GwB 101/ 147–48.

19. GwB 105/153.

20. GwB 105/152.

21. GwB 101/148.

22. GwB 102/148.

23. GwB 105/153.

24. GwB, the whole of page 104/151.

25. GwB 104/152.

26. GwB 101/147.

27. The French word *dispenser* admits the same ambiguity as one finds in *délivrer*.

28. GwB 104/151.

29. Thomas Aquinas, *S.Th.* I,1,8 ad.2.

30. Hence Heidegger's *Geviert, Geschick, es gibt.*

31. GwB 105/152. Being is appropriation (*conatus*); distance is a "violence."

32. GwB 105/152.

33. Cf. GwB 101/148: "Being/[the] being is distracted . . . (*L'Etre/étant s'affole . . .*)"

34. GwB 107/155. Here, Marion himself is involved with our powerlessness to remain apart from "agapè." In our view, this is another point where he moves too quickly over a necessary step.

35. One thinks, for example, of the Kantian question of whether thinking, as the acquisition of knowledge, can go beyond the world of experience.

36. From the "Inleiding" by Jozef Keulartz, to Wilhelm Dilthey, *Kritiek van de historische rede* (Amsterdam: Boom, 1994), p. 27.

37. Cf. Urbain Dhondt, "De temming van het oneindige verlangen. Over rite en ethiek in de religie" (The Taming of Infinite Desire: On Rite and Ethics in Religion), in E. Berns, P. Moyaert, and P. Van Tongeren, eds., *De God van denkers en dichters. Opstellen voor Samuel Ijsseling* (Amsterdam: Boom, 1997), p. 228.

38. This is so whether as *regeneration* of pure dispersal or as *repentance* at a "fall" into pure exteriority and dispersal. In this latter case, *proodos* could also be understood as *abandon* and *epistrophè* could be understood as *pardon*.

39. At the same time, it *is* a middle-point that religion has given all manner of symbolic locations and in turn all sorts of symbolic names. Hence in Judaism do all prayers ascend to heaven through "Jerusalem," and for both Orthodox and Catholic Christians they ascend via the "Mother of God."

Derrida and Marion

Two Husserlian Revolutions

John D. Caputo

Jacques Derrida and Jean-Luc Marion have each undertaken to extend or radicalize Husserl's phenomenology, to push his phenomenology to its limits—indeed beyond its limits—all the way up to the breaking point, all the way to the possibility of what is impossible in phenomenology. But they have done so in radically opposing ways. They each may be viewed as radical post-Husserlians who go back to Husserl's distinction in the *Logical Investigations* between "intention" and "fulfillment" but with fundamentally antagonistic results.

For Husserl, consciousness "intends" an object as a totality, but this intention can only be partially fulfilled since the object can be "given" in intuition only within the limits of possible or actual experience, meaning that its total givenness will always be held out as a regulative ideal, an Idea in the Kantian sense, that guides subsequent experience.[1] We intend the whole thing, but not wholly (*totum non totaliter*), as the medieval philosophers used to say. One of the claims that made Derrida's *Speech and Phenomena* famous is his argument that by means of this analysis—and contrary to Husserl's express intentions— Husserl both discovered and repressed the structural capacity of the signifier to function in the absence of the fulfilling intuition, a result that Derrida described as the "the emancipation of speech as nonknowing."[2] Husserl unearthed the hollowness of the signifier precisely in order to bury it beneath the mounting accumulation of intuitive givenness. But Derrida turns this analysis around and argues that Husserl had discovered the capacity of the signifier to travel light, to trim the weight of givenness that binds the signifier down to the actuality of the present and thereby impairs the effectiveness of the signifier, restraining its range and reach. In what follows, I will argue that Derrida is undertaking a "messianic" reading of Husserl's distinction, to borrow a term from his more recent work. His analysis of Husserl is not meant to confine us, negatively, to a hollow and empty play of signifiers, as the more alarmist among the Husserlians thought, but to release the signifying power of the sign, to allow the signifier to head for the future, for the unfilled and unfulfillable coming of something that eye has not seen, nor ear heard. In this way, Derrida's reading of Husserl reflects the biblical discourse of memory and expectation, of hope and promise. To speak, for Derrida, is always to be caught up in a promise.

Marion, on the other hand, pursues a completely opposite and, as I will argue, more Neo-Platonic reading of Husserl, a Christian Neo-Platonism, to be sure, with a Messiah who has indeed arrived (whereas Derrida refers approvingly to the Messiah in Blanchot's *Writing of the Disaster*, who is always and structurally "to come").[3] For Marion, Husserl's phenomenology has allowed itself to be preoccupied with what Marion calls "poor" or commonplace phenomena[4] in which the intention exceeds or outreaches the givenness, whereas Marion analyzes the possibility of a phenomenon that is impossible on Husserl's terms, where the givenness exceeds the intention, swamps and saturates it with givenness and leaves it groping for words (meanings, significations). This is Marion's well-known "saturated phenomenon," which leaves the intention, meaning, or signification bedazzled, stunned, and amazed by the advent of givenness.[5] Where Derrida feels around in the dark for the most radical implications of the emptiness of intentions, where intuitive givenness is structurally off-limits, Marion pursues a phenomenon whose givenness goes beyond the limits of any possible intention, a phenomenon than which nothing more given could be intended or conceived.

The differences that divide Derrida and Marion over their interpretations of the gift and of mystical theology, and even their differences over the Messiah, if I may say so, are clearly foreshadowed by the different directions in which they each seek to radicalize Husserlian phenomenology.[6] The differing ways they hear Husserl's dry and technical distinction between intention and givenness structure the very lively debate between them. Derrida and Marion share a revolutionary love of the impossible, of a possibility that Husserlian orthodoxy declared impossible, but they differ on whether that impossibility is to be found in a givenness that can never be intended or in an intention that can never be given. It is these opposing ways of radicalizing Husserlian phenomenology that I wish to explore here under the description of two differing "revolutions" in phenomenology, for it is always in the name of what is or seems impossible, of an impossible dream, that revolutions are launched.

I. Husserl

In the *Logical Investigations*, First Investigation, §15, and in the Fourth Investigation, Husserl describes the conditions of meaningful signs in terms of his theory of pure or a priori grammar. Derrida follows his use of two examples of completely meaningless signs, signs that Husserl accuses of being *Unsinn*, viz. "*Grün ist oder*" ("green is or") and "abracadabra."[7] The latter is an illustration of gibberish or jabberwocky—it has no meaning content—while the former fails because it violates the laws of meaning formation (*Bedeutungslehre*), that is, it fails formally; while each of its components is meaningful, the components cannot be combined in this way.

Husserl elaborated a continuum of possibilities of meaningful speech that ranges from the sphere of meaning (*Sinn*) at the top, through contradiction (*Widersinn*), all the way down to non-sense (*Unsinn*). At the top of the chain stands a true assertion that is intuitively filled in the present. Thus, if I say "Boston played an important role in the American revolution" while I am visiting Boston and touring its historic sights, I say something meaningful, true, and more or less intuitively fulfilled. If, after I have gone home, I say "Boston played an important role in the American revolution," I say something meaningful and true but fulfilled by memory or a memorial intuition, which is a lesser mode of intuition. If I utter the sentence without ever having laid eyes on Boston, the sentence is meaningful and true but more empty than fulfilled, because I am relying upon secondhand accounts from teachers and in books, films, photographs, paintings, and my imagination, which are weaker and more derivative modes of fulfillment.

If I say "Boston did not play an important role in the American revolution," I am mistaken, but my speech does not fail to be good speech. It is meaningful but false and unfulfilled. I continue to make good sense or good speech even if I depart the sphere of actuality and make an imaginative assertion, like "Sleepy Hollow is the land of Ichabod Crane," which is good speech and true, but only imaginatively fulfilled.

I continue to make good speech, Husserl says, even if I leave the land of *Sinn* (meaning or sense) so far as to say something contradictory (*Widersinn*). So if I say "Boston played an important role in the American revolution, but then again it did not" or more simply "the circle is square," the utterance is false, unfulfilled, and unfulfillable, but it still belongs to the sphere of *Sinn* for Husserl, namely as a contrary *Sinn*, a *Widersinn*. The reason for this is that such assertions are in good logical form, form that admits of valid substitution instance. So when I say "the circle is square," the statement is of a logical form that allows me to substitute "the circle is a plane figure," which is true. Even a contradiction is good diction, for Husserl.

But when I say *"Grün ist oder"* ("green is or"), I have set sail from the shores of *Sinn* once and for all, and have definitively bid sense adieu, having embraced a perfect *Unsinn*. That assertion is neither true nor false, neither fulfillable nor unfulfillable, because it fails to be an intention or assertion on formal grounds. That is because there is no valid substitution instance of this form. "Yellow is or" or "green is and" are no less an *Unsinn* than "green is or." The fault here is formal and categorial, having to do with the "categories of meaning": we cannot thus combine a nominative, a verb, and a conjunction. We cannot thus combine these "categories of meaning." The violation here is a violation not merely of the laws of the empirical grammar of a natural language but of the a priori grammar of any possible language. We might also see Husserl as describing the field of possible speech, that is, of possibility and impossibility themselves. Thus the field of *Sinn* has to do with what is possible and actual, with *Widersinn*, which stretches intention to a merely formal possibility, and with *Unsinn* with describing what is absolutely impossible.

II. Derrida

It was just these prohibitions that Derrida sought to test in *Speech and Phenomena* and "Signature, Event, Context."[8] Derrida thought—in a vintage example of a "deconstruction"—that Husserl had simultaneously made a great discovery and that he had in the same act repressed what he had discovered. For the importance of Husserl was to have emancipated speech from "intuitionism" or the "intuitionistic imperative,"[9] that is, from the demand that every signifier be fulfilled by intuition or givenness. Like the Boston patriots whose defiance of British oppression must have inspired Derrida in the year he spent at historic Harvard, Derrida protested the unfair taxation that the crown of intuitionism levies on the signifier. But if the Boston patriots said no taxation without representation, Derrida would say there can be no taxation—no demands for intuitive fulfillment—with representation. For if the function of the signifier is to represent, to operate *für etwas*, that is, to stand in "for something" that is not present, by what perversity does Husserl then go to measure signifiers by the degree to which they are fulfilled by the fulfilling presence of what they signify? If Husserl has shown that the power of the signifier is precisely its capacity to function in the absence of intuitive fulfillment, then why measure signifiers in terms of presence rather than of absence? Why not say that signifiers function all the more perfectly in their unique and distinctive role as signifiers when they are not fulfilled, and even more perfectly still when they are, in principle, not fulfillable? From the point of view of Derrida's revolution, Husserl turns out to be a royalist, still loyal to the royal crown of presence and suspicious of representation and of the democratic freedoms it grants signifiers. Should we then say that, by declaring his independence of the royal road of intuitionism, of the crown of givenness, Derrida confirms that deconstruction is America?

After all, it would not take much to find a sense for "green is or." One could, for example, in the course of explaining the rules of a new board game in which the conjunctions are color coded, go on to explain that in this game "and is yellow, but is orange, and green is or." Or one could insert the sentence as the response to the command "Produce a string of three English signifiers." Or one could cleverly insert the string as a line in a verse composed by Lewis Carroll and have Alice exclaim that the language they speak here is impossibly difficult but is oddly beautiful. And so on. There really is no limit to the multiple ways in which the sentence could be recontextualized in order to make sense or to be enjoyed for its other effects, non-semantic ones, purely graphic or phonic effects that are produced outside the reign or the rule of logical meaning.

At this point I think we can also see the extent to which Derrida's theory of *différance* converges with Rorty's notion of recontextualizability.[10] Both Rorty and Derrida think that there is no assertion that cannot be rendered true if it is false, or false it is true, or meaningful if it is meaningless, by altering its context. Sentences or phrases do not have some sort of *an sich* meaning that stands up against any possible recontextualization. Among other things, the possibility of using coded language, or of mentioning rather than using words, or of assuming roles in dramatic productions, makes it possible to say anything, or to unsay it.

To be sure, the orthodox Husserlian would respond that if I say "green is or" in the course of explaining a game in which conjunctions are color coded, then "or" is not functioning as a conjunction but as a nominative (the word *or*) and so I have not found a counter-example to the laws of a priori grammar. But Derrida's point is that the laws of a priori grammar are themselves a subset of the play of signifiers and do not have final authority over the signifiers, which can play various "categorial" roles depending on their context. As there is nothing about signifiers qua signifiers that submits them to the laws of intuition or givenness, so there is nothing about them that subjugates them to an a priori grammar, which is a demand introduced from without, as an imperative of formal logic, or, as Derrida said in those heady days of deconstruction and the "Yale School," a "logo-centric" demand.

Consider how much the liberation of the signifier from the demands of intuitive redemption—where intuitive fulfillment or givenness is impossible—makes possible. It explains the possibility of non-Euclidean geometry, that is, of a formal mathematics where intuition is impossible, which has been of no small importance in the history of mathematics. It also makes possible the highest reaches of the unintuitable structures of theoretical physics. Physics is forced to make use of mathematical formulae governing phenomena that intuitively behave as both particles and waves, thus constituting a science that can proceed only by suspending the rule of intuition, the demand to fulfill its signifiers. Thus, *pace* Alan Sokal, who has made a living by denouncing what French philosophers say about science,[11] deconstruction seems to me singularly helpful on this point. Again, it is precisely the suspension of the demand for intuitive fulfillment that explains the poetry of writers like Stéphane Mallarmé or James Joyce, in whose sheer phonic and graphic resonance we all rejoice (re-Joyce).

When we shift from the early Derrida to the late, we discover that this same radicalization of phenomenology is at work in the ethico-religious phenomena that have lately drawn his attention. The structural impossibility of non-appearing belongs to the essential structure of the *tout autre* and friendship, of faith, the gift, hospitality, and the messianic. It was Husserl's famous Fifth Cartesian Meditation that taught us that the other (alter ego) as other is constituted by unintuitability, that this non-intuitability is not a limit that we tolerate but the positive and constructive condition that we affirm, the necessary condition under which the other is "given" as other. The other is "given" in such a way that its own proper conscious lifestream is not given, not present, absent. That insight, appropriated in ethical terms by Levinas, becomes in turn the basis of Blanchot's and then Derrida's analysis of the "friend" who "appears without appearing":[12]

> [T]he other appears as such: this is to say, the other appears as a being whose appearance appears without appearing, without being submitted to the phenomenological law of the originary and intuitive given that governs all other appearances, all other phenomenality as such. The altogether other, and every other (one) is every (bit) other (*tout autre est tout autre*), comes here to upset the order of phenomenology.

The model is generalizable to all the phenomena that interest Derrida in his later writings. For faith is faith, Derrida says precisely when it has to do with what is not seen, not intuitable, with what eye cannot see or foresee, with what is not given but promised, with what is given enigmatically, through a mirror (I *Cor.* 13:12), through a glass darkly. The more visible, intuitable, clear, and credible a phenomenon is, the less it has to do with faith. Faith is faith, is most itself, just when what we are expected to believe seems impossible, just when we are blinded as to its possibility and are forced to go it by faith alone. Just so the gift: the more visibly plenitudinous, the more given the gift, the more the gift succumbs to the effects of self-annulling, whereas the gift is gift, is most itself as a gift, when something happens without setting in motion the lines of debt and gratitude that bind us back to the giver. Again, with hospitality, the more the coming of the other is plannable and foreseeable, the more hospitality is the coming of the same, not of the other. But such structural emptiness and unintuitability is a scandal and a stumbling to Husserl himself, and this despite the fact that Husserl also discovered the pre-eminent phenomenon of non-appearing, the appearing of the other, whose very appearing as other requires an absolutely unintuitable non-appearing.

Most interestingly, and this is why I have called Derrida's radicalization of Husserl "messianic," the entire analysis of the Messiah is foreshadowed by the early analysis of the unfulfillable signifier, the sign whose time never comes but is always coming, for whose coming we pray and weep, which keeps us open to the future without binding us to the present, which allows us to see the present as a kind of idol vis-à-vis the messianic age. The deconstruction of the rule of intuition over the signifier is thus like the hammer that Moses took to the golden calf in which Aaron tried to trap the divine. The deconstructive effect is to release the messianic possibilities of our words, of our best words— words like *the gift, friendship, hospitality, justice* and *democracy*—with which we first, in an initial gesture, associate ourselves, for we always begin where we are and have inherited no better words, but from which we also, in a second gesture, disassociate ourselves in an act of messianic longing for their unfulfill-able possibility. These words are hollowed out by messianic longing, by the very promise that constitutes language, a promise that opens up whenever we open our mouths. "From the moment I open my mouth, I have already promised; or rather, and sooner, the promise has seized the I which promise to speak to the other, to say something . . ."[13] They harbor within themselves the structure of messianic expectation, which requires that they will never be "given," that no existing person or historical institution, nothing actual or present, could ever pose or pass itself off as justice itself, or as democracy itself, which would result in the worst tyranny and oppression. This is not to say that there is no justice, democracy, or gift, but rather that these things, *s'il y en a*, transpire in the madness of the moment (*Augenblick*), of a momentary "event," which is all too soon enclosed again by the flood waters of the present, which oppress the unquiet of our heart (*inquietum est cor nostrum*).

Finally, as this reference to Augustine reminds us, I would say that this messianic reading of the structural unintuitability of an intention is the reason why the name of God is so important for Derrida, for the name of God is the name of the possibility of the impossible. The name of God is perhaps the most important name of all because it is the name of what we desire, and what we desire is impossible, the impossible, which is why we love it so. This desire keeps the future open, so that we are always asking with St. Augustine, "what do I love when I love (my) God?" Derrida's radicalization of Husserl is thus all at once democratic and American, but also a little Jewish and Augustinian and messianic.

III. Marion

For Jean-Luc Marion, the radicalization of Husserlian phenomenology takes the form not of liberation of the phenomenon from the demands for givenness, but of releasing the given phenomenon from the demand to be measured by the reach of the intention or signification. If Derrida mounts a resistance to the "intuitionistic imperative," Marion mounts a resistance to the imperative of signification or intention, to the rule of intentional meaning. The challenge facing Marion's phenomenological revolution is to let that which gives itself be given from itself, not merely "within the limits in which it is given," which is the limit that Husserl put upon the principle of all principles (*Ideas I*, §24), but to go to the limit of what gives itself without limits and unconditionally, to prepare oneself for the possibility of the impossible.[14] Marion gives various examples of the "saturated phenomenon," including intensely packed and vivid historical events, events of great personal moment, like birth or death, love or betrayal, and the experience of the work of art. But the analysis reaches its peak with religious phenomena, with the transforming and bedazzling appearance of Christ who transforms himself before the disciples, leaving them stunned and blinded, or the Christ who when approached by the soldiers in the garden of Gethsemene says "I am" (*ego eimi*) and they fall back before the power of his words (*John* 18:6). The experience of the impossible, of the phenomenon par excellence, is likewise found in the *aliquid quo majus nequit cogitari*, the thought we cannot think or identify, conceive or contain, the givenness beyond concept, category, identification, or intention. He is focused on the infinite givenness of what cannot be an object and does not have to be, God without being, an experience testified to in the tradition of Christian Neo-Platonic mystical theology, which is the invisible hand guiding his reading of Husserl's famous distinction.

If Derrida's revolution lay in declaring the independence of the signifier from the royal reign of presence or givenness, we might say that Marion's revolution is a little counterrevolutionary, a royalist revolution that reaffirms the Husserlian rule of givenness, the divine right of *Gegebenheit*. If for Marion we have to do with an excess of givenness, for Derrida, we have always to do with what is always yet to be given, a givenness to come, a givenness that is never given, something, *s'il y en a*, whose givenness is structurally impossible of "being given" (*étant donné*). For Marion it is a question of admitting an impossible givenness (*donation*), an impossible event, for which we lack both the name and the thought. For Derrida, it is a matter of the advent (*ad-veniens*) of the impossible, the unforeseeable coming of something *tout autre*, whose coming (*venue*) or incoming (*in-veniens*) we cannot see or foresee or conceive.

Marion's argument reaches its summit precisely with such religious phenomena, with the experience of the power and glory of Christ in the New Testament, with the God of mystical theology, which he explicates in terms of what he calls the "saturated phenomenon." For Kant and Husserl, every idea or intention is an "infinite" idea or intention, a regulative ideal, an "idea in the Kantian sense," because no finite complex of intuitive content would ever be fully adequate to any *eidos*. For Husserl and Kant, "God," as an intention of an "infinite being," which has no perceptual content at all and no hope at all of every acquiring any, is the very paradigm of such an idea. Marion's revolution is to turn the Husserlian analysis on its head and say that, on the contrary, in the case of religious phenomena, say the God of mystical theology, God "is— or better, God gives"—an overflowing intuitive content that "saturates" the intention, an excess of *givenness* (*Gegebenheit*) which the idea, intention, or concept simply cannot contain.[15]

Husserl's distinction between intention and fulfillment lies at the basis of the distinction between idol and icon in *God without Being*.[16] The idol "with its visibility fills the intention of the gaze, which wants nothing other than to see." (10–11). The "gaze" is an intentional act, a wanting to see the divine in something visible, which is sated and fulfilled by the glow of what it sees, where it comes to intuitive rest, where it "lets itself be filled" (11). The idol, in turn, "saturates it [the gaze] with visibility," "bedazzles" and "ravishes" it with its splendor. But the idol produces only a first, imperfect and finite saturation, one real enough but still a "low water mark" (14), even a slightly indolent saturated phenomenon, one that suffers from "fatigue." For here the intentional aim allows itself to rest in the visibility, and has no taste for transcendence, for aiming higher (*invisable*), for the invisible beyond (*invisible*) (13). In the idol, the intention has the initiative, but with the icon the grip of the intention is broken because the visible is broken into by the invisible. All this visibility is itself "saturated" by the invisible (17), so that rather than arising from an intentional aim that grows lazy with visibility, the icon awakens the aim from its indolence by way of a genuine and infinite saturation, provoking the intentional gaze beyond itself, opening it to something unenvisageable, that gives itself to be seen from out of itself (24). The movement of phenomenology at work in the idol is reversed with "precision": instead of intending (see), we are intended (seen), and instead of being a mirror in which the intentional gaze beholds itself, we become a mirror of the infinite (21–22)— "by dint of being saturated beyond itself from that glory." It should not go unnoticed, however, that something of the bedazzlement of the idol is recuperated in the New Testament accounts of Christ, where the power and glory of the Messiah bedazzles the disciples or the soldiers who have come to arrest him.

Making use of his revolutionary reading of Husserl, Marion can thus recast the "three ways" of mystical theology in a more radical phenomenological way.[17] (1) The mystical way of affirmation is redescribed in terms of phenomenological fulfillment or confirmation: it is possible to assert that "S is P" on the basis of the fulfilled or given sense of these terms in experience. Thus the attribution of goodness to God in the assertion "God is good" depends upon the finite fulfillment of the intention "good" in our experience of good things, which can confirm, albeit incompletely, the infinite goodness of God. (2) The second way of mystical negation is redescribed in terms of phenomenological inadequation: the assertion that God is good in mystical theology goes hand in hand with also denying goodness of God, with saying that "God is

John D. Caputo

not good" in any of the ways that the intention of goodness is given in experience, which offer too ordinary or impoverished an experience to be adequate for the way in which is God is good. (iii) But both of these ways remain within the orthodox framework of Husserl's determination of the relationship between a limited fulfillment and an intention that overreaches it. It is only with the third way of mystical eminence that Marion reverses this relationship and invokes his idea of a phenomenological excess, of the saturated phenomenon, where givenness overflows meaning and passes over into another order entirely. It must be emphasized that for Marion this is of a performative or pragmatic order, an order not of higher predication but of praise, where saying "God is good" takes the form not of "S is P," but of "Hallelujah!" "Glory be to God," a little bit like someone down in Louisiana at a pentecostal meeting filled with the Holy Spirit shouting "Thank you, Jesus." Marion likes to think that deconstruction only gets as far as the second way of mystical theology, the way of negation, which would leave us twisting in the winds of negation and even atheism, so that contrary to Derrida's claim that deconstruction is affirmation—*viens, oui, oui*—Marion regards Derrida as a master of negation. Still, it is true that Derrida "quite rightly passes for an atheist," and what he affirms is not infinite givenness.

In the essay "In the Name," Marion makes much of his argument turn on distinguishing presence and givenness. That, to be sure, is a legitimate distinction, as we have all learned from Husserl's Fifth Cartesian Meditation, where we "intend" the other precisely insofar as the other is not present, where the "givenness" of the other is a function of the non-presence of the intentional stream of the other ego. But that, as we might expect, is not the use that Marion intends to make of this distinction, because the whole thrust of his Husserlian revolution is not to pursue intentions that are not fulfilled but rather to pursue a fulfillment that cannot be intended. Marion thus insists that the "presence" referred to in the expression "metaphysics of presence" has to do with a givenness whose parameters are set by the intentional act, a givenness that is marked off a priori by the limits of the intention to which it is never adequate. That is why Marion can say that in orthodox Christian theology, the metaphysics of presence is actually a heresy, a form of Arianism, which denies the incomprehensibility of God.[18] When Marion rejects the charge that mystical theology represents a "metaphysics of presence," he has redefined the metaphysics of presence as an undertaking held captive by the higher idolatry of the concept. In the metaphysics of presence, God is cut to fit the size of the concept, cut down to size and made a proportionate object of "onto-theo-logic"—which is really what Marion means by the "metaphysics of presence"—instead of allowing human thought to be thrown into a higher mystical confusion, "bedazzled" by Christ's transfigured flesh, or by God's uncontainable, unidentifiable plenitude. When Marion says that mystical theology is not a "metaphysics of presence" but a "theology of absence,"[19] we must be careful to understand what he means and to keep in mind the difference between the two revolutions we are describing here. Marion does not mean that God *in propria natura* is "absent" from mystical theology the way the alter ego is absent from the self in the Fifth Cartesian Meditation, that is, structurally inaccessible to our intention, which is what Derrida means by both God and the *tout autre*, which in turn is why he can say *tout autre est tout autre*. Marion means that God is "absent" from mystical theology because God is given beyond our conceptual grasp, given in a way that is greater than anything that can be conceived (intended), so that Anselm and Christian Neoplatonism hover in the background of this claim, not Husserl's Fifth Cartesian Meditation. God is "absent" by excess, not defect. God is absent from conceptual thinking for Marion, not because God is withdrawn from and inaccessible to human thought in a radical and structural way, like the alter ego in the Fifth Cartesian Meditation. He means that conceptual thinking "misses" God, rather the way someone who is insensitive to painting or music does not "pick up" what is going on there and misses the beauty of the work, even though it is "given," even as the one who responds to what is genuinely given is lost for words. For all practical purposes, God's "absence" in the "theology of absence" amounts to a more eminent presence. That leads me to my conclusion.

IV. Conclusion: Deconstruction, Intuitionism, and the Kingdom of God

I contend that Marion's revolution fails and that Derrida's succeeds. Furthermore, I hold that, contrary to Marion's tendency to associate deconstruction with negation and atheism and to associate his phenomenology with giving "relief" to theology, it is rather more Derrida (who rightly passes for an atheist) than Marion who can be of help to any possible phenomenology of religion. I hold to this view for two reasons.

(1) What Marion is defending is, I think, a phenomenological version of Christian Neo-Platonism that falls prey to Derrida's critique of hyper-essentialism. It is, if not a "metaphysics of presence" in the straightforward sense, a "meta-metaphysics of hyper-presence." For after all, when Derrida criticizes the rule of presence, the presence he is speaking of is not limited to what is presented by a concept, and it would certainly include the hyper-presence of something whose presence is not restrained by a concept that Marion describes as givenness. By redescribing the God of mystical theology in terms of givenness rather than presence, Marion simply redescribes what Derrida calls "hyper-essentialism" in terms of givenness rather than of presence in the narrow sense. But Marion's givenness, or hyper-givenness, is no less hyper-essentialistic, and this because it is rather boldly a mode of absolute rather than conditional presence. The "hype" that surrounds the *hyperousios* in mystical theology, all the eminence that heightens its *ousia*, is, for Marion, a reflection of the fact not that it is absent but that it is too present, present beyond presence, for any concept to take its measure. That is why, in a context in

which he is not trying to observe this distinction, Marion is perfectly comfortable referring to "the absolute mode of presence" (*le mode absolu de la présence*) of the saturated phenomenon.[20] The distinction he is drawing between presence and givenness amounts, in fact, to a distinction between a limited, conditional, and relative presence (determined by concepts) and unlimited, unconditional, "absolute" presence. This is not the distinction we can draw from Husserl's Fifth Cartesian Meditation, where the givenness of a phenomenon is a function of its structural withdrawal or absence; this is a distinction that arises rather from the history of mystical theology or from a reading of the New Testament. Derrida recognized this as early as "Violence and Metaphysics," when he pointed out that Levinas is in a difficult position, because Levinas, for whom language supplies the very proximity of the distance of the other, cannot make the standard move of mystical theology, which is to say that it has been visited by something so eminent and unlimited, by a presence that is so absolute, that it is lost for words to describe it.[21] Of course, it is perfectly true that the experience described by mystical theology has abandoned the form of metaphysics, that it does not take the form of concepts, judgments, and arguments. But it is no less true that it is still metaphysical as regards its content, metaphysical in a way that crowns metaphysics with a presence beyond presence, with an unlimited and unconditional presence, with the gift or present of a presence of which the metaphysical concept dare not dream, with a "meta-metaphysical, meta-ontological" presence.[22] The best way to save the name of God is to say that God is everything save what we say or conceive.

But Marion cannot succeed simply by defining metaphysics to mean the presence that is presented by the concept. That succeeds only in saving, excepting, the surplus of givenness, the absolute presence of the *hyperousios*, from a narrowly redefined sense of metaphysics and from "onto-theo-logical" and "representational" thinking, but not from a higher or hyper-essentialism. For hyper-essentialism means hyper-presence, super-presence, absolute, unlimited, and unconditional presence beyond the limited presence whose horizons are set by the concept. When a Christian Neo-Platonic mystic like Meister Eckhart speaks of the Godhead beyond God, and when Marion speaks of God without Being, they both give words to what Derrida calls the dream of presence without *différance*, a dream that "must vanish at daybreak as soon as language awakens."[23] The dream of givenness without presence is the dream of the transcendental signified, of a givenness without violence, without or beyond language, without conditions or limits, without even the elementary "archi-violence" of the trace. But Derrida thinks dreaming is a work of language that transpires within language, that takes the form of the dream provoked by language, by the promise contained within language for the *tout autre*, the dream expressed in the "*viens, oui, oui*" directed toward an absolute future, something absolutely to come. For as soon as we open our mouths, we speak words that ache with messianic longing, words whose power derives from the fact that they are hollowed out and emptied by the expectation of things to come, words that are "filled" only with "promise." To speak is to make promises to ourselves, or rather, to speak is to respond to a promise made to us by language. To speak is a structurally messianic and prophetic act, which calls for things to come.

(2) This Neo-Platonic hyperessentialism comes home to roost on Marion when he concedes that the saturated phenomenon is too dazzling for phenomenology to say or decide what it is bedazzled by. Hyperessentialism stresses phenomenology to the breaking point. At the end of *Étant donné* (§29), Marion takes up the paradoxical "conditions" that are imposed upon the response to and reception of something "unconditional." He describes an "immanent decision," where we are "condemned to decide about a saturated phenomenon,"[24] solicited to decide for the saturated phenomenon, to make ourselves responsive to it. While we cannot give the saturated phenomenon to ourselves, or constitute it for ourselves, still we are responsible for being responsive to its call. While we cannot set down prior conditions for its self-giving, we can and must—this is a necessary condition—give ourselves to its unconditional giving. He describes an existential aporia in virtue of which we must give ourselves lovingly to a pure love that gives us the power to love and the power to give ourselves in the first place. Otherwise the absolutely given (*donné*) might be left entirely in abandon (*abandonné*).

We have to do here with a hermeneutical circle from which we must not try to escape but rather learn to enter by way of love and trust and faith. This decision ultimately requires the love and trust and faith that what we have to do with here, in the saturated phenomenon, is the face of love, and not nothing, or not something else, like a blind play of faceless forces. That is why, on Marion's rendering, phenomenology itself can only render a description of a formal possibility or "revealability" of God or absolute love, while it falls to an actual historical "revelation"—an historical confession of faith—for this phenomenon to be actually given.[25] By "possible" I think Marion means that phenomenology discovers something "determinable," something (an excess) in need not exactly of actualization but of determination (an excess of *what*?). What interests me is that for Marion the bedazzling event of the saturated phenomenon, the event in which the *étant donné* turns to love, is finally the work of revealed theology, of the historical actuality of a divine revelation. If the phenomenologist comes upon phenomena of excess, of surpassing givenness, it is only the believer who by the "gift of faith"—that is, the historical tradition one has inherited—is able to say what it is that is given so excessively, to say that we have to do here with a love that surpasses all understanding and not the *khora*. Historical Christianity plays the role of the *Concluding Unscientific Postscript* relative to the *Philosophical Fragments*: it gives this pure possibility its historical name.

I think that Marion is right about that, but my point is that Marion is landed by this rather "critical" and even Kantian analysis of the relative borders of phenomenology and theology right back where Derrida says we are all along, back with faith, back with inherited vocabularies, back with seeing through a glass/glas darkly. We are right back with the necessity of interpretation, the inescapability of construing shadows (or dazzling lights). Now, from the point of view of Husserl, we are right back with an intention that is not fulfilled. For once we put a construal on the saturated phenomenon in terms of an historical faith, once we give it an historical name, once we say it is God and not *khora*, the transfigured Christ and not a Nietzschean play of forces, supereminent love and not a desire for our mommy or not a cerebral hemorrhage brought on by falling off my horse, we no longer remain within the limits of givenness but have gone on to put a "take" on it, which is what Husserl calls an *Auffassung*, an intentional apprehension or "taking as." This historical confession is an intentional act, a confession or affirmation of faith, whose value and power is precisely its capacity to function in the absence of a clarifying fulfillment. You have believed because you have seen, Thomas, but blessed are those who believe and have not seen. If something is given but I know not what, then I am proceeding by faith, which is an empty intention, if I say that it is infinite love that has been given. Something has happened, but it is my historical tradition that gives it a name. I am in love, even in love with God, but I have not escaped the question, "what do I love when I love my God?"

Now that, from Derrida's point of view, is something of a *quod erat demonstrandum* in which Marion comes around to confessing that givenness requires an intention that intends something not given that we can and must believe, that we also trust and love. Faith, hope, and love are intentional acts of intending what we cannot see, which is exactly what happens when something is given but we do not know what.[26] It is worth pointing out that Derrida and Marion agree that faith is not ultimately a cognitive act at all but a deed, not a way of knowing but a way of doing something—of loving and praising, for Marion, and of doing the truth, of making the truth happen, *facere veritatem*, of doing justice, for Derrida.

For Derrida, faith is a prophetic faith, a way of bearing witness to a truth that eludes us, to something that is neither conceptually present nor superconceptually given, but rather structurally coming or promised, something precisely not given, for whose "coming" we hope and long, pray, and weep. Our words are filled with eschatological promise, not phenomenological givenness; they set off sparks of memory, hope, and expectation, not of saturating givenness. Let us listen once again to what Derrida says in *Speech and Phenomena* about the "originality" of Husserl's conception which—against Husserl's own purposes—breaks the grip of "intuitionism," but this time with a religious ear, or with an ear for what Derrida later on called a religion without religion:[27]

"One can speak without knowing. And against the whole philosophical tradition Husserl shows that in that case speech is still genuinely speech, provided it obeys certain rules that do not immediately figure as rules for knowledge."

By a "speech without knowing" Derrida had in mind, in those days, primarily the uncontainable graphic and phonic effects of poetic language of the sort one finds in Mallarmé or Joyce. But nowadays, that is how he is thinks about the *tout autre*, the friend, hospitality, justice, democracy, the gift, forgiveness, the yes, faith, witness—and the Messiah. Indeed, I would argue, although this would require another format, that by resisting the "intuitionistic imperative," the rule of intuition, presence, or givenness, Derrida remains loyal to a biblical discourse of memory, expectation, and promise, and, in so doing, he goes some way toward describing what we mean by the "rule" or "reign of God," whom no one has seen.

NOTES

1. E. Husserl, *Logical Investigations*, trans. J. N. Findlay, 2 vols. (New York: Humanities Press, 1970), vol. 2, *Investigation VI*, pp. 675–706.

2. J. Derrida, *Speech and Phenomena and Other Essays on the Theory of the Sign*, trans. D. Allison (Evanston, Ill.: Northwestern University Press, 1972), p. 97.

3. J. Derrida, *Politics of Friendship*, trans. G. Collins (London and New York: Verso, 1997), pp. 37, 46 n.14.

4. J.-L. Marion, *Étant donné* (Paris: P.U.F., 1997), pp. 309–14.

5. J.-L. Marion, "The Saturated Phenomenon," trans. T. A. Carlson, in *Phenomenology and the Theological Turn* (New York: Fordham University Press, 2000).

6. See *God, the Gift and Postmodernism*, eds. J. D. Caputo and M. J. Scanlon (Bloomington: Indiana University Press, 1999), for the debate between Derrida and Marion, entitled "On the Gift," pp. 54–78; Marion's lecture "In the Name" and Derrida's response, pp. 20–53; and my account of their differences in "Apostles of the Impossible: Derrida and Marion," pp. 185–222.

7. Husserl, *Logical Investigations*, vol. 2, pp. 510–26. By confusing the French *ou* with *où*, the English translation of *Speech and Phenomena* mistranslates the German *"Grün ist oder"* as "green is where" (pp. 92, 99), which completely undoes Husserl's example of non-sense.

8. J. Derrida, *Margins of Philosophy*, trans. A. Bass (Chicago: University of Chicago Press, 1982), pp. 307–30.

9. Derrida, *Speech and Phenomena*, p. 97.

10. I have defended this point in my *More Radical Hermeneutics: On Not Knowing Who We Are* (Bloomington: Indiana University Press, 2000), pp. 105–12; for Derrida on recontextualization, see his *Margins of Philosophy*, pp. 317–18.

11. See J. Bricmont and A. Sokal, *Fashionable Nonsense: Postmodern Intellectuals' Abuse of Science* (New York: Picdor USA, 1998). It must be said that Bricmont and Sokal do concede that Derrida is not implicated in what they call "nonsense" (*Fashionable Nonsense*, p. 8); but they never take the time to see what positive implications are harbored by Derrida's theory of signs.

12. Derrida, *Politics of Friendship*, p. 232.

13. J. Derrida, "How to Avoid Speaking: Denials," trans. K. Friedan, in H. Coward and T. Foshay, eds., *Derrida and Negative Theology* (Albany: State University of New

John D. Caputo

York Press, 1992), p. 84. For Derrida, language is constituted by the promise; see pp. 82–85, 97–98.

14. On this point, see the remarkable and felicitous summary of the argument of his complicated book in J.-L. Marion, *Reduction and Givenness*, trans. T. A. Carlson (Evanston, Ill.: Northwestern University Press, 1998), pp. 203–205.

15. See the final paragraphs of Marion, "Saturated Phenomenon," in op. cit. (note 5, above).

16. J.-L. Marion, *God Without Being*, trans. T. A. Carlson (Chicago: University of Chicago Press), especially chapter 1.

17. J.-L. Marion, "In the Name," in *God, the Gift, and Postmodernism*, pp. 24–28.

18. Ibid., 34–36.

19. Ibid., 37–39.

20. J.-L. Marion, "Metaphysics and Phenomenology: A Relief for Theology," trans. T. A. Carlson, *Critical Inquiry*, 20 (Summer 1994): 589.

21. J. Derrida, *Writing and Difference*, trans. A. Bass (Chicago: University of Chicago Press, 1978), p. 116.

22. J. Derrida, *On the Name*, ed. T. Dutoit (Stanford, Calif.: Stanford University Press, 1995), p. 68.

23. Derrida, *Writing and Difference*, p. 151.

24. Marion, *Étant donné*, p. 422.

25. Marion, "Metaphysics and Phenomenology," pp. 589–91.

26. An intention lacks fulfillment not only by being simply empty, as when I encounter the name of something about which I lack the most elementary information, but also when something is given but unclearly, in which case I lack a clarifying fulfillment. If something is given, but there are conflicting construals of it, then my intention lacks fulfillment. See Husserl, *Logical Investigations*, Investigation VI, pp. 701–706. If something is given but I do not know what, I might well be motivated to accept someone else's interpretation. When a physician shows me an x-ray and says "here is the problem," and points to a dark spot on the x-ray that I do not understand, my intention is more or less unfulfilled and non-intuitive, even though something is given, and I am proceeding by a certain faith if I go along with what the physician says.

27. Derrida, *Speech and Phenomena*, pp. 89–90.

The Universal in Jewish Particularism

Benamozegh and Levinas

Richard A. Cohen

I. Overview

A flame needs a candle as much as a candle needs a flame. Judaism finds the universal, the holy—the "image and likeness" of God—not in another world, a heaven hovering above or a "soul" or "spirit" detached from matter here below. Rather, holiness is found here and now in the unending divine–human partnership of *sanctification*. The world's ascent is God descent. To sanctify is to make the profane holy. Passion becomes compassion. "The so-called profane," Martin Buber said, "is only the not yet holy." The Hebrew term usually translated as "law," *halakhah*, in fact means "walk," "path," or "way." The Jewish path creates, nurtures, enhances, and preserves the holy on earth. Thus Judaism is a religion of *incarnation*, holiness on earth, the sanctification of life and of all of creation. While Jews know the heights of personal salvation, they prefer the collective endeavor of universal redemption. Holiness is separation—the pure from the impure, and also the pure from the vulgar, the sacred from the profane, the clean from the unclean, the pure from the vulgar—but it is not exclusion. Everything—from birth to death to mourning, from morning to night, from work to rest, from the bathroom, kitchen, dining room, bedroom, office, farm, factory, dance, song, government, and army, to school, science, synagogue, and Temple—is to be transfigured and made holy. Transcendence and immanence meet in the refinement of a covenant exclusive of nothing. Judaism is thus one—not the only one, but unique— expression of the religious paradox of humanity co-creating God's created universe.

Judaism is not a religion, however, if by religion one means a compartment of life dedicated to God in contrast to other compartments of life with other devotions. Rather, like being a Hindu, or being Chinese, to be a Jew is to participate in a vast and ancient civilization. It is a civilization as old as civilization itself, and for much of its history it has been as dispersed as the globe itself. Like any civilization, then, it is far more than a rational "system" or a consistent "worldview." It cannot without distortion be reduced to a simple formula, a principle, a thesis, or even a set of basic concepts. Its coherence is less the unity of a philosophical or theological system, than the integrity of a history, a narrative, or a life. Judaism, like any civilization, cannot without distortion be summed up or boiled down. Knowing Judaism—whether for the first time or after a long time, whether from inside its vast precincts or outside—is always a matter of highlighting, emphasizing, choosing an angle or perspective, and selecting from a multiplicity of foci that that flow from and feed into one another. Neither an artificial unity nor a set of unrelated fragments, the coherence of Jews and Judaism is the variform integrity of life itself, unique individuals joined together as a unique people growing organically—in complexes of actions, with reactions at once internal and external—across historical time.

II. Jewish Universalism in Elijah Benamozegh and Emmanuel Levinas

With this overview in mind, the thesis of this paper is that Judaism is a universal religion. This thesis strongly contrasts with and contests the perennial Christian misrepresentations of Judaism as a merely carnal, tribal, or nationalist cult. Even more profoundly, it strongly contrasts with and contests certain modern, and often Jewish, misrepresentations of Judaism that would relegate most of historical Judaism to the same small teapot of parochialism. The thesis of this paper, in other words, is that old-fashioned, unregenerate, as it were, traditional, rabbinic, or Talmudic Judaism—label it "orthodox Judaism," if you will—is a universal religion.

This claim could be justified on the basis of many Jewish thinkers, past and present. One could even go all the way back to the Hebrew prophets, and farther still. Here, however, this claim will be approached through the works of two outstanding modern Jewish thinkers: Rabbi Elijah Benamozegh (1823– 1900), of Livorno, Italy, and Emmanuel Levinas (1906–1995), born in Kovno, Lithuania, and Parisian by choice.

It may seem odd to juxtapose two thinkers who, although both Jewish and both philosophically minded, flourished in different centuries, hailed from very different parts of Europe (and even more so from "Jewish Europe"), and lived in quite different social and cultural milieus. If these differences do not seem divisive enough, consider also that Benamozegh served as a community rabbi, and was both a Talmudist and a Kabbalist,[1] while Levinas was qualified in none of these ways.[2] Levinas, for his part, quite unlike Benamozegh, studied under two of the most influential professors of philosophy of the twentieth century: Edmund Husserl, founder of phenomenology, and Martin Heidegger, renovator of ontology. Levinas earned advanced academic degrees in philosophy from two French universities, the University of Strasbourg and the University of Paris-Sorbonne, and became a professor of philosophy at three: the University of Poitiers, the University of Paris-Nanterre, and the University of Paris-Sorbonne. Benamozegh, in contrast, had none of these attainments. These are all surely significant differences. In addition, the thought of Levinas is now fairly well known, while that of Benamozegh, like Benamozegh himself, is almost unknown.

What links these two thinkers, however, is far more profound and consequential. I will briefly mention some factors that are of particular relevance to the concerns of the present paper, without delving into nuances or eventual qualifications. First, the level or rank of their achievements distinguishes them. Both were privileged to articulate profound, comprehensive, and original philosophies. Second, both were fully engaged with western civilization as a whole. Their respective philosophies are not only concerned with western civilization, but are written in its idiom; they have thus appropriated and engaged the great texts and spiritual creations of western civilization. Third, and without contradiction of the previous point, both Benamozegh and Levinas were faithful to Jewish traditional sources, to the Talmud above all. Fourth, both found the heart and soul of Judaism in its commitment to morality and justice for all. Both understood that Judaism's elevated and elevating commitment to holiness demands a redemptive praxis oriented by the divine commands of morality and justice. In sum, both Benamozegh and Levinas acceded to the authority of Jewish tradition by creating original ethical philosophies in dialogue with western civilization as a whole. Both thinkers gave voice to the Hebrew spirit in Greek letters.

Benamozegh and Levinas understood that the ancient and perennial Jewish concern for morality and justice is pivotal for Jews in relation to their own Judaism, to be sure. But they also recognized that this concern is no less pivotal in the relation of Jews and Judaism to humankind. And, even beyond that, they understood that the redemptive enterprise, as understood by normative Judaism, remains critical to the relation of Jews and Judaism to the cosmos as a whole, to all of creation. From these preliminary considerations alone, it should be clear that universal morality and justice—dismissed by today's sophisticated cynics as illusion, ideology, super-structure, willful and constructed products of "modern," "Enlightenment," or "humanist" subjectivism—are, for these two thinkers, inextricably bound at once to Judaism's unique experience and to the highest hopes of a pluralist humanity.

It is particularly important, in the often imperial and missionary environment—subtle yet crude—of Christendom, to underline the universality and the pluralism of Judaism's holy mission. The ethical zeal to make the world a better place, a zeal that inspires Levinas and Benamozegh in their Judaism, is the very same zeal that inspires them to insist upon the multiplicity of paths that can lead to the fulfillment of the commands of an infinite God. Faithful to their own tradition, hence faithful to the one God of all humanity, neither thinker is limited by an exclusionary imperialism that would require the conversion of everyone to Judaism in the manner that Christian evangelizing aims to convert the world to Christianity. Many genuine paths—each one absolute and authoritative for the believer—lead to the infinite God. Chosen by such a God, Judaism is a religion not of tolerance, if tolerance means that one grits one's teeth and provisionally endures alternatives. Rather, it is a religion whose divinely revealed teachings of universal morality and justice aim to produce not a mirror image of itself, but a righteous humanity, whatever the denominational affiliations of that humanity. With the same breath with which Benamozegh and Levinas insist upon the fundamental and irreducible relevance of Judaism for Jews as Jews, they also insist, to the same Jews—without any diminution, condescension or duplicity—on the irreducible relevance, the universality, of Judaism for all of humanity. To be chosen is to be responsible for each and everyone, Jew and non-Jew alike, "widow, orphan, and stranger."

Both refuse the ideology of secular modernity.[3] For neither thinker is Judaism conceived as a "religion" in the narrow sense, that is, a restricted "ecclesiastical" zone or compartment of life.[4] One is not French, Italian, or American first, and Jew second. One is French, Italian, or American as a Jew. That is to say, contra Spinoza, but in line with America's "founding fathers," what France, Italy, and America do must measure up to the high moral standards of Judaism, must be judged according to an "inalienable" right and not merely according to the passing demands of power, success, or popularity. Not a "religion," Judaism is a way of life. It is manifest in denominational forms of piety such as prayer and communal worship services, to be sure, but also and no less authoritatively is it manifest in the so-called "secular" dimensions of life, in the familial, social, civic, economic, and political aspects of life.[5] In this way, for both Levinas and Benamozegh, the particularity of one's own tradition and the universality of morality and justice need not stand in conflict with one another. Indeed, the reverse is true. The elevation demanded by ethical universality is rooted in the particular, just as the aspiration of particularity requires and demands universality. Such is Jewish singularity, the Jewish notion of election. Each is elected for all. The universality of Judaism is no less universal for being Jewish and no less Jewish for being universal. Or, in the words of Benamozegh: "the voice from Sinai addresses all humanity."[6] Embracing and guiding Jews, but also humanity and all creation, these thinkers see in the most specifically Jewish conception of universality rooted in particularity, or the most specifically Jewish conception of particularity rising to universality, "the highest conceivable form of universalism."[7]

In contrast to modern Enlightenment notions of universality, based ultimately in a mathematical conception of truth (as is evident in Descartes), the ethico-metaphysical universalism of Judaism retains it universality without sacrificing the particular, singular, or unique. Indeed, standing against modern objectified forms of universality, and for an older tradition sensitive to the humanity of the human, Judaism demands precisely the reverse: respect for the unique, the singular, the particular. The identity of the unique, which requires pluralism, and the identity of unity, which erases difference, are not reducible to one another. Faithfulness to the orthodoxy of traditional Judaism requires the recognition, in Benamozegh's words, "that God's face assumed many expressions at Sinai."[8] The universality espoused by Benamozegh and Levinas is wedded to the historical particularity of texts, rituals, legislation, customs, and traditions, which have been handed down and developed as the heritage of a long Jewish history. Paradoxical as it may seem, it is not despite its universality but rather *because* of it that Judaism remains fully Jewish. This universality joins the Judaism of today to its long history and ancient traditions, promulgating neither a de-natured or abstract universality, as did the Enlightenment reformers of Judaism, nor a triumphant and exclusionary universality, as did the Church, but rather producing what Levinas names a "Jewish humanism" or a "biblical humanism."[9]

This route, via the concrete universality of tradition, however, and paradoxically at first glance, claims to be more enlightened than the Enlightenment. Benamozegh and Levinas confront modernity and modern Reform Judaism in precisely those terms, and on precisely those grounds—ethics and universalism—that the modern enlightenment perspective used in its attempt to critique and overthrow traditional Judaism. But they show, contrary to the Enlightenment and contrary to the Reformers, that "positive religion"—religion in its particularity, that is to say, in its history, its texts, its traditions, and so on—is indeed positive, the ground and source of a universal humanity.

For almost two centuries, it has been standard fare in the history of ideas—in Jewish studies a history dominated by the unacknowledged biases of German *Wissenshaft* Judaism—that the central conflict within modern Judaism is (as within all modernity) the struggle between the particular and the universal, between the "positive" and the "natural" or "rational." According to this narrative, the forces of the particular would be fragmenting and hence reactionary expressions of a narrow-mindedness, of the merely partisan and parochial, throwbacks to the merely national or ethnic. Orthodoxy and particularity in this negative sense would be equated—in order to be combated, by a self-proclaimed enlightened or liberated universalism. In this narrative, the "good guys" would be the Reformers. They would be the enlightened, cultured, fraternal bearers of the illuminating, liberating, and hence progressive forces of the *universal*, of reason, guided by the ideal of humanity united under reason.[10] But the truth is, in fact, otherwise.

All forms of Judaism, with a few minor exceptions, have always defended an ethical universalism. And all forms of Judaism, again with minor exceptions, have opposed particularism. To take one obvious example: ethical universalism has clearly been a core motif of Judaism since the days of the biblical prophets, which is to say, for more than three thousand years, so it can hardly be the discovery of an enlightened modern Judaism alone.

My thesis, then, made in the name of Benamozegh and Levinas, is that the central conflict in modern Judaism is not a struggle between particularity and universality, nationalism versus humanism, ethic versus ethnic, but rather, and more deeply, *a struggle between different versions of Jewish universalism.* To make this thesis clear, in the following I distinguish and locate Benamozegh and Levinas within a typology of three versions of universalism. Let me also say, right from the start, that useful as I think this typology is—indeed I think it is of sufficient heuristic value to grasp and contextualize the essential character of Benamozegh's and Levinas's Jewish universalism—it is not perfect. It requires further refinement and qualification,[11] and I look to readers to contribute toward making these improvements. That being said, philosophy and wisdom must make distinctions. It is important to recognize, first, that there *are* different types of universalism, and, second, to be clear about their differences.

III. Particularity and Three Types of Universality

It seems to me that appropriate name for the universality promoted by Benamozegh and Levinas is *concrete universalism*, because it remains tied to particularity. Or one could call it, compressing the title of this paper, *universal particularism*. The universality of the Reformers, and of an enlightened modernity more generally, I name *abstract universalism*, because Benamozegh and Levinas would criticize it—in contrast to the concrete universalism they identify with traditional Talmudic/rabbinic Judaism—precisely for its abstractness. The third kind of universalism, which is prevalent in Christian triumphalism and in all imperial politics, but is also occasionally present in Judaism, I name *exclusive universalism*, because Benamozegh and Levinas criticize it for its exclusivity, again in contrast to the genuine or non-exclusive universalism of traditional Talmudic/rabbinic Judaism. Finally, it almost goes without saying, all forms of universality must be distinguished from the perspective—-or non-perspective—of brute particularity.

A. Particularity

The perspective of a brute particularity is difficult to define precisely because particularity resists the universality inherent in definition itself. Definition works by specification within a genus. But particularity is precisely what defies genera and generalization. Defined negatively, then, we can say that particularity is an indifference to the universal. It is an original fragmentation without possible cohesion, an original pluralism without possible unity, the exception without a rule. It is constituted, one might also say, as an indeterminable set of monads without windows. Pure particularity is incommunicable and hence unintelligible. Even a bump or a groan in the night, to the extent that such events, however radically *hic et nunc*, would establish a communication, a contact, a commonality, however minimal, they would thus already undermine the purity or absoluteness of brute particularity. Such was Hegel's enduring insight articulated at the start of both his *Phenomenology* and his *Logic*. Particularity, then, is an ideal limit, but as the reverse side of all idealism, it is the dark side.

All forms of Judaism, and not just Reform Judaism, oppose the outlook of particularity. It is the outlook—or the tendency supported by the outlook—that Levinas identifies with idolatry and mythology, and sees as Judaism's fundamental and implacable enemy. Indeed, the very mission of Israel is to destroy the perspective of—or to reverse any direction toward—particularity. "Judaism," Levinas writes, "appeals to a humanity devoid of myths—not because the marvelous is repugnant to its narrow soul but because myth, albeit sublime, introduces into the soul that troubled element, that impure element of magic and sorcery and that drunkenness of the Sacred and war, that prolong the animal within the civilized."[12] Or, more succinctly and emphatically, he calls "the Torah itself, the book of anti-idolatry, the absolute opposite of idolatry!"[13] Benamozegh, because he is a Kabbalist who subscribes to the cosmological doctrines of the "broken vessels" and the "retrieval of the sparks," finds holiness in all things. But this perspective is not equivalent to antinomianism, and in no way means that he sanctions or condones evil. Benamozegh, like Levinas, opposes the particularity or polytheism of paganism precisely because, and to the extent that, it does not rise to the ethical universality of either "Mosaism" (i.e., Judaism) or "Noachism" (i.e., the minimum standard of righteousness for all nations). In his great work *Israel and Humanity*, he recalls the following words of the Talmudic rabbis: " 'Whoever renounces idolatry is a true Jew,' and 'Whoever renounces polytheism thereby affirms the entire Law.' "[14]

B. Universality

In contrast to the particularity—noise, and ultimately silence—of pagan idol worship, polytheism, and mythology, Judaism is in all its historical forms an ethical monotheism, and on this basis it espouses universality. Most broadly, "universality"—what logicians today call a "universal quantifier"—is the reference made by the "all": that which unifies and applies to every member of a particular set. Whether it is function of language alone, as nominalists claim to believe, or whether it has to do with the essence or nature of the real, as realists think, or whether it is some combination of the two, in every case universality is

Richard A. Cohen

that which is the same in difference. For example, when the Greek philosopher decides that "Man is a rational animal," or when the Bible declares that man was "created in the image and likeness of God," both are making what are formally universal claims. Whether true or false, both claims identify something that is the case—"rational," "image and likeness of God"—for those being and only those beings that are (that are in this way defined as) "human."

In religion, more specifically, the issue of universality applies primarily to relations between God and individual human beings and between God and individual organized religions. This is because individuals, whether humans or religions, differ from one another. Do God's love and providence apply to everyone and all groups equally, or to some more than others? Are God's revelation, redemption, and salvation meant for all humans equally, or for some more than others? And if the latter, for some only, is this because God's revelation, redemption, and salvation are already given (through grace, predestination, reincarnation, etc.) or subsequent to some chosen activity (faith, morality, repentance, enlightenment, etc.)? Regarding the various institutionalized religions, is only one, or are only some, or are all religions equally linked to God? What I am calling *exclusive, abstract,* and *concrete* universality are three distinctive but all universal answers to these fundamental religious questions.

1) Exclusive Universality

The term *exclusive universality* appears to be an oxymoron, since *exclusive* and *universal* seem to exclude each other. But it is precisely this exclusion that makes for this type of universality. It is the perspective of a part—a partisan— that, in its partiality, takes itself to be the whole. Maintaining itself in partiality, hence in the opacity of matter or body rather than in thought or spirit, it is the effort to achieve universality by physically or violently excluding everything else other than itself. It is the "one for all," where the one alone counts instead of all others. Its exclusiveness and its universality, then, are inseparable. This is because its universality is achieved only by excluding or negating difference. Thus it is an imperial and totalitarian universalism, because a part, as a part, takes itself to be the whole, which can only mean that it must take the place of the whole. By annihilating all difference, whether by violent obliteration or by sweet conversation, whether with or without the consent of the (merely provisional) other, here a part becomes the whole, and hence the "all," the universal.

One religious version of "exclusive" universality occurs in Christian triumphalism. It appears in a Roman Catholic version, in the doctrine of "salvation through the Church alone," and in a Protestant version, in the doctrine that salvation can be achieved solely through faith in Jesus Christ. This version explains the otherwise paradoxical militant Christian missionary fervor in the name of love that will only be satisfied when it has forever eliminated all other paths to God. This form of universality has never been normative for Judaism,

142

though it has nonetheless been found there. Whether true to authorial intention or not, one might find instances of it in the *Kuzari* of Yehuda Halevi; in certain commentaries of Nachmanides (e.g., to *Deuteronomy* 18:19, stating that prophecy would be limited to the Land of Israel and to Jews only); in the Zionism of Rabbi Tzvi Yehuda Kook (1891–1982);[15] and in the mystical ideology of contemporary Chabad Chassidism.[16]

Benamozegh, Levinas, and Reform Judaism especially, criticize all forms of this universalism—in Judaism, in Christianity, in politics, and elsewhere—as merely particularism in disguise. Because its universalism can only be achieved by totalizing a part, hence by means of totalitarianism more or less masked, its elimination of alternative paths is inevitably achieved, according to these critics, unjustifiably and hence violently. While one must admit, in principle, that is to say according to an abstract logic or theo-logic, that an infinite God can do whatever He wants, and hence could have provided all of humanity only one very specific path to salvation, a path known and proclaimed by only one religion, such a view, when approached from a slightly less abstract perspective, is fraught with insuperable difficulties. For one, its distribution of the damned and the saved, even from very simple chronological and geographical points of view, contradicts any intuitively obvious sense of God's Benevolence. Further, such a view challenges not only belief in God's goodness, but also belief in the reasonableness of his very act of creation, that is to say, the act of producing a multiple world. Finally, the logic of exclusive universality contradicts the express views of God's own revealed and hence sacred scriptures, which—without transparently self-serving interpretive gymnastics—nowhere set such limits to God's approachability.

Critics of exclusive universality see in its efforts to eliminate all other paths to God the violence of a leveling that is really nothing other than another expression of the intolerance of all parochialism, however rhetorically dressed up in a cloak of a (post facto and hence imaginary) universality. I cite Benamozegh, referring not to Christian or Jewish exclusivism, but to one of its political manifestations in ancient Roman imperialism: "The establishment of *jus gentium* ["law of the nations," or "international law"] has been credited to the Romans, but incorrectly, for the Romans regarded their empire as co-extensive with the world. The truth is that historically, Moses was the first to affirm its essential principle, and from a philosophical standpoint, it is clear that the very doctrine of universal Providence contained the germ of *jus gentium*; for if God rules the peoples of the world according to inviolable laws, nothing could be more natural or more just than that the peoples in their mutual relations should themselves be held responsible for the observance of these laws."[17] Or, to take second example from one of the many he finds of Christian exclusivity, Benamozegh writes that for Judaism, as seen by the Kabbalists, "the work of redemption is assigned not to a single individual, even a man-god, but to all humankind."[18]

Reform Judaism went further than Benamozegh or Levinas. It saw not only in Christian triumphalism and political totalitarianism, but also in traditional Judaism itself nothing less than the same anti-humanism of a parochial exclusivity. Thus it attacked Talmudic and rabbinic Judaism for its particularism. And thus, in its stead, Reform Judaism proposed an enlightened, rationally purified, progressive, humanist, universalist Judaism.

2) Abstract Universality

Enlightened, rational, or, as I call it, "abstract" universality, in contrast to exclusive universality, is the "all for one," where the *all* takes the place of the *one*. Truth or value lies not in what is singular or unique, but in what is common and the same. Causality replaces casuistry. Principles replace principals. What counts is the essence at the expense of existence, the law or rule rather than the instance or the circumstance. The particular, therefore, lacks significance. The enlightened universal, then, is the perspective of thought or spirit independent of extension and body. It is the universalism of modern science, of logical and mathematical relations, the perspective of reason, of non-contradictory and objective knowledge. Such a universalism tends naturally and necessarily toward the unified coherence of a system, the system *mathesis universalis*.

Like all the forms of universalism, abstract universalism is also dynamic. Because it is not based in the divisibility of extension, however, its dynamism is not manifest as overt violence, the war of one part against all other parts. Rather, its effort is to eliminate particularity and partisanship altogether, but to do so rationally, through intellectual agreement. Since only the universal is real, true, and valuable, particularity can only be unreal, untrue, and worthless. Hence, partisanship of any kind (except, inexplicably, that in favor of the universal!) can only be parochial, special pleading, mere privilege. Here is the universal of Spinozism, Hegelianism, and Marxist dialectic, as well as of all assimilationist ecumenicalism in religion. It is also the universalism of Paul, writing to the Galatians (*Gal.* 3:28): "There is neither Jew nor Greek, there is neither slave nor freeman, there is neither male and female; for you are all one in Christ Jesus."[19] Reformers of Judaism, of course, did not deny Jewish tradition in the name of Jesus, but rather in the name of a universal ethics, an ethics rationally purified of all particularity.[20]

Benamozegh and Levinas reject this type of universalism precisely because it is abstract and therefore reductive. Very simply, it reduces away not the partiality of the particular, as it thought, but the uniqueness of the singular—the singularity, for example, of family, community, nation, and tradition. For a genuine humanism, these are not simply the manifestation of a more primitive ignorance and unjustifiable special pleading. The particular is not an obstacle to a genuine humanity, but a necessary and irreducible dimension of its expression.[21] Ethics, Benamozegh and Levinas both insist, can never be efficacious if its idealism is merely angelic, a spiritualism divorced from the flesh and blood concerns and commitments of real people. Humans and humanity are not constituted by abstract essences alone, but in the sociality of families, communities, nations, and the like.

Benamozegh makes a powerful and deep observation: "Variety is not arbitrary or accidental, but something necessary and organic, with roots in the depths of human nature."[22] Variety is not some sort of ontological error, an affront to philosophers. It is the real; indeed, it is more real than the simplifications of a coherent thought. Benamozegh could have learned this from Vico, to be sure, but no less did he experience it daily as a rabbi, a Talmudist, a community leader, and a Kabbalist—*and*, let us add, as a son, a father, and a grandfather. Social life and its requirements of love, morality, and justice do not fit neatly into neat intellectual categories. Referring to a pagan philosopher's observation that there are many paths to the divine, Benamozegh comments: "Nothing could be more true or profound. Monotheism can become universal only with this understanding: unity in diversity, diversity in unity."[23] Elsewhere, in a summation that surely is meant as an attack on Kantian ethics, he sums up the Jewish ethical position vis-à-vis partiality and universality: "two parts of a single system. . . . *Interest by way of virtue and virtue by way of interest:* this is the teleological formula of society."[24]

Levinas, for his part, has devoted long and careful philosophical analyses—in his two major works, *Totality and Infinity* (1961)[25] and *Otherwise than Being of Beyond Essence* (1974),[26] and in many other shorter works, as well as in the analyses of his no less subtle and penetrating exegetical writings—his many "Talmudic Readings,"[27] and his many "Essays on Judaism"[28]—to show at the closest quarters that the transcendence of a genuine ethics is repressed in the tyranny of an abstract intellectualized totality. Thus, for a seductive cognitive abstractness, he will criticize the rationalism of Spinoza's metaphysics, the conceptualism of Hegel's philosophical history, and the representational prejudice of Husserl's phenomenology. No less will he criticize the totalitarian tendency of their alleged reversals, which tend toward the exclusivity of the particular: Nietzsche's fragmenting will to power, Heidegger's fundamental ontology, and Derrida's semiotic deconstruction. In the space of this essay, I can do little more than recommend to the reader Levinas's masterful critiques of the imperial totalizing not only of the exclusive universal, in its opaque brutality, but also of the more subtle and sophisticated violence perpetrated intellectually and spiritually in the name of the abstract universal.

3) Concrete Universality

In contrast to the "one for all" of exclusive univeralism (the one instead of the all), and the "all for one" of abstract universalism (the all instead of the one), concrete universality is the "one and all": the all integrally united with the one. Here the universal and particular—mind and body, spirit and letter—are inextricably bound to one another. Universalism is achieved neither by one part masquerading as a whole, while in fact violently eliminating alternative parts, nor by a universal pretending angelically to surpass particularity, while in fact ignoring or suppressing its own material conditions. Rather, from the integral perspective of the concrete universal, the exclusive and abstract forms of universality are revealed as based upon and reproducing a constructed dualism—whether political or epistemological—of mind and body, spirit and letter, apart from one another and hence only artificially linked.

Based neither in mind nor in body abstracted from each other, the concrete universal is rooted in the integral unity of moral praxis, lived as a temporal existence penetrated by the obligations and responsibilities of a pluralist (familial, communal, social, political, economic), multivalent, and historical world. The *all* of the exclusive universal is the *only*; the *all* of the abstract universal is the *every*; the *all* of concrete universal is the *each*. Neither purely subjective, the part taking the place of whole, nor purely objective, the whole annihilating the part, its meaningfulness—and the meaningfulness of Judaism—is always already *in medias res*, a present always already the product of a past and always projecting toward an unforeseeable future. Genuine universality depends on and requires particularity. In Levinas's words: "Its truth is universal like reason; its rule and moral institutions, Judaism's particular support, preserve this truth from corruption."[29]

My thesis, it may now be said, is that both Benamozegh and Levinas understand Judaism in terms of concrete universality, and second, that what they criticize in alternative interpretations of Judaism (and in Christianity) is precisely exclusivity and/or abstractness. Of course, too, they also both attack particularism.

For Talmudic or rabbinic Judaism, God, creation, and humanity are interwoven. To use Benamozegh's expression, humanity is in "partnership" with God, just as God is in "partnership" with humanity. To be sure, the relation is asymmetrical: God is above, and humanity moves upward, but true humanity and true divinity lies in, and not elsewhere than, these relations. For both thinkers, humanity's partnership with God is constituted in an interpersonal morality and social justice that are together the *sacred* work of redemption. Religious life for Judaism lies neither in an "other world" that will be, nor in "this world" as it is. Hence, it requires neither a blind and blinding faith nor a false and falsifying contentment with being. Rather, Judaism lives in the positive work of transforming the real into the good—the work of sanctification. In the concrete everyday labors and details that conserve and develop morality and justice on earth—hence in a piety that is equivalent to righteousness—lies the path of the divine. "The vision of God," Levinas writes, "is a moral act."[30] What Levinas calls a "biblical" or "Jewish humanism," as one instance of the "wisdom of love,"[31] is "a difficult wisdom concerned with truths that correlate to virtues."[32] Or, as Benamozegh expresses the biblical and rabbinic perspective: "They call just men *partners* of holy God."[33] "The just person," he continues, "whom the Talmud proclaims to be greater than the heaven and earth, and the saint, whom the rabbis call the partner of God, are superior not only to nature but also to the angels and the gods."[34]

Concreteness thus means never to neglect the neighbor for sake of the true or the spiritual. It is not God in the other that one respects, and through this respect makes one's relationship "religious," but rather because one respects the other—through moral and juridical service—one is aiming at the divine. The good—the prescriptive—is the ground of the real and the true. The good is found neither in the sky nor in the mind, but in the transcendence of the face-to-face relation and, no less, then, in the plurality of social and interpersonal relations. That is to say, goodness is found—concretely lived—in moral kindness and just institutions. This is what Benamozegh calls a "Hebraic cosmopolitanism,"[35] one that takes into account the individuality of the individual, the specificity of the community and nation, as well as the importance of time and place, without, for all that, relativizing either God or the transcendent ideality of the good. Speaking of Divine providence and referring to Paul's letter to the Galatians, Benamozegh writes these remarkable words: "Unlike Paul, we do not say of this Providence that it knows neither Jews nor Greeks, for that implies an inadmissible leveling of differences, a suppression of all nationality. We affirm, rather, that Providence recognizes equally Jews, Greeks, and Barbarians—in a word, all races and peoples, who ought to be perceived as one though without losing their individual identities."[36] Jew is not Greek and Greek is not Jew, nor even is one Jew another Jew, or one Greek another Greek, yet *each* Jew and all Jews, just as *each* Greek and all Greeks, are beholden to the same imperatives of morality and justice. "For the Jews," Benamozegh writes, "national feeling is never separated from their commitment to mankind. . . . [Judaism] affirms that Divine Providence extends without distinction over all of mankind, that God is the universal judge of nations as well as of individuals."[37] Thus Benamozegh's stunning and fundamentally pluralist proposition: "variety is not arbitrary or accidental, but something necessary and organic, with roots in the depths of human nature."[38] The virtue of variety, indeed, the necessity of variety—of the difference between one and another—for virtue, is precisely what the Reformers of Judaism, in their zeal for the abstract universal, did not grasp, or refused to grasp. Needless to say, defenders of exclusive universality are also blind to the fundamental virtue of pluralism.

But let us ask how, more specifically, do Benamozegh and Levinas find in Jewish concreteness—in specific rituals, prayers, history, books, traditions, and so on—and not only in its universally recognized moral legislation, such as most of the ten commandments—*how specifically do they find universality in Jewish concreteness?* I have already given the answer: they both find the unity of the particular and the universal in morality and justice. But their approaches nonetheless differ, because Benamozegh and Levinas differ in background, family, language, training, social environment, audience, and immediate spiritual context.

Because I want to conclude this brief presentation with Benamozegh, I will here turn to Levinas first. No doubt in part because of his university training, his devotion to philosophy, and the fact that most of his writings were published for an educated and cultured but non-Jewish audience, Levinas will often characterize Judaism's concrete universalism in terms of method. More specifically, he contrasts the ethical orientation of rabbinical exegesis, as found in the Talmud, and in his own exegetical writings, to the epistemological and ontological orientation of abstract rationality. That is, he finds in Judaism's Talmudic and rabbinic hermeneutics—in its attention to both the letter and the spirit of texts to discover the sacred, and to discover it in a moral and juridical social context—the meeting place of the concrete and the universal. I cite Levinas:

> I wish to speak of the Torah as desirous of being a force warding off idolatry by its essence as Book, that is, by its very writing, signifying precisely pre-scription and by the permanent reading it calls for—permanent reading or interpretation and reinterpretation or study; a book thus destined from the start for its Talmudic life. A book that is also by that very fact foreign to any blind commitment that might think itself virtuous because of its decisive-ness or stubbornness. . . . The Talmudic life and destiny of the Torah, which is also an endless return, in its interpretation of several degrees, to particular cases, to the concreteness of reality, to analyses that never lose themselves in generalities but return to examples—resisting invariable conceptual en-tities . . . renewing, though continual exegesis—and exegesis of that exe-gesis—the immutable letters and hearing the breath of the living God in them. A liturgy of study as lofty as the obedience to the commandments that fulfills the study.[39]

For Levinas, it is "through continual exegesis—and exegesis of exegesis," that Judaism finds spirit in letter, in all registers, no matter how particular they may seem—in prayer, family life, eating habits, manners, holidays, tradition, and so on. For it is in the concrete that an ethical universal finds its genuine, if never final, manifestation. Such is the universal and u-topian vision of Judaism.[40]

Benamozegh, by contrast, explicates the indissoluble integrity of particu-lar and universal in rabbinic and Kabbalistic terms, in terms of Jewish priest-hood and the two dimensions/orientations of Mosaism and Noachism. Bena-mozegh affirms the unity of God, of humanity, and of Providence, but rejects an abstract universalist account of them, because "we would have an appar-ently universal religion, but one whose very constitution would tend to pre-clude Jewish individuality."[41] Rather, Benamozegh affirms "a religion of truly universal character [which] would embrace all of mankind, even while pre-serving Jewish individuality," and he continues, rejecting exclusive univer-sality, by adding: "nor would this be an Israel to whom all the other peoples were subordinated."[42] The bond that unites the particular and the universal in Judaism is the bond that unites its Mosaic and the Noachide dimensions globally, namely, "the hierarchical organization of the human race into priests and laymen."[43] That is to say, the particular is harmonized with the universal when the particular, like the priest in relation to the layman, *serves* the universal. Thus, like Levinas, ethical monotheism—service to and for the other, the other before the self—lies at the basis of a concrete or Jewish universalism.

I conclude with a striking citation from Benamozegh's *Israel and Humanity*, in which he highlights a rabbinical commentary on the praise and priority Jews give to Israel, the chosen land—so seemingly particularist—in universalist terms. Benamozegh writes:

> It seems to us that the strikingly universalist idea which the sages derive from this text, which is apparently so exclusive in its implication, beautifully characterizes the authentic spirit of Judaism. A country which finds itself chosen to be a means of grace and blessing for the entire world, but is in no way licensed to hold others in contempt: This is the dominating concept of the entire Law, written and oral, beginning with Abraham, in whom all races should be blessed, and finishing with the Messiah, who will bring both deliverance for Israel and the knowledge of truth for all peoples.[44]

The universal is thus found not outside the particular, or despite the particular, but precisely because of, and in view of the particular. It is found neither in an epistemological nor in an aesthetic rigor, but in the stringency of an ethics through which humanity is constituted: in the moral obligations and responsibilities of one for another, and in the demand for justice that these obligations and responsibilities exert on each for all.

NOTES

1. Elijah Benamozegh (1823–1900) is unfortunately still too little known today, even in Italy, and even in Jewish intellectual circles. He was the rabbi of the important Italian Jewish community of Livorno, and an intellectual leader of nineteenth-century Italian Jewry. Although he wrote prolifically, for the most part in Italian and Hebrew, two of his works written and published in French have been translated and published in English: *Jewish and Christian Ethics* (1867; English trans. Emmanuel Blochman [San Francisco: E. Blochman, 1873]), and *Israel and Humanity* (1914, posthumous; English trans. Maxwell Luria [New York: Paulist Press, 1995]). An excellent recent book on his thought, *Philosophie et Cabbale*, by Alessando Guetta (Paris: L'Harmattan, 1998), is presently being translated for publication in English. See also, e.g., "Elie Benamozegh," by J. Jehouda (trans. A. Propp), in L. Jung, ed., *Jewish Leaders (1750–1940)* (New York: Bloch, 1953), pp. 233–46; D. Novak, *The Image of the Non-Jew in Judaism* (Lampeter: Edwin Mellen Press, 1983), pp. 361–64; and *La Rassegna Mensile di Israel*, vol. 43, no. 3 (September–December 1997), on "Elia Benamozegh, Livorno 1822–1900: Un Maestro in eta moderna," ed. L. Franchetti Naor and M. Silvera.

2. Although Levinas delivered many addresses published under the name of "Talmudic Readings," he was the first to admit that he was not a "Talmudist." This title is reserved for those pious Jewish scholars whose authority derives from have mastered significant portions or all of the vast legal (*halachic*) dimension of the Talmud, something Levinas not only did not and never claimed to have accomplished, but an authority to which he several times publicly deferred. For example, at the start of his commentary to the Talmudic tractate *Shabbat* 88a–88b, in a lecture entitled "The Temptation

of Temptation," Levinas makes the following prefatory remarks: "Finally, I am a bit embarrassed that I always comment on the aggadic texts of the Talmud and never venture forth into the Halakhah. But what can I do? The Halakhah demands an intellectual muscle which is not given to everyone. I cannot lay claim to it." In E. Levinas, *Nine Talmudic Readings*, trans. A. Aronowicz (Bloomington: Indiana University Press: 1990), p. 32. Or, another example, Levinas's prefatory remarks to his commentary to tractate *Sanhedrin* 36b–27a, in a Talmudic reading entitled "As Old As the World?": "As in all previous years—and this is not merely a formal excuse—I feel inadequate to the task entrusted to me. The public, responding to these commentaries so favorably as to intimidate me, has in its midst many people who know the Talmud infinitely better than I do." In Levinas, *Nine Talmudic Lectures*, p. 71. Again, the opening sentence of his commentary to *Baba Metsia* 83a–83b, in a Talmudic reading entitled "Judaism and Revolution": "As always when I begin my Talmudic readings at this colloquium of intellectuals, I fear the presence in the room of people who know the Talmud better than I do. That is not a difficult feat but one which places me in a state of mortal sin, the sin of the student holding forth before his master." In Levinas, *Nine Talmudic Readings*, p. 96. These expressions are not false, misleading, or ironic gestures. And Levinas knew the Talmud quite well!

3. While much has been written on the topic of modernity and secularization, the *locus classicus* no doubt remains the debate between Hans Blumenberg, in *The Legitimacy of the Modern Age*, trans. R. M. Wallace (Cambridge, Mass.: MIT Press, 1985), original German publication in 1966, and Karl Lowith, in *Meaning in History* (Chicago: University of Chicago Press, 1949), original German publication in 1953.

4. Thus Levinas and Benamozegh stand against both Blumenberg, who argues for the irreducibly secular character of modernity, and Lowith, who argues that the secularity of modernity remains a tranfigured form of religion (Christianity), to which it is reducible. Blumenberg would be wrong to think that secularity is irreducibly independent of religion, and Lowith would be mistaken to think that secularity can be reduced to religion. For Levinas and Blumenberg, in contrast, the "secular"—without reduction—is already religious. Of course, this means conceiving religion differently than either Blumenberg or Lowith conceive it.

5. In his introduction, entitled "Les politiques du salut," to the recently republished book by Elie Benamozegh, *Morale juive et morale chretienne* (Paris: In Press Editions, 2000; 1st ed., 1867), Shmuel Trigano comments on the pernicious effects of the divorce between religion and politics found in Christianity; see pp. 7–12.

6. Elijah Benamozegh, *Israel and Humanity*, trans. L. Maxwell (New York: Paulist, 1994), p. 297. (Henceforth, IH.)

7. IH 326.

8. IH 302.

9. Emmanuel Levinas, "For a Jewish Humanism," in E. Levinas, *Difficult Freedom*, trans. S. Hand (Baltimore: Johns Hopkins University Press, 1990), p. 275. Understanding Jewish universalism not only in terms of ethics but no less in terms of Talmud and Jewish tradition, Benamozegh and Levinas join and continue the earlier labors of Rabbi Samson Raphael Hirsch in opposing Liberal or Reform Judaism. I would also like to link the name Abraham Joshua Heschel to the traditionalist defense of Jewish ethical universalism that unites Hirsch, Benamozegh, and Levinas.

10. On Benamozegh and the German Reformation of Judaism, see A. Guetta, *Philosophie et Cabbale* (Paris: L'Harmattan, 1998), pp. 184–92.

11. Other types or mixed types of universalism might also exist. For example, the slogan (sometimes heard in American "Conservative" (Masorti) Judaism: "Be a Jew at home and a citizen outside," might be seen as a hybrid of concrete universalism at home (and presumably at the synagogue, Mikvah, and Talmud Torah) and abstract universalism in the public sphere. Whether such a hybrid is faithful to either concrete universalism or to abstract universalism, however, is debatable.

12. E. Levinas, "Being a Westerner," *Difficult Freedom*, p. 49.

13. E. Levinas, "Contempt for the Torah as Idolatry," in E. Levinas, *In the Time of the Nations*, trans. M. B. Smith (Bloomington: Indiana University Press, 1994), pp. 58–59.

14. IH 257 (citing *Megillah* 13a, and *Kiddushin* 40a).

15. See D. Samson, *Torat Eretz Yisrael: The Teachings of HaRav Tzvi Yehuda HaCohen Kook* (Jerusalem: Torat Eretz Yisrael, 1991).

16. See A. Ravitzky, *Messianism, Zionism, and Jewish Religious Radicalism*, trans. M. Swirsky (Chicago: University of Chicago Press, 1996), pp. 181–206.

17. IH 128.

18. IH 203.

19. On Paul and his transformation of Judaism, see the remarkable scholarly study by H. Maccoby, *The Mythmaker: Paul and the Invention of Christianity* (New York: Harper and Row, 1987); and, brilliantly emphasizing the literary strategies of Paul's abstract universality, see D. Boyarin, *A Radical Jew: Paul and the Politics of Identity* (Berkeley: University of California Press, 1994).

20. Not only Reformers, however, have been defenders of an abstract universality in Judaism. I think a persuasive case can be made that the late Professor Yeshayahu Liebowitz (1903–1995), and many of his present-day disciples, defended an abstract universalism in the name of Jewish orthodoxy. Jewish law would be obeyed "for its own sake" and not for the self and social perfection it effects. It would thus be a form devoid of content, or, at least, a form whose peculiar content—whatever that might be, perhaps pure obedience?—would have to be supplemented by external considerations of morality and justice. The fact is not surprising, then, that Liebowitz's academic expertise was in chemistry and neurophysiology (though of course it must be said also that not all scientists who happen to be Jewish and orthodox share his beliefs about the abstract nature of orthodox Jewish law).

21. This defense, by the way, was also and precisely the point Moses Hess made against Karl Marx, namely, that nations are not simply ignorant obstacles to a global proletarian, but rather an integral part of what it means to be human. See K. Marx, "On the Jewish Question" (1843); M. Hess, *Rome and Jerusalem* (1862); and, more generally, on the modern dissolution of intermediary groups between individuals and an allegedly more rational global humanity (which in fact means, the State), A. Gehlen, *Man in the Age of Technology*, trans. P. Lipscomb (New York: Columbia University Press, 1980). H. Bergson, interestingly enough, also admits "the requisite moral conformation for living in groups" between the solitary individual and humanity in general, in *The Two Sources of Morality and Religion*, trans. R. Ashley Audra and C. Brereton (New York: Doubleday, no date given), p. 95. The defense of the singular also lies at the heart of Vico's *New Science* in contrast, say, to Hegel's *Science of Logic*.

22. IH 315.

23. IH 315. Benamozegh invokes Symmachus (late 2nd c.), who had said: " 'It is because the mystery is so great that it is impossible to reach it by a single path.' "

24. IH 294–95.

25. E. Levinas, *Totality and Infinity*, trans. A. Lingis (Pittsburgh: Duquesne University Press, 1969).

26. E. Levinas, *Otherwise than Being; or, Beyond Essence*, trans. A. Lingis (The Hague: Martinus Nijhoff, 1981).

27. For most of Levinas's "Talmudic Readings," see E. Levinas, *Nine Talmudic Readings; Beyond the Verse*, trans. G. D. Mole (Bloomington: Indiana University Press, 1994); *In the Time of the Nations* and *New Talmudic Readings*, trans. R. A. Cohen (Pittsburgh: Duquesne University Press, 1999).

28. Many of Levinas's "Jewish essays" are found in the following collections by Emmanuel Levinas: *Difficult Freedom*, trans. S. Hand (Baltimore: Johns Hopkins University Press, 1990); *Beyond the Verse; In the Time of the Nations*.

29. E. Levinas, "For a Jewish Humanism," *Difficult Freedom*, p. 274.

30. Ibid., 275.

31. E. Levinas, *Otherwise than Being*, p.162.

32. E. Levinas, *Difficult Freedom*, p. 275. For a fuller explanation of this phrase—"a difficult wisdom concerned with truths that correlate to virtues"—see the translator's introduction to E. Levinas, *New Talmudic Readings*, pp. 1–46; or my book, *Ethics, Exegesis and Philosophy: Interpretation After Levinas* (Cambridge: Cambridge University Press, 2001).

33. IH 198.

34. IH 201.

35. IH 151.

36. IH 133. Also see note 18 above.

37. IH 206. This is also Benamozegh's perspective in *Jewish and Christian Ethics, with a Criticism of Mohamedism*, trans. E. Blochman (San Francisco: E. Blochman, 1873).

38. IH 315.

39. E. Levinas, *In the Time of the Nations*, pp. 58–59.

40. Because of space limitations, let me simply refer readers to one more of Levinas's shorter articles on Jewish universalism, which, like "For a Jewish Humanism," is also found in Levinas, *Difficult Freedom*—namely, "Israel and Universalism," pp. 175–77.

41. IH 237–38.

42. IH 238.

43. IH 239.

44. IH 318.

The Kingdom and the Trinity

Kevin Hart

I

The principal motifs of Christianity are the Kingdom and the Trinity, and the main difficulty that Christianity has faced, still faces, and will continue to face, is how to relate them. I realize that this is a statement in need of commentary at every level, and that it would take volumes to justify it in satisfying detail. Each word, *Kingdom* and *Trinity*, is nested in related problems that, if they seem to have become more clear with the advent of modernity, still remain pressing for moderns and postmoderns alike. To speak about either the Kingdom or the Trinity is to be involved in the relations between experience and revelation, scripture and theology, history and truth, and to realize that we share these tensions with Judaism. All I can do in this brief essay is clarify the statement with which I started, beginning with some of its key words. My title reverses the one that Jürgen Moltmann chose for the first volume of his "systematic contributions to theology" that, taken together, form a distinguished example of redirecting liberalism in the wake of neo-orthodox criticism.[1] I will try to rein in an unruly topic by engaging Moltmann from time to time, a conversation that is part of a wider discussion between theological modernity and theological postmodernity.

Principal poses too many difficulties to be the first word in line for comment, so I will begin with a less assertive one. I have chosen *motifs* over *dogmas* mainly to underline the incommensurality of talk about the Kingdom and the Trinity. That there are specific and highly detailed dogmas about the Trinity that are binding on all Catholics is well known. Yet there is no dogma of the Kingdom: one can read Henry Denzinger's *Enchiridion Symbolorum* from beginning to end without encountering a reference to it. The preaching of the Kingdom strikes us from the first as resisting reduction to propositions; it concerns something that is "already but not yet," and the parables about it are notoriously hard to harmonize. In order to let this preaching resonate as deeply and as widely as possible, it is best to retain the Greek βασιλεια and let its strangeness aid our thinking. This was the word the LXX chose to translate the Hebrew words for Yahweh's reign and dominion, and we do well to recall that, for all its originality, Jesus' image of the βασιλεια also draws on the Jewish idea of Yahweh as King.[2] To translate βασιλεια as *regnum, Reich, royaume* or Kingdom, as is usually done, is to reveal facets of the Greek and Hebrew while allowing the image of a fully realized and observable state to veil what is at issue.

Of course, if we say that the dogmas of the Church (as "holy, catholic, and apostolic") answer eschatologically to the preaching of the βασιλεια we will be right, as we would be if we said the same thing about the communion of saints. Yet neither dogma captures what is at risk in Jesus' parables, sayings, and prayer about the βασιλεια; and the relationships between βασιλεια and Church, βασιλεια and Heaven, have tensions that need not distract us here. The former is especially challenging, since it is every Christian's responsibility to help make βασιλεια and εκκλησια one, and although I will make some passing remarks on the relation of βασιλεια and the Church I will focus on the more primitive element to which the Church must always answer. In my understanding, talk about Church and Trinity takes place on the same theological plane, namely that of dogma. Now, dogmatic theology has its own complexities, but it also has a fundamental unity as goal. My theme, the βασιλεια and the Trinity, takes hold otherwise, if it can be said to take hold at all. For the two terms exist on different theological levels, and at least initially this situation perplexes how they can be related and how they can be said to be "principal" motifs of Christianity.

Perhaps the word *motif* has an additional claim to our attention over and above the word *dogma*, though, insofar as Christianity is always much wider than its formulations in conciliar definitions or as embodied in the magisterium. It is in the nature of Christianity to exceed any idea of it itself. At its best, the Church's framing of revealed truths is rational, conducted with close reference to scripture, and attentive to the historical deposits of faith. Who would wish it otherwise? One of the most forceful of all witnesses to this understanding of revealed truth is St. Thomas Aquinas, who tells us that the faith has a propositional structure. What we are to believe is distinctly stated in the creed, he says, and the faithful are expected to affirm these propositions through the proper exercise of faith and reason.[3] Yet Thomas did not teach that everyone should have an explicit understanding of the faith, and certainly never taught that there is an indisputably Christian basis for choosing to think about God in a propositional manner. Not all of our relations with God—in prayer and study, sacraments and acts of love, the routines of daily life and mystical ecstasy—can be captured in propositions. Revelation is never given *as such*, in a moment of full presence that can be intuited and translated into constative statements; it enters the world by way of the incalculable and never yields that dimension of its reality, even in dogmatic formulations. More generally, there is no good reason to consider acts of theoretical consciousness always to benefit the faithful more than affection, desire, imagination, and touch. Christianity is a way of life before it is a mode of reflection.

This is not to say that the formulation of dogma is a second-order reflection on Christian experience, for there is no continuous line between first- and second-order levels in Christianity.[4] One would be hard-pressed to say where testimony ends and dogma begins in the New Testament. As St. Anselm observes, "he who does not believe will not experience, and he who has not had experience will not know."[5] Inevitably one recalls St. Augustine: "faith seeks, understanding finds."[6] Nothing in that formula prevents us from retaining a childlike faith, but it stops that faith from being childish. Without a dialogue of faith and understanding we could not enter any of the mysteries, let alone the trinitarian nature of God that is the deepest of them all. This dialogue helps to protect the believer from mystifications of God's self-revelation while retreating before the mystery of that revelation. That said, dogma is not the sole mode of reflection available: the arts can exist in dialectical relationships with faith, and offer ways of clarification and illumination, though they never result in *articuli fidei*. Nor is reflection the only dimension of Christian life outside faith. For faith draws on what precedes it while eluding dogmatic definition, and here I am thinking once again of the βασιλεια.

The Trinity exceeds dogma; the βασιλεια precedes it. The one is a motif of Christianity because the most orthodox formulations insist on their inadequacy with respect to it, while the other is a motif because it informs dogmas without ever quite becoming one itself. No claim is being made, then, that the Trinity and the βασιλεια exist on the one theological plane or are comparable in any way. If this begins to clarify why I am calling the βασιλεια and the Trinity motifs of Christianity, it does not account for the judgment that they are principal motifs of the faith. That must be done in another way, and if it is to be done well it must take account of the fact that the judgment would have sounded odd to many followers of Jesus over the centuries.

A historian would struggle to find times when the faithful, priests, bishops, and theologians were all equally concerned with both the βασιλεια and the Trinity. It would be far easier to find periods when the one was of interest and the other was not. Certainly the Jesus movement, consisting of ordinary folk who heard the parables or prayed the "Our Father," would have thought the βασιλεια was Jesus' central message. There is even testimony that Jesus preached it after Easter Sunday (*Acts* 1:3). The gospels represent Jesus before he went to Jerusalem in relation to the Father and the Spirit, although there is no mention of him preaching the Trinity after Easter. Yet the resurrected Christ commanded his disciples to baptize "in the name of the Father, and of the Son, and of the Holy Ghost" (*Mt.* 28:19). The sole glimpse the gospels give us of the Trinity occurs in liturgy and is likely to have preceded the formation of the New Testament.[7] We move toward a soteriological understanding of the Trinity only in St. Paul's epistles to the Corinthians, Ephesians, and Romans.[8] If there is little theology of the Trinity in Paul, there is even less of the βασιλεια, and it is mainly taken up with Paul's distinctive christocentrism. What Jesus calls with respect to the righteous "the kingdom of their Father" (*Mt.* 13:34) becomes for Paul "the kingdom of Christ and of God" (*Eph.* 5:5). Had he also spoken of "the kingdom of the Spirit." we might have witnessed a trinitarian theology beginning to formulate itself by way of the βασιλεια.

Paul did not take that path, nor was it a direction many of the Fathers chose to follow. Theophilus, Justin Martyr, and Tertullian began to develop the doctrine of the Trinity without reference to the βασιλεια. Meanwhile, the βασιλεια was mostly interpreted in its own terms, which were either developed from New Testament sources, spiritualized, or accommodated to changes in society.[9] Irenaeus envisaged a divine reign on earth after the general resurrection.[10] Origen, however, saw Christ himself as αυτοβασιλεια.[11] Eusebius declared Constantine to have ushered in the kingdom, thereby allowing βασιλεια and μοναρχια to be identified.[12] And Augustine maintained that εκκλεσια and βασιλεια form a unity here and now, although they are not yet identical.[13] Of all the major Catholic theologians, only Augustine gives sustained emphasis to both the βασιλεια and the Trinity, although relating them was not a concern for him. Centuries later, Thomas has much to say about the Father, Son, and Spirit but for political reasons of the day, God's reign did not become one of his major themes.[14]

Understanding God as Trinity became the index of Nicean orthodoxy; and along with the christological doctrines with which it is intimately related, it has remained so. The dogma of the Trinity has not always been of deep interest to theologians, however, as is silently attested by those Catholic histories of the doctrine that pass from Thomas to Bernard Lonergan and Karl Rahner without a whisper about the intervening seven hundred years.[15] In the eighteenth century, when scholars began to focus on the βασιλεια, the doctrine of the Trinity was at its lowest ebb, especially in the Protestant churches. Immanuel Kant tartly observed in a late work, "Whether we are to worship three or ten persons in the Divinity makes no difference."[16] He regarded the Trinity "merely as a representation of a practical idea" yet vigorously recast Jesus' preaching of the βασιλεια along the axis of ethics as the Kingdom of Ends.[17] In the wake of the Enlightenment, the Trinity continued to fare badly.

Friedrich Schleiermacher may have concluded *The Christian Faith* (1821–1822) with an account of the Trinity but did so by pointing out that the doctrine, as ecclesiastically framed, "is not an immediate utterance concerning the Christian self-consciousness, but only a combination of several such utterances."[18] Ernst Troeltsch kept faith with Schleiermacher in many respects, although he did not hesitate to say in his 1912–1913 lectures that "all of theology can be expressed" in terms of the Trinity.[19] In this, as in other things, he was ahead of his time. Schleiermacher may also have observed that "the consciousness of God is always related to the totality of active states in the idea of a Kingdom of God," but the βασιλεια thereafter remains in the background of his theology.[20] By and large, though, the βασιλεια received far more attention than the Trinity in the nineteenth century. In 1819, Johann Sebastian Drey, one of the founders of Catholic theology at Tübingen, declared it to be "Christianity's supreme idea," while in his *Rechtfertigung und Versöhnung* (1870–1874), Albrecht Ritschl developed that idea so thoroughly that it became virtually identical with the gospel.[21] By the time Adolf von Harnack lectured on the question "What is Christianity?" (1899–1900), we find liberal theology affirming that talk of the Trinity obscures Jesus' authentic teaching, which is centered on the βασιλεια.[22]

Of course, the βασιλεια and the Trinity have been leagued together, and doubtless in ways that Paul would never have imagined. Gregory of Nyssa stressed that the Holy Spirit is King, just as the Father and the Son are, although he does not explore the theme that the Kingdom of God is trinitarian.[23] Many centuries later, Joachim of Fiore (1130–1202) developed the view of three historical kingdoms, each distinctive yet involved in the others, and each occurring under the sign of a divine person. The Jews had already experienced the kingdom of the Father; Christians had lived until now in the clerical kingdom of the Son; and the kingdom of the Spirit, to be associated with monasticism, had already been announced in the life of St. Benedict. Joachim reached this conclusion by a mixture of prophetic exegesis and philosophical theology. Arguing against Peter Lombard's teaching that the divine unity is "true and proper," Joachim suggested it is "collective and similar." This account of the divine unity was declared heretical by the fourth Lateran Council (1215), which upheld the Lombard's teaching.[24] Yet the council did not condemn the theology of history that is consistent with the heretical understanding of the divine unity. That was left to the provincial council of Arles (1263). By then, the expectation of a *tertius status*, an age of the Holy Spirit, had been taken up by the Franciscan Spirituals, among others; and although Joachism was opposed by the Church, the energies it had unleashed contributed to the ferment of the Reformation. Indeed, as Moltmann points out, Lutherans and Calvinists adapted Joachim's schema in their threefold distinction of *regnum naturæ*, *regnum gratiæ* and *regnum gloriæ*.[25] It is an adaptation, Moltmann stresses, not a simple translation. Protestantism regards the rules of nature and grace as belonging to this world, and the rule of glory as belonging

Kevin Hart

to the world to come, and in so doing it elides Joachim's speculation that there will one day be an earthly kingdom of the Spirit.[26]

Moltmann himself adapts Joachim's understanding of the Trinity and the βασιλεια, and I will explore his point of view as well. However, at this point I simply wish to let him remind us that my conjunction of βασιλεια and Trinity might seem strange not only historically but also politically. For Moltmann urges that there are strong threads tying monotheism and monarchy so that God has been figured as a divine patriarch whose absolute rule in heaven is replicated in the world in ways that are profoundly oppressive.[27] Only by radically thinking God as irreducibly trinitarian, Moltmann argues, can we recognize that Christianity is not at heart committed to monarchy or pa-triarchy but is a religion of freedom. Appealing as this "social doctrine" of the Trinity is, there are difficulties with it. One must be careful when affirming the triune God not to imply that Yahweh, the God of the Jews, is a thoroughly oppressive deity.[28] Equally, one must proceed slowly when criticizing the link between monotheism and monarchy, for the Fathers often used the two words interchangeably.[29] Besides, the appeal to plurality is not in itself reassuring: everyone can give examples of both a benign monarch and a violent junta. Other problems with social trinitarianism will become apparent as my argu-ment develops.

Finally, if there are historical and political reasons why the conjunction of βασιλεια and Trinity can cause flickers of concern, there are also conceptual worries. I have said that the βασιλεια and the Trinity exist on distinct theologi-cal planes, and that, in very different ways, they are principal motifs of Chris-tianity. The conceptual difficulty is that each of the βασιλεια and the Trinity can lay claim to being the whole of theology. That they do this in different ways is to be expected, although because the one informs doctrine while the other has doctrine quietly confess its inadequacy, they have something in common. The word *motif* captures only part of this, and my sense is that βασιλεια and Trinity also impinge on us other than as distinctive features of Christianity. It is as though they act as vanishing points of the faith, and to make some sense of that I will ponder each in turn, beginning with the βασιλεια.

II

In calling the βασιλεια a vanishing point of the faith, I am not thereby agreeing with Rudolf Bultmann that "*The message of Jesus* is a presupposition for the theology of the New Testament rather than a part of that theology itself."[30] To be sure, the gospels are concerned to testify that Jesus is the Christ; and doubtless, as Bultmann and his school showed by form and redaction criticism, the gospels were shaped in different ways and to different ends. Yet transmission analysis need not draw a firm line between Jesus and the Christ. It can help us to hear Jesus in those testimonies of faith in Christ. Writing a generation after Bultmann, Joachim Jeremias states in his theology of the New

Testament that "Our starting point is the fact that the central theme of the public proclamation of Jesus was the kingly reign of God."[31] I agree; but it also needs to be stressed that Jesus' *actions* also testify that the βασιλεια is at hand. His sayings and his doings cannot be separated. What Jesus tells us about God, in word and deed, occurs in and through the βασιλεια. It is the vanishing point that orients us with respect to our ultimate horizon, God. It is what allows action on the plane of experience to be called "Christian."

This remark can be taken in two ways. On the one hand, we can regard the βασιλεια as a part of theology. After all, it tells us nothing about creation and apocalypse, nothing about the Trinity, and not much about christology. Its concern is limited and intense: to declare the nearness of God's reign, and to provoke conversion; to induce faith that the Father will rule in power and judge with authority; and to spread conviction that his dominion is growing here and now. On the other hand, the βασιλεια can be regarded as giving the whole of theology. Not only does it declare God to be sovereign creator and lord of history, but also, in being preached by Jesus, it reveals the intimacy of the Father and the Son, through whose relation we can discern the Spirit. The kingdom of the Father is, as Paul saw, also the kingdom of Christ, which gives us a basis for christology. Chances are that those who try to derive all theology from the βασιλεια will argue that it is eschatological in one sense or another (as "consistent," "inaugurated," "realised"), and accordingly they would develop a soteriology and adduce a doctrine of the Church.[32] Depending on how we define *eschatology*, we might also be able to outline a doctrine of the apocalypse.

A similar story could be told about the Trinity. Seen from one vantage point, it can be regarded as a part of theology, certainly the most mysterious but perhaps for many Christians not the most important for daily life. (Hence the old jibe about the Trinity having five notions, four relations, three persons, two processions, one nature, and no proof.) The doctrine speaks of God's internal relations—Father and Son as communicating, and the Spirit as communicated—but, as Kant, Schleiermacher, and Harnack have suggested, it is abstract, speculative, and insufficiently grounded in scripture. Seen from another vantage point, the Trinity appears to contain the whole of theology. Paschal trinitarians tell us that the Trinity is best thought by way of Jesus' crucifixion and resurrection, and that this complex event bespeaks his earthly life, while looking forward to the apocalypse.[33] If we add Karl Rahner's formula that the economic Trinity is the immanent Trinity, as Paschal trinitarians usually do, it is possible to see the whole of salvation history, from creation to apocalypse, in trinitarian terms.[34]

Therefore, both the βασιλεια and the Trinity can be seen as principal motifs of Christianity in the sense that the whole of the faith can be deduced from either. Yet can Christianity have two principals, especially two that compete for the whole of the faith? Doubtless they are not the only motifs for which such a claim can be made. For example, Louis-Marie Chauvet has

Kevin Hart

recently argued that sacramental theology "cannot be viewed as just another sector in the field of theology" since it is "a *dimension* that recurs throughout the whole of Christian theology." Consequently, "the *entire* field of theology . . . is to be rethought according to this constitutive dimension of the faith."[35] Chauvet is quite right: sacramentality runs through the whole of theology. In prizing the βασιλεια and the Trinity, though, I have not been thinking of them as dimensions of the faith but as dominant ideas whose authority answers to their status as vanishing points of Christian experience. Only by defining "principal" in this way, perhaps, can one keep the claims of the βασιλεια and the Trinity in balance. Such would be the hypothesis that imposes itself on us now, of Christian experience coming into perspective only with the βασιλεια calling us on the left and the Trinity on the right. What would be important, it seems, is not that the βασιλεια and the Trinity exist on different theological planes, but rather that they organize the entire plane of Christian experience.

Anyone defending this hypothesis would have to reject the idea that Christianity has just the one vanishing point, whether it be the βασιλεια or the Trinity. The arguments to be raised are easily imagined. If we orient the faith wholly by way of the βασιλεια, it becomes eschatological, ethical, or mystical. Consistent eschatology has proven to be indefensible and, as Albert Schweitzer showed, ethics is the "negative theology" of its failure.[36] Unless one incorporates Jesus' preaching into the life of God, as happens in the doctrine of the Trinity, even a sense of the βασιλεια as inaugurated eschatology would become no more than an open-ended ethics. The remaining solution is that of Marcus Borg, for whom the βασιλεια is a symbol for "the experience of God" and Jesus a mystic: a view I find difficult to reconcile with scripture.[37] At the same time, to ground the faith exclusively in the Trinity, even in Paschal trinitarianism, is quietly to bypass the acts and preaching of Jesus. In the last fifteen years or so, we have become more sanguine that Schweitzer ever was about hearing the voice of the historical Jesus, and a sense of the Nazarene's vision of God's rule is crucial for any program of Christian social justice. This last point reminds us that we need to keep βασιλεια and Trinity in play so that we may keep faith with the confession that Jesus is the Christ. The torture and execution of Jesus tells us that to preach the βασιλεια is to accept the possibility of unmerited suffering, while the resurrection confirms our faith in the one who preached and reveals him in relation to the Father and the Spirit.

On the hypothesis under consideration, both the βασιλεια and the Trinity are required as vanishing points if experience is to be represented as Christian. Now if we inquire into our guiding metaphor, we will find that it can be taken in two ways: either the vanishing points shape what counts as Christian experience but cannot themselves be experienced, or anything that counts as Christian experience must refer to the βασιλεια and the Trinity. In its very ambiguity, the hypothesis captures dominant versions of the theology of experience. Conservatives who prize tradition over the individual tend to regard experience as shaped by an understanding of the faith as historically received. Christian experience, for them, is construed as the renunciation of experience and the affirmation of faith.[38] Liberals argue a different case: that experience requires us to modify tradition. The βασιλεια, for instance, comes to us in our experience of community. This might be seen as a late flourishing of a theology of correlation; if so, those proposing it will be convicted of nostalgia. For it will be said that cultural pluralism has increasingly become an impediment to harmonizing faith and life. In all likelihood, when we talk of experiencing the βασιλεια in our social group or even our church, we are quietly ignoring many who are not part of that group and who do not wish to join us, even were it easy to do so. Yet this recognition of the failure of correlation can be a spur to experience the βασιλεια in terms of mutual otherness. Indeed, one could say that such difference is the condition of social experience.

To introduce the word *experience* in theology is to be required to make some remarks about method. Since the enlightenment, an emphasis on human experience has been co-ordinate with a theology that grants revealability a methodological privilege over revelation. There has been revelation, so the story goes, only because there is faith, and we must elaborate revelation by way of this faith. Against this, those who grant priority to revelation urge that to limit God to the conditions of human experience is already to have made him into an idol. This dispute is commonly represented as the contradiction of opposing schools (Bultmann and Barth, Rahner and von Balthasar), and it has paralyzed theology for some time. Rahner proposed an ingenious resolution of the dispute in suggesting that categorical and transcendental schemas converge, although his God seems never to interrupt the world, and this sits oddly with much biblical narrative.[39] Properly seen, however, this dispute does not take the form of a contradiction but an aporia. The revelation that Jesus is the Christ occurs as an absolutely singular event that interrupts the world in a decisive way. Yet the very fact that one can confess "Jesus is Christ" presumes that the revelation was always and already able to be experienced: accepted or rejected, explored in and through a tradition that would fray more than once.

Grasped in this way, the Christian revelation can be analyzed both "from above" and "from below," and a bitter theological division can be overcome. Considered "from above," as Hans Urs von Balthasar would wish, God fully reveals himself in his Son, the "absolutely singular" human being.[40] Yet the very fact that this revelation can be perceived, with increasing clarity over time, means that the *absolute* character of the Son's singularity is erased in his incarnation or, if you like, his life and the testimonies concerning it. (The virgin birth and the immaculate conception are attempts to arrest this erasure at the level of dogma.) We are left with the singularity of Jesus in whom, by grace, the faithful discern the trace of God. Considered "from below," one hears the message of Jesus, and on the basis of testimony comes to believe that God has acted decisively in his life, suffering, and death. Recast in an existential register, the aporia can be characterized as follows. A believer is always and

Kevin Hart

already caught between a call to correlate faith and experience, and a call to recognize that the βασιλεια breaks into and reorganizes our experience of the world. The situation need not be paralyzing; it can be energizing; but it propels one forward without any deep assurance that, at any given moment, one is doing the right thing.[41]

An aporia has been called a *negative form* because the affirmations it brings forth can never lodge in a present moment.[42] From the position of everyday Christian life, it generates a negative theology more true to the faith than that diagnosed by Schweitzer and more recognizable to most Christians than that professed by the great mystics. If the believer is always caught in an aporia, it follows that neither the conservative nor the liberal theology of experience is entirely right. We must go further if we are to go anywhere at all.

III

Good theology seems to occur in an impossible place, where it can be conducted both "from above" and "from below." We long for a theology in which God can be God. Yet all that we know of God is imbricated in our languages and our customs. This is not a regrettable circumstance: it is a consequence of Christianity being an incarnational faith. Christians see God most clearly when they look at Jesus; however, they see only traces of him, and even were it otherwise, no gaze can contain divinity. When Christians confess that Jesus is the Christ, that perception of Jesus in the synoptic gospels must vie with the faith those gospels elicit. If it is to avoid the seductions of Gnosticism, christology must begin "from below," and if it is to *be* a christology, it must gradually ascend and make sense of Christ's relations with the Father and the Spirit. It would be a mistake, however, to talk about trinitarian theology as though it were done only "from above": the economic Trinity is involved with all life, and this recognition calls into play a theology "from below." No doubt it would be wrong to infer from the formula "the economic Trinity is the immanent Trinity" that we can speak meaningfully of the deep mystery of God's nature; its proper function is to assure us that while everything divine is mysterious, nothing divine is withheld from us. There is no God beyond God.

A long meditation on the proposal that "the economic Trinity is the immanent Trinity" would surround it with many qualifications.[43] I will consider just one. Bruno Forte tells us that the formula is valid *"on the plane of the experience of God,"* meaning, I take it, that the immanent Trinity is given to us in our historical experience of salvation.[44] The old problem of whether it is indeed possible for a finite being to experience an infinite one is not addressed here, and I presume this is because Forte accepts the solution proposed by Hegel, and reworked by Rahner, that human beings are always and already graced.[45] Rahner argues on the basis of the unity of the two trinities that we experience each of the divine persons "in his own personal particularity and diversity," although he stresses that these "three self-communications are the self-communication of the one God in the three relative ways in which God subsists."[46] We experience God as triune but not as three absolutely distinct subjects. This is theologically correct, of course (I refrain from entering the debate about Rahner's alleged modalism), yet precisely "on the plane of experience" it is perplexing. After all, for Rahner our experience of God is transcendental and pre-reflective; and we are left wondering what a pre-reflective transcendental experience of three relative modes of subsistence might consist in. Yet the claim is not without biblical support. Think of Paul writing to the Ephesians: "There is one body, and one Spirit, even as we are called in one hope of your calling; One Lord, one faith, one baptism, One God and Father of all, who is above all, and through all, and in you all" (*Eph.* 4:4–6). Commenting on this passage, Gordon D. Fee observes that it puts into credal form "the affirmation that God is *experienced* as a triune reality."[47] Elsewhere, he notes that while there is little trinitarian theology in Paul, his epistles "are full of presuppositions and assertions which reveal that he *experienced* God, and then expressed that experience, in a fundamentally trinitarian way."[48]

The least clear word in these remarks is the one that Fee emphasizes so strongly. He tells us, in a formulation of his own rather than Paul's, that "By the presence of the Spirit, God's love, played out to the full in Christ, is an experienced reality in the heart of the believer."[49] Certainly the indwelling of the Spirit involves the self-communication of the Father and the Son, although I add that this is mediated at all levels by scripture and tradition. This is an important qualification; otherwise, people would seek a particular sort of experience, which they associate with the Father or the Spirit or the Son. God does not usually give himself in this way. Returning to scripture for a moment, I think J. D. G. Dunn is right to say that although Paul holds the Spirit to be "the medium for Christ in his relation [. . .] no distinction can be detected in the believer's experience" between Christ and the Spirit.[50] And for patristic support, one could do no better than to cite St. Gregory of Nyssa: "All providence, care, and attention of all [. . .] is one and not three, kept straight by the holy Trinity."[51] I would emphasize Augustine's insight that belief leads to experience, which means, in this context, that our faith in Jesus' preaching of the βασιλεια leads us to experience God's love in our relations with one another. It is only through reflection that we may in faith call that experience "God's love."

Because the word *experience* has been used too loosely and too often with reference to the Trinity, some theologians have preferred to speak of the Trinity "from above" rather than "from below."[52] Dialectically at least, it is easy to ascend to the heavens: we pass from the economic to the immanent Trinity. Moltmann shows us how when observing that "The expression 'experience of God' [. . .] also means God's experience with us."[53] Here we see a Hegelian philosophical theology meeting a biblical theology. Moltmann tells us that we truly experience God when coming to see that he is the living God who has already loved and suffered, for in recognizing that history, we enter into a personal relationship with him. This sociality becomes the basis for Moltmann's doctrine of the Trinity. "God suffers with us—God suffers from us—God suffers for us: it is this experience of God that reveals the triune God."[54] (One can only wonder what would happen to this prepositional theory of the Trinity were Moltmann to find a way in which God suffers in us or through us.)

Moltmann's quarry here is Schleiermacher's theology of experience that, as we have seen, regards the Trinity as a derivative dogma. In reacting against it, he seeks recourse to the biblical narrative of God's relations with his people. Another dialectical move is possible, however—one that would appeal to a theologian working "from above." For if we believe that God is triune, we can always ask what is God's experience of himself. Schleiermacher's future opponent at Berlin, G. W. F. Hegel, had asked himself that very question as a young man in 1807. "The life of God," he wrote, is "love disporting with itself." He then immediately added that "this idea falls into edification, and even sinks into insipidity, if it lacks the seriousness, the suffering, the patience, and the labor of the negative."[55] What maintains the dignity of thinking God as love is, for Hegel, the recognition that the economic Trinity can be glimpsed in and through the negativity of history. At no time, though, does Hegel simply identify the economic and the immanent trinities. Lecturing as an older man in Berlin in 1831, he asserted that the immanent Trinity precedes history. He called it the kingdom of the Father, and saw history in terms of the kingdom of the Son that would be reconciled to the kingdom of the Father in and through the kingdom of the Spirit.[56] Thus, Hegel affirms that the suffering and death of Jesus enter eternally into the life of the Trinity: "Otherness, the negative, is known to be a moment of the divine nature itself."[57]

One would think that no theologian would be entirely comfortable with Hegel's account of the Trinity because the dialectic seems to constrain God's actions. God must be free to be God. Yet this freedom constitutes itself in love. Beyond being and non-being, the Trinity nonetheless freely ties itself to what it has created. It does so because it *is* love: among other things, the doctrine of the Trinity means that God's very act of being is social. When we confess that the Son proceeds eternally from the Father, and that the Spirit proceeds eternally from the Father and the Son, we are saying that God is always and already in relation with himself as other and the same. God's revelation is always a self-communication; and since his selfhood is beyond "being" in the sense that it is always and already "being-with," the revelation of God is the founding of being-in-relation with others, and first of all with himself. This is a "social Trinity," to be sure, although I wish that judgment to be read as a gloss on I John 4:16, by way of Richard of St. Victor. In his *De Trinitate*, Richard argues that we must recognize that love is perfect not when it is between two persons, but when it is shared with a third.[58] The third completes love (and the fourth has the status of a third: such would be Richard's answer to Kant on plurality in God).[59] Now it must be kept in mind that the divine persons are relations, not subjects. Even when this is understood, difficulties can arise, especially when the Trinity is approached from the viewpoint of the βασιλεια.

Moltmann rightly rejects Joachim's theology of history, and seeks an understanding of the trinitarian kingdoms that is not governed by periodization. "We shall instead interpret the history of the kingdom in trinitarian terms," he writes, continuing with "the kingdoms of the Father, the Son and the Spirit mean continually present strata and transitions in the kingdom's history."[60] Creation, liberation, and community follow and involve one another in a joyous movement whose end is the glorification of God as triune. The βασιλεια and the Trinity remain related in and through a theology of history. What troubles me about this position are the assumptions that there is a "history of the kingdom" (rather than a history of representations of the kingdom), and that history is the medium through which a Christian relates to the kingdom.[61] That the βασιλεια was breaking into the world since John the Baptist is announced in the gospels (Mt. 11:12, Lk 16:16), and this late in Christian history it would be hard to admit there has been no discernible realization of the βασιλεια. It does not follow, though, that the βασιλεια offers itself to historical perception; and it is unclear how one would go about writing its history. The kingdoms may be "continually present," but since they do not present themselves to human consciousness in ways that can be registered, their mode of presence remains enigmatic.

More generally, Moltmann stands accused of not being clear whether the βασιλεια and the Trinity are linked because we participate by grace in the Trinity or because we regard the Trinity as a model of the βασιλεια.[62] This sort of confusion is not uncommon in social trinitarianism. By contrast, Leonardo Boff is plain: "the Trinity is our true social program," he says.[63] Yet there is reason for concern. How can created beings be asked to take the inner life of the uncreated God as our social program? We can never aspire to the divine perichoresis, and to do so would be to slight the excellence we enjoy as creatures of flesh and blood. I do not say this in order to argue for participation in the divine life. In my view, we explore in grace the relations that God has opened up for us in both creation and revelation: a time when God interrupted what is not, and a time when he interrupted what is.[64] Rather than saying that our true social program is the Trinity, it would be more telling to say it is the βασιλεια. Yet the New Testament witness is clear that it is God who primarily brings on the βασιλεια, not men and women, and so we cannot call it "our true social program" unless we offer a nuanced understanding of "our" and "program." That done, we could begin to recognize that, because the βασιλεια is preached by the Son, in the Spirit, and brought on by the Father, it is trinitarian through and through.

IV

Perhaps it makes sense to speak of the βασιλεια and the Trinity as vanishing points on the plane of being. On my reading, it makes little sense on the plane of experience. Only God fully knows what it is to be a Christian; we must make our way as pilgrims in the only medium we know, ordinary experience, aware all the time that the most banal events are fraught with eternal significance.

In our mortal lives, Christian experience has just the one vanishing point, the βασιλεια. To hear the preaching of Jesus—in his parables, sayings and prayer—is to apprehend God's rule breaking into this world, and to recognize it as a sociality beyond all society. It is not a utopia but will be the most profound reality. We help God to bring it about by acts of gentleness, by demanding justice, by attending mass, by writing poems, by giving away money and resources we do not really need, by praying in secret, by being ourselves, by protesting against the desecration of creation, by caressing those we love, by forgiving those who want to hurt us, by celebrating beauty. . . . There has never been a limit on how we can help God to bring about the βασιλεια. God calls us to be creative in this as in everything. We are creative because we are created in God's image.

The βασιλεια is never fully present here and now; it is a seed. There is no doubt that, in the parables of growth, Jesus taught that the βασιλεια can be witnessed; yet while God's rule may "already" be here for those with eyes to see, it is "not yet" here in decisive strength. It will never be fully present to mortal consciousness: God's mystery can never be contained in a present moment or a moment of presence. So, strictly speaking, we never experience the βασιλεια. What we seize is not "an experience" but rather a new structure of experiencing, one in which God is absolutely central to how one lives (*Jn* 3:3). This can yield the convert new experiences by virtue of his or her allegiance to Jesus, and it can realize the peril at the heart of experience (*Jn* 21:18), but it does not necessarily lead to a different sort of experience. Christianity does not solve life's problems; it raises them to a higher level. One can have a fleeting awareness of the new structure of experiencing, and this reflexivity is a part of what cannot be turned into knowledge from an event. Yet faith tells us that it is not all of what is risked in experience.

Jesus tells us that wherever two or three are gathered in his name, he will be there (*Mt.* 18:20). What we have in our everyday encounters with one another is none other than Jesus. Do we experience him there? Only prereflectively, in faith, and through our experience of others. Do we experience the βασιλεια? Only in moments of growth or interruption. Perhaps it is enough, for human beings are created in the image of God—our being is "being with"—and so perhaps we have a fleeting sense of the βασιλεια both inside and outside of ourselves. Were we to have more than that, we could content ourselves with a "social gospel." Were we to have less than that, we would not call on God when protesting against injustice. We desire more not only because we want to live in an equitable society but also because we long for God to caress all creation. I think that this desire finds expression in the formula that the economic Trinity is the immanent Trinity. For in saying that, we say that God, as he truly is, is in the world. Considered christologically, the formula is profoundly incarnational; it encourages us to hear Jesus preaching the βασιλεια to recognize that it bespeaks both the Father and the Spirit, and to see in faith that the immanent Trinity is there as well.

I can best capture this thought by saying that the βασιλεια is the trace of the Trinity. In terms of the metaphor I have been using, the Trinity abides "behind" the βασιλεια and gives itself to us in co-operating with God in bringing about his rule. This is why I have reversed the title of Moltmann's book *(The Trinity and the Kingdom)*: the Trinity comes to us in and through the kingdom. Usually there is no "experience of the Trinity" except reflectively in concrete social events that aid the coming of the βασιλεια, and there is no longing for the βασιλεια that is not also pleasing to the Trinity. Strictly speaking, we cannot say that the Trinity comes through the βασιλεια, for the βασιλεια does not offer itself to experience in quite that way: it is both here and still to come. This eschatological character of the βασιλεια means that the Trinity also is always to come. In saying that, I am not agreeing with Wolfhart Pannenberg's contention that the deity of God is "dependent upon the eschatological coming of the kingdom."[65] Not at all: I am merely saying that the Trinity is not offered to experience in the present moment. It offers itself, rather, as a trace that passes through those experiences that help bring on the βασιλεια.

This understanding leads to two adjustments in Rahner's theology. In the first place, it introduces an asymmetry into his trinitarian theorem. To be sure, the economic Trinity is the immanent Trinity: there is no God beyond God. Yet to say that the immanent Trinity is the economic Trinity is to say more than we can know or need to know. Even a theology that is firmly oriented toward soteriology must make room for doxology in order to be theology. In the second place, relating the βασιλεια and the Trinity as I do makes us question Rahner's view that transcendental experience refers, by dint of structural necessity, to the subject. Rather, it would refer by way of the subject to the transcendental, intersubjective community. There is no work that helps bring on the βασιλεια that is not also pleasing to the Trinity. I think this is what Rahner perceived in his doctrine of anonymous or implicit Christianity, although I suspect he confused the language of Christianity with the language of the theology of religions. We can begin to clarify the issue by saying that people of all faiths seek the kingdom of God, and that Christians recognize that kingdom as the trace of the Trinity.

I realize that I am proposing a belated understanding of the *vestigium trinitatis*, and I know that it has long since lapsed from favor in Catholic circles and has been sharply rejected by many Protestants.[66] Augustine pondered the possibility that there were traces of the Trinity in the "inner man" in *De Trinitate*, XI, and others have sought to find such traces in nature. More recently, Boff has found *vestigia trinitatis* in co-operation and collaboration when they appear in social groups.[67] My case differs from these in that I do not argue from the world to God. Earlier, I considered von Balthasar's description of Jesus as "absolutely singular," and I maintained that the incarnation of Jesus, his very life, erases the "absolute" character of his singularity. Were this not so, Jesus would have been invisible. Or, were this so, our relation to Jesus as the Christ would not be one of faith. I think the New Testament tries to record the trace of that absolute singularity, although in doing so it often replaces a trace by signs. The virgin birth, the voice heard at Jesus' baptism, the miracles, the resurrection, the uncreated Λογος in John's stately proem: different as they are, these are all signs of Jesus' absolute singularity. We talk of a "gospel of signs" embedded in John, but in truth all the evangelists wrote gospels of signs.

The evangelists also wrote gospels of a trace, and this is more difficult to find on the printed page of a Bible. At times it is legible, for some traces can be signs. More generally, I maintain that it passes through Jesus' parables, sayings, and prayers relating to the βασιλεια, and in his actions designed to call it to people's attention. These are not all of a piece, and in passing from exegesis to theology we should be conscious of the ability the parables have to unsay themselves. Jesus' mission was to preach the βασιλεια; his resurrection was both the confirmation of that preaching and an extension of its significance. Jesus preached the kingdom of the Father, the final communion to which we are called, and which is brought about only by the Spirit. The trace of the Trinity therefore passes through the βασιλεια. It passes through; it is not caught there. This βασιλεια is neither an event nor an institution; it is a structure of experiencing, one that reveals human being to have the character of "being with." John Zizioulas is right to emphasize that we discern this structure in the eucharist where many become "one bread and one body" (I *Cor.* 10:17).[68] It is indeed the *structure* of the βασιλεια we perceive there, not the βασιλεια itself, for if it is already in the Church it is not yet here fully.

Jesus taught that outcasts and sinners are close to the βασιλεια, and we should remember that the Trinity is not only a perfect community, one we cannot emulate, but also a community that is largely indifferent to our ideas of purity and perfection. God does not ask us to be other than created beings; he asks us to help him rule in strength, and to recognize that his reign is growing here and now. We approach the Trinity in letting God bring on the βασιλεια. We call "saints" those people who identify themselves wholly with the divine reign, who serve it in extraordinary ways, that is, by their awareness that when serving God ordinary deeds are charged with the extraordinary. At times, the saints seem to us like willful children who, for no good reason, run madly across a field toward the horizon. Yet they never vanish there, and to them it doubtless seems as though they run all day and come no closer to their goal.

What they do not realize at any given moment is that, in taking the βασιλεια as the sole vanishing point of their existence, the Trinity has already rushed out to meet them. In their slightest act of helping to bring on the reign of love, they are embraced by the Trinity, deeply and for ever.

NOTES

An earlier version of this paper was first delivered as the 2000 Cardinal Knox Lecture at Catholic Theological College in Melbourne. I am grateful to the Master of the College, Fr. Austin Cooper, for honoring me with the invitation. I would also like to thank some friends for their comments on the earlier draft: Mark Brett, Andrew Hamilton, and Tony Kelly.

1. J. Moltmann, *The Trinity and the Kingdom: The Doctrine of God*, trans. M. Kohl (San Francisco: Harper and Row, 1981).

2. See R. Schnackenburg, *God's Rule and Kingdom*, trans. John Murray (New York: Herder and Herder, 1963), Part I. Bruce Chilton argues that Jesus was influenced by the Targumic expressions "the kingdom of God" and "the kingdom of the LORD." See his *God in Strength: Jesus' Announcement of the Kingdom* (Sheffield: JSOT Press, 1987).

3. I explore this in more detail in "'Fides et Ratio et . . .'" in *The American Catholic Philosophical Quarterly*, 76:2 (2002): 199–219.

4. On this question, as well as on the nature of a dogmatic statement, see K. Rahner, "What is a Dogmatic Statement?" *Theological Investigations*, V, trans. K.-H. Kruger (London: Darton, Longman and Todd, 1966).

5. Anselm of Canterbury, "On the Incarnation of the Word," in his *Trinity, Incarnation and Redemption: Theological Treatises*, ed. J. Hopkins and H. Richardson, rev. ed. (New York: Harper and Row, 1970), p. 10.

6. Augustine, *On the Trinity*, trans. Arthur West Haddan, in *The Works of Aurelius Augustine*, 15 vols., ed. M. Dods (Edinburgh: T. and T. Clark, 1873), VII, p. 378.

7. Such is the argument of Heinrich Schlier, "Kerygma und Sophia: Zur neutestamentlichen Grundlegung des Dogmas," in his *Die Ziet der Kirke* (Freiburg: Herder, 1966).

8. See G. D. Fee, *Paul, the Spirit, and the People of God* (Peabody, Mass.: Hendrickson, 1996), pp. 38–46.

9. Schnackenburg gives an exhaustive account of the different ways in which the βασιλεια has been interpreted in *God's Rule and Kingdom*, 114–16. Not all these were taken up by the Church Fathers, needless to say.

10. Irenaeus, *Against Heresies*, 5.33.3.

11. Origen, *Comment. in Matthaeum*, Tomus XIV, 622 (Migne, 13-G).

12. It is easy to find passages in Eusebius's *In Praise of Constantine* that suggest that βασιλεια and μοναρχια could be identified; it is more difficult, however, to read their rhetoric with care. I do not think that Eusebius identified with two states without qualification, although his phrasing allowed his listeners and readers to do just that. Thus the following passage: "Thus outfitted in the likeness of the kingdom of heaven, he pilots affairs below with an upward gaze, to steer by the archetypal form. He grows strong in his model of monarchic rule, which the Ruler of All has given to the race of men alone of those on earth." H. A. Drake (ed.), *In Praise of Constantine: A Historical Study and New Translation of Eusebius' Tricennial Orations*, University of California

Publications: Classical Studies, vol. 15 (Los Angeles: University of California Press, 1976), III, 5.

13. Augustine, *City of God*, 20.9; 18.29.

14. Joachim's theology of history was firmly rejected by Thomas Aquinas. See *Summa Theologiæ*, 1a2æ, 106, 4. Doubtless the controversy over Joachim's theology of the βασιλεια made Thomas cautious about engaging in extended commentary on it.

15. See, for example, the article "Trinity, Holy" in *New Catholic Encyclopedia* (New York: McGraw-Hill, 1967). For a more recent instance, see G. O'Collins, *The Tripersonal God: Understanding and Interpreting the Trinity* (New York: Paulist Press, 1999), §§ 7–8. Scholarly attention to the history of the dogma of the Trinity is largely confined to its origins and initial developments. See, for instance, J. Lebreton, *Histoire du dogma de la Trinité*, 2 vols. (Paris: Gabriel Beauchesne, 1910–27).

16. I. Kant, *The Conflict of the Faculties*, trans. M. J. Gregor (New York: Abaris Books, 1979), p. 67.

17. I. Kant, *Religion within the Limits of Reason Alone*, trans. T. M. Greene and H. H. Hudson (New York: Harper and Row, 1960), p. 133. See my essay "Kingdoms of God," forthcoming in P. Rothfield, ed., *Kant after Derrida* (Manchester: Clinamen Press, 2002).

18. F. Schleiermacher, *The Christian Faith*, 2 vols., ed. H. R. Mackintosh and J. S. Stewart, intro. Richard R. Niebuhr (New York: Harper and Row, 1963), II, 738.

19. E. Troeltsch, *The Christian Faith*, ed. G. von le Fort, trans. G. E. Paul (Minneapolis: Fortress Press, 1991), p. 105.

20. F. Schleiermacher, *The Christian Faith*, I, 43. Karl Barth, however, indicates that Schleiermacher spoke of the βασιλεια in his sermons. See his *The Theology of Schleiermacher: Lectures at Göttingen, Winter Semester of 1923/24*, ed. D. Ritschl, trans. Geoffrey W. Bromiley (Grand Rapids, Mich.: William B. Eerdmans, 1982), §1.

21. J. S. Drey, *Brief Introduction to Theology: With Reference to the Scientific Standpoint and the Catholic System*, trans. and intro. Michael J. Himes (Notre Dame, IN: University of Notre Dame Press, 1994), § 60. Also see §§ 71, 268, 275.

22. See A. von Harnack, *What Is Christianity?* trans. T. Bailey Saunders (Philadelphia: Fortress Press, 1957), p. 144.

23. Gregory of Nyssa, *On the Holy Spirit*, in *A Select Library of Nicene and Post-Nicene Fathers of the Christian Church*, 2nd series, ed. Henry Wace and Philip Schaff, vol. 5 (Oxford: Parker and Co., 1893), p. 321.

24. H. Denzinger, *Enchiridion Symbolorum*, rev. Karl Rahner (Freiburg: Herder, 1954), pp. 431–32.

25. T. Moltmann, *The Trinity and the Kingdom*, 206. Moltmann returns to this theme in his *The Coming of God: Christian Eschatology*, trans. M. Kohl (Minneapolis: Fortress Press, 1996), pp. 143–145. The influence of Joachim extended far beyond his times. See Karl Löwith's reflections on this in "Modern Transfigurations of Joachim," *Meaning in History* (Chicago: University of Chicago Press, 1949), pp. 208–13.

26. It must be noted, however, that Joachim does not simply propose a triadic pattern. He develops interrelated patterns of twos and threes. See M. Reeves, *The Influence of Prophecy in the Later Middle Ages: A Study in Joachism* (1969; reprint, Notre Dame, Ind.: University of Notre Dame Press, 1993), pp. 19–20.

27. See T. Moltmann, *The Trinity and the Kingdom*, pp. 131, 163.

28. See W. Brueggermann, *Theology of the Old Testament: Testimony, Dispute, Advocacy* (Minneapolis: Fortress Press, 1997), Part IV, chapter 21. Ben C. Ollenburger

argues that "The notion of God as king in the context of Zion symbolism . . . is counter to any human form of dominion in which the prerogatives of God are contravened and humankind itself is seen to be both the executor of power and the legislator who determines the norms of its execution." *Zion, The City of the Great King: A Theological Symbol of the Jerusalem Cult* (Sheffield: JSOT Press, 1987), p. 159. Also see Regina Schwartz's fine study, *The Curse of Cain: The Violent Legacy of Monotheism* (Chicago: Chicago University Press, 1997). In her criticism of Jewish monotheism Schwartz takes care to uncover a tradition of generosity in the Jewish scriptures as well as a tradition of violence.

29. See G. L. Prestige, *God in Patristic Thought* (London: Heinemann, 1936), p. xxv.

30. R. Bultmann, *Theology of the New Testament,* trans. Kendrick Grobel, 2 vols. (London: SCM Press, 1952), I, 3. Nevertheless, Bultmann conceded with regard to the historical Jesus that, "Little as we know of his life and personality, we know enough of his *message* to make for ourselves a consistent picture," *Jesus and the Word,* trans. L. Pettibone Smith and E. Huntress (London: Ivor Nicholson and Watson, 1935), p. 12.

31. Joachim Jeremias, *New Testament Theology,* 2 vols., trans. J. Bowden (London: SCM Press, 1971), I, p. 96.

32. The main exception here is of course Ritschl. More generally, those who argue for a non-eschatological account of the βασιλεια, such as C. H. Dodd and Marcus J. Borg, tend not to make such large claims. In my judgment, attempts to construe the βασιλεια as non-eschatological do not fit the biblical evidence. The strongest case for a non-eschatological βασιλεια is proposed in M. Borg's *Conflict, Holiness and Politics in the Teaching of Jesus* (New York: Mellen, 1984). For a powerful exegetical defense of the βασιλεια as eschatological, see John P. Meier, *A Marginal Jew: Rethinking the Historical Jesus,* 2 vols. to date, II: *Mentor, Message, and Miracles* (New York: Doubleday, 1994), chapter 15. Chilton convicts Borg of self-contradiction in his *Pure Kingdom: Jesus' Vision of God* (Grand Rapids, Mich.: William B. Eerdmans Publishing Co., 1996), p. 18.

33. See, for instance, T. Moltmann, *The Crucified God: The Cross of Christ as the Foundation and Criticism of Christian Theology,* trans. R. A. Wilson and J. Bowden (London: SCM Press, 1974), 240; E. Jüngel, *God as the Mystery of the World: On the Foundation of the Theology of the Crucified One in the Dispute between Theism and Atheism,* trans. Darrell L. Guder (Grand Rapids, Mich.: William B. Eerdmans Publishing Co., 1983), p. 184; and D. Coffey, *Deus Trinitas: The Doctrine of the Triune God* (Oxford: Oxford University Press, 1999), p. 18. A good introduction to paschal trinitarianism is given by Anne Hunt in her *The Trinity and the Paschal Mystery: A Development in Recent Catholic Theology* (Collegeville, Mich.: The Liturgical Press, 1997).

34. See K. Rahner, *The Trinity,* trans. Joseph Donceel (London: Burns and Oates, 1970), p. 38.

35. L.-M. Chauvet, *Symbol and Sacrament: A Sacramental Reinterpretation of Christian Existence,* trans. P. Madigan SJ and Madeleine Beaumont (Collegeville, Mich.: The Liturgical Press, 1995), pp. 159–60.

36. A. Schweitzer, *The Quest of the Historical Jesus: A Critical Study of the Progress from Reimarus to Wrede,* 3rd ed., trans. W. Montgomery (London: Adam and Charles Black, 1954), p. 396.

37. Borg, *Conflict, Holiness and Politics,* p. 261.

38. See, for example, Hans Urs von Balthasar, "Experience God?" in his *New*

Elucidations, trans. Sr. M. T. Skerry (San Francisco: Ignatius Press, 1986). Of course, the matter might be considerably more complicated than this. Bernard Lonergan, for instance, in no way rejects experience yet he regards it as only the first stage of an ascent to knowledge that includes both understanding and judgment. See his *Insight* (San Francisco: Harper and Row, 1958), p. 357.

39. See K. Rahner, "Observations on the Concept of Revelation," in *Revelation and Tradition*, by K. Rahner and Joseph Ratzinger, trans. W. J. O'Hara (London: Burns and Oates, 1966). Also see my essay " 'The Experience of God,' " in J. D. Caputo, ed., *The Religious* (Oxford: Basil Blackwell, 2001).

40. Von Balthasar and Ratzinger, *Two Say Why: Why I Am Still a Christian and Why I Am Still in the Church*, trans. John Griffiths (London: Search Press, 1973), p. 27.

41. The point has been made strongly by Jacques Derrida in "Force of Law: The 'Mystical Foundation of Authority,' " *Cardozo Law Review*, 11: 5–6, 961, 971.

42. I take the description of an aporia as a "negative form" from Derrida, *Aporias*, trans. T. Dutoit (Stanford, Calif.: Stanford University Press, 1993), p. 19.

43. See, for instance, W. Kasper, *The God of Jesus Christ*, trans. Matthew J. O'Connell (London: SCM, 1984), pp. 273–77, and Y. M.-J. Congar, *Je crois en l'Esprit Saint*, 3 vols. (Paris: Éditions du Cerf, 1980), I. 2.

44. B. Forte, *The Trinity as History: Saga of the Christian God*, trans. P. Rotondi (New York: Alba House, 1989), p. 9 (Forte's emphasis).

45. See G. W. F. Hegel, *Lectures on the Philosophy of Religion*, 3 vols., ed. P. C. Hodgson, trans. R. F. Brown et al. (Los Angeles: University of California Press, 1984–85), I, 322, and K. Rahner, "Concerning the Relationship between Nature and Grace," *Theological Investigations* I, trans. C. Ernst (London: Darton, Longman and Todd, 1961).

46. K. Rahner, *The Trinity*, pp. 34–35.

47. G. D. Fee, "Paul and the Trinity: The Experience of Christ and the Spirit for Paul's Understanding of God," S. T. Davis, D. Kendall, SJ, and G. O'Collins, SJ, eds., *The Trinity: An Interdisciplinary Symposium on the Trinity* (Oxford: Oxford University Press, 1999), p. 55 (Fee's emphasis).

48. G.D. Fee, *Paul, the Spirit, and the People of God*, p. 38 (Fee's emphasis). Also see Fee's magisterial *God's Empowering Presence: The Holy Spirit in the Letters of Paul* (Peabody, Mass.: Hendrickson, 1994), p. 827.

49. G. D. Fee, *Paul, the Spirit, and the People of God*, p. 42.

50. J. D. G. Dunn, *Christology in the Making*, 2nd ed. (London: SCM Press, 1989), p. 146. The point was made earlier by R. S. Franks in his criticism of Leonard Hodgson's *The Doctrine of the Trinity: Croall Lectures, 1942–1943* (London: Nisbet and Co., 1943). See Franks, *The Doctrine of the Trinity* (London: Gerald Duckworth and Co., 1953), pp. 196–97.

51. Gregory of Nyssa, "Concerning We Should Think of Saying That There Are Not Three Gods to *Ablabius*," in *The Trinitarian Controversy*, trans. and ed., W.G. Rusch (Philadelphia: Fortress Press, 1980), pp. 156–57.

52. James P. Mackey, for instance, titles a book, *The Christian Experience of the Trinity* (London: SCM Press, 1983), yet offers no remarks at all about "experience." A more careful approach is maintained by Anthony Kelly, *The Trinity of Love: A Theology of the Christian God* (Wilmington, DE: Michael Glazier, 1989), § 2.5.

53. T. Moltmann, *The Trinity and the Kingdom*, 4.

54. Ibid.

55. G. W. F. Hegel, *The Phenomenology of Mind*, trans. J. B. Baillie (New York: Harper and Row, 1967), p. 81.

56. See G. W. F. Hegel, *Lectures on the Philosophy of Religion*, III, 362.

57. G. W. F. Hegel, *Lectures on the Philosophy of Religion*, III, 326.

58. 'Vides ergo quomodo caritatis consummatio personarum Trinitatem requirit, sine qua omnino in plenitudinis sue integritate subsistere nequit', Richard of St. Victor, *De Trinitate*, III. xi. 40.

59. Richard's insistence on *three* as the fundamental number for love, and presumably for ethics as well, would also constitute his answer to Emmanuel Levinas who, despite his recognition of "the third," prizes *two* as the basic unit of ethics. Not that Levinas values "love" in any simple or straightforward way. See, for instance, his remarks on the topic in *Autrement que savoir* (Paris: Orisis, 1986). I reserve this topic for another essay.

60. T. Moltmann, *The Trinity and the Kingdom*, p. 209.

61. The authoritative history of the representations of the βασιλεια is E. Staehelin, *Die Verkündigung des Reiches Gottes in der Kirche Jesu Christi*, 7 vols. (Basle: Friedrich Reinhardt, 1951–1965).

62. See R. Bauckham, "Jürgen Moltmann's *The Trinity and the Kingdom of God* and the Question of Pluralism," K. Vanhoozer, ed., *The Trinity in a Pluralistic Age: Theological Essays on Culture and Religion* (Grand Rapids, Mich.: William B. Eerdmans, 1997), p. 160.

63. L. Boff, *Trinity and Society* (Maryknoll, N.Y.: Orbis, 1988), p. 16.

64. See my essay, "'Absolute *Interruption*': On Faith," in J. D. Caputo, ed., *Questioning God* (Bloomington: Indiana University Press, 2001).

65. W. Pannenberg, *Systematic Theology*, trans. G. Bromiley, 3 vols. (Grand Rapids, Mich. William B. Eerdmans, 1991), I, 331.

66. The fullest account is given by Karl Barth, *Church Dogmatics*, I. i §8.3. Also see Jüngel, *God as the Mystery of the World*, 348–49.

67. L. Boff, *Trinity and Society*, pp. 119–20.

68. J. D. Zizioulas, *Being as Communion: Studies in Personhood and the Church*, trans. J. Clarke et al. (Crestwood, N.Y.: St Vladimir's Seminary Press, 1985), p. 206.

Ultimacy and Conventionality in Religious Experience

Joseph S. O'Leary

To what extent is mystical experience shaped by language? To what extent does it touch on an absolute, immediately given, beyond the grasp of language? This is a tired old question, but we can perhaps renew it and make it fruitful by drawing on the Indian topos of the two-fold truth (*dva-satya*), taken as a theory of how conventional historical religious languages can serve as vehicles for insight or revelation having the quality of ultimacy. I shall use *ultimacy* freely here as a phenomenological term, meaning that which is recognized as supremely, undeniably, unsurpassably real. It does not have the metaphysical implication of terms such as *absolute* or *transcendent*, nor does it have, as these do, the status of a unitary principle. It is more adjectival than substantive, in that it can attach to a great variety of experiences. Yet it is not merely subjective, but is recognized by the subject as irreducible bedrock reality. A question that will occupy us in the following pages is the degree to which not merely the conventional languages of religion, but even the ultimacy of which they are a vehicle, can be conceived of as a pluralistic, culturally contextual phenomenon.

Mâdhyamika Buddhism connects the lighting up of ultimate reality (*paramârtha-satya*) to the skillful deployment of a given conventional set-up (*samvrti-satya*): "Without a foundation in the conventional truth, the significance of the ultimate cannot be taught."[1] All the realities of our world have a merely conventional existence; the ultimate truth about them is their emptiness; yet the truth of emptiness is realized only in constantly dismantling the delusions of substantiality to which the conventional world gives rise. As Mâdhyamika reflection advances, the ultimate truth becomes increasingly elusive, so that in the end we seem left with little more than a skillful play with conventions. The two-truths theory is a logical and historical quagmire; even within Mâdhyamika there is an endless variety of interpretations of its meaning.[2] Still, I believe the theory can free up our thinking on the historical and textual embeddedness of mystical experience. Or rather, it abolishes the entire idea of "mystical experience," which is all too redolent of a fixated clinging to a reified ultimacy. The idea of "the emptiness of emptiness" thwarts any tendency to cling to emptiness itself as a privileged object of a special experience, and sends us back instead to engagement in the world, an engagement that has become free, vital, and creative because emptied of fixations.

In the present essay I shall not enter into any details of Buddhist debate, but merely allow a general sense of the interplay of the two truths to guide my reflections. I shall argue that the embeddedness of religious experience in a given historical, cultural, traditional, and linguistic context means that that experience cannot be treated as a pure delivery of ultimate reality. Certainly any attempt to formulate it as such is immediately compromised. Ultimacy can only be indicated obliquely by the torsions of a manifestly non-ultimate language. Even silence, situated at the end of a traversal of speech, is always located as a signifier within a certain cultural context: a world separates the silence of Vimalakîrti from that of the Pseudo-Dionysius. Ultimacy is encountered situationally, as confirmation and fulfillment of a pre-given language but also as revelation of its inadequacy. At the very point where the conventional web of religious discourse is most charged with a sense of the ultimate, it is also shown up in its thinness, almost to the point of breaking. Here the text will start using the negative terminology of ineffability or incomprehensibility, or will burst into poetic metaphor or nonsensical paradox, mantras, glossolalia. In the past there was a certain security in such apophatic rhetoric, for the writer was securely situated in prayer before the divine incomprehensibility. Today our religious metaphors are more likely to have a spectral quality, as remnants and quotations from an historical repertory.

Very interesting to the theologian are those figures, such as Plotinus and Augustine, who after experiencing a powerful encounter with ultimate reality turn back to the realm of conventional language, which they revise in light of the encounter. Mysticism thus impresses its mark on language. The comprehensive critical labors of the Neo-Platonists or the Mâdhyamika thinkers are a clearing of the pathways of thought and language that lead to and from the breakthrough to ultimacy. These include the pathways of established religious tradition, Hellenic or Indian, now purged of representations that have become obstacles to insight, and given a relativized and more functional status. Today the movement of history brings breakthroughs to a simpler vision of what matters in religion, and these breakthroughs, though more of an existential than a mystical order, are our cues for reappropriating the radicality and clearsightedness of the classic mystical texts. Reassessing conventions in light of ultimacy takes on today an historical depth. We measure the entire sweep of religious traditions by the orientation to ultimacy manifest in classic mystical texts, and in so doing we gain a new sense of the radical contingency and conventionality of religions as historically constituted. This allows us to acquire a free relation to the tradition, so that instead of being a prison that blocks out all sense of ultimacy, the tradition becomes a repertory of skillful means (*upâya*) that can serve in varying manners to orient the religious quest to its ultimate goal.

It might be objected that this critical enterprise can proceed on the basis of modern theological common sense and that there is no need to invoke the luxuries of mysticism. But if mysticism is really nothing more than a matter of seeing things as they are, and thus filling in the central piece in the puzzle of existence, then theology at its moments of highest lucidity may find itself rejoining the insights of those contemplatives who grasped most clearly the phenomena that are religion's concern. However, there is a more serious objection to harping on ultimacy and mystical breakthroughs—namely, that it misses the point of the biblical revelation. If God has come to humanity, incarnately, in a generous outpouring of the Spirit, then mysticism and contemplation are no more than a registering of this reality, within the context of the total response to it constituted by the multi-faceted life of the people of God. To talk of the ultimate or of religious experience is to cut across the breadth and wealth of biblical language and lifestyle, intruding on them an alien and narrow concern. Philosophers of religion are quite likely to project a warped theology in their preoccupation with such matters as religious experience and mysticism. The theologian cannot, in any case, ignore the heritage of mystical texts, but will bring to them critical discernment, even suspicion, as for example Luther did in esteeming Augustine and spewing out the Pseudo-Dionysius. Luther was able to read Augustine's contemplative texts as revealing an entire lifestyle, both individual and ecclesial; perhaps those of Dionysius could have been read in the same way if Luther had been attuned to the lifestyle of the Eastern Church. Perhaps one may say quite generally that mystical experience gains its meaning and validity only within the total context of the way of life that secretes it. The fleshliness of the biblical world is then not the exception but the rule. Even mystical purists such as Plotinus, if looked at closely, may be found to be engaged in wide-ranging communal praxis, within which the rare encounters with the One acquire their full significance.

The cozy frequentation of approved classics is no doubt a narrow and old-fashioned approach to religious experience. But it can be argued that the enduring classics of religious articulation offer our best defense of sanity and rationality in the religious sphere, and that these qualities are even more important than mysticism at a time when civilization is threatened by religious irrationality. The classic status of certain contemplative breakthroughs in the history of religion, which realize in a ripe and illuminating form the spiritual potential of the tradition within which they arise, and in turn serve as the foundation for further developments of the tradition, has usually been secured by a correspondingly great literary text—such as the *Bhagavad-gîtâ*, the *Enneads*, the Epistles of Paul, and the Zen koan collections. As an object of study such a text can be more fruitful than any phenomena of real life, not only because of the vast historical reach of the classic text, but also because the textual inscription reveals that the mystical witness is involved with all the conventionalities of a given culture, and in addition exposes it to the various treacherous features of textuality rehearsed so dramatically by Jacques Derrida at one time: dissemination, citationality, iterability, and all the other dimensions of *la différance*.

The achievement of the religious classics is that they succeed in disposing the resources of their cultural context toward the dimension of ultimacy, allowing it to react on that context with critical and illuminative force. A mystical text empties out conventional language before the ultimate, burns the language like straw, but in such a way that it then functions as a burning bush, indicating the contours of the numinous real by its stammerings and silences. This eloquent breakdown of the conventional before the ultimate is favored by cultural crisis or by a meeting of cultures, a fusion of horizons, in which conventional frameworks are enlarged and broken open. The traumata of the twentieth century have enabled artists to approximate to the dynamic of mystical expression: I venture to mention Anton Webern and Paul Celan. To read a mystical text, one has to be attuned to the contemplative wavelength of its author; that is the reason why for most of us, most of the time, mystical texts are not the most attractive reading. Of course, countless mystical texts fail to communicate at all, either because they merely repeat the conventional spiritual jargon of their time or because they flounder helplessly in their effort to articulate the ineffable.

The Case of Augustine

Though Augustine of Hippo was a very busy ecclesiastic and a very productive intellectual, his works are steeped in a steady contemplative awareness, which at times blossoms into direct testimony to experiential encounter with the divine. It was at the time of his conversion, in 386–387 (C.E.), that mystical aspirations gripped him most; his experiences of that time are written up in glowing colors in the *Confessions* (401 C.E.), but the mystical does not retain the central place in his preoccupations. It had given him just enough light to illumine the great public mansion of his thought, without withdrawing him

Joseph S. O'Leary

into an esoteric sphere. In contrast, Plotinus, whose writings kindled Augustine's mystical period, was single-minded in pursuit of direct encounter with
the One. Porphyry tells us how "that God appeared who has neither shape nor
any intelligible form. . . . To Plotinus 'the goal ever near was shown': for his end
and goal was to be united to, to approach the God who is over all things. Four
times while I was with him [in Rome, 263–270 c.e.] he attained that goal, in
an unspeakable actuality and not in potency only." Porphyry himself "drew
near and was united" only once in his sixty-eight years (Porphyry, *Life* 23).
Plotinus himself tells us: "I have come to that supreme actuality, setting myself
above all else in the realm of Intellect. Then after that rest in the divine, when I
have come down from Intellect to discursive reasoning, am puzzled how I ever
came down" (*Enn.* IV 8, 1). Plotinus's circle was a laboratory of the spirit, and
in Milan Augustine frequented a circle modeled on it. But already in his own
circle in Cassiciacum, the wider world of the Church was shaping spirituality
in a more homely, communal, down-to-earth manner.[3]

A fusion, or mutual cracking open, of cultural horizons (Gadamer's *Hori-
zontverschmelzung*) underlies the spiritual synthesis that Augustine wrought.
The classical world and its values had entered a twilight zone of incertitude,
intensified by the barbarian menace, whereas the Christian church, having
secured its basic dogmas, was crossing a new threshold of self-conscious lucidity. In Augustine's thought, classical values are Christianized wholesale;
most notably, the Platonic tradition of philosophical eros, which ascends to the
ecstatic vision of Beauty and, beyond that, to a mystical contact with the One,
is transformed through encounter and synthesis with the New Testament mysticism of the divine agape poured forth in our hearts as a gift of grace descending to our fleshly, historical world. The mutual transformation of the two
horizons is not only philosophical, but is lived out in contemplative experience. Augustine had appropriated two languages, two cultures, which were
already intersecting in the previous Christian tradition. Milan in the 380s was
the site of a repristination of both traditions. The Latin reception of Plotinus
and Porphyry revealed an unsuspected spiritual majesty in Greek thought.
The Latin appropriation of the spiritualizing, Origenian approach to Scripture, represented by Ambrose, made the biblical tradition equally fresh and
exciting. Augustine steeped himself in these currents. His mystical experience
is inconceivable apart from them, and represents his internalization of them,
his appropriation of the existential possibilities they opened up. The traditions
prepared the ground for his breakthrough to an ultimate level, and this in turn
permitted him to retrieve the traditions with a lucid mastery which is not
merely intellectual but is constantly referred to that encounter with ultimacy
as to its foundation.

Disentangling himself from Manicheanism, Augustine was plagued by
dualistic and reified conceptions of the world of spirit. His confusion on this
account had become a nagging koan. The words of Plotinus, like those of a
perceptive Zen master, cut these knots and kindled an enlightened awareness:

Et inde admonitus redire ad memet ipsum intravi in intima mea duce te et potui, quoniam factus es adiutor meus; "And being thence admonished to return to myself, I entered even into my inward self, with you as my guide: and I was able, for you had become my Helper."[4]

The taste of ultimacy here is also a taste of spiritual freedom. In Buddhist terms, it is an experience of emptiness: his mind is emptied of the reified conceptions of self on which a deluded and superficial self-consciousness battened, and he is freed to rejoin the pre-reflexive awareness that precedes the construction of that rather opaque object we call *I* and *me*. Consciousness, Sartre says, in words that resonate suggestively with Buddhist themes, is *"l'existant absolu à force d'inexistence."*[5] This "non-substantial absolute" also resonates with Plotinus: "He has nothing and is the Good by having nothing. But then if anyone adds anything at all to him, substance or intellect or beauty, he will deprive him of being the Good by the addition" (*Enn.* V 5, 13). Contemplative awareness is intrinsically empty of substantiality, empty of being. It opens up at the "absolute near side" (Keiji Nishitani). It is a joyful unfolding of the light of the phenomena such that distinctions between subject and object do not arise. The self that clings to itself, that projects itself as a solid substance, then clings to objects, gives them substantiality too. The ego, as Freud and Lacan show, is a projection of our deep-rooted needs, an objectification of self that, by masquerading as the true subject, actually shelters us against true subjectivity and alienates us from our original empty freedom. Such an ego will cling also to fetishized objects in the world around it. But the self that has discovered its emptiness also lets objects go in their emptiness and abides in a state of pure experience in which subject and object have not arisen.

Augustinian *caritas* opens up at this radical level; it is not, originally at least, an objectified psychic construct: "to place interiority before one is necessarily to give it the weight of an object. It is as if it shut itself up, offering us only its external aspects, an interiority closed on itself."[6] However, it is true that *caritas* gives an interiorizing and spiritualizing inflection to biblical agape and is shaped and limited by a kind of Platonic self-containment. Lutheran scholars such as Anders Nygren have pointed to the task of finding the way back from this enclosure to the open horizons of agape. *Caritas*, for Augustine, was supreme reality, the inner light of love. Yet after centuries of *caritas*-thinking—one could list, in the manner of Von Balthasar, figures such as Bernard, the Victorines, Dante, Petrarch, Pascal, Fénelon—we can see that the regime of *caritas* is a product of cultural conditions, which could function within a medieval regime of truth as a useful convention for attunement to a gracious ultimacy, but which is less immediately functional within modern horizons of thought. Charity and grace are indeed ultimate and unconditioned realities, yet there is a specifically Augustinian staging of their emergence. Augustine's conventional world, with its notions of the human psyche,

Joseph S. O'Leary

of temptation and sin, and its residual Platonist preoccupations and structures, belongs to a past epoch, so that we cannot fully assume it as coterminous with our own world. The style in which he figured the presence of the divine as *gratia* and *caritas*, is no longer ours. We must seek the ultimacy specific to our present conventional world, the specific way in which our world signals its limits, its emptiness. Here we sight a paradox of the intrication of ultimate and conventional in religious experience: Augustine broke through to the pneumatic immediacy which is the milieu in which one can begin to apprehend the divine, yet the ultimacy of this experience comes to us now shackled by the time-bound conventions of thought and language that once were its perfectly efficacious vehicle.

Augustine's earliest references to the enlightenment he experienced in Milan on reading the *libri Platonicorum* (*Contra Academicos* II 5; *De Beata Vita* 4) are more nakedly Plotinian than the account in *Confessions* VII, without the rich biblical harmonics of the later text. Thus such expressions as *quoniam factus es adiutor meus* (Ps. 29:11) may refer less to the phenomenology of the original quasi-Plotinian experience than to a retrospective recognition of divine providence and grace at work in it.[7] The borderline between experience and interpretation, already problematic at the heart of the experience itself, becomes more so in the case of the remembered experience. The joy and light of Milan and Ostia had their own irreducible reality, but their articulation in words, the interpretation of their theological and metaphysical implications, and their placing within the total edifice of his vision required many years of further study and reflection. At least in Augustine's case, breakthroughs to ultimacy are inseparable from the long processes of interrogation and interpretation that precede and follow them. The classic religious vision is, by the same token, inseparable from its classic literary expression in the text of the *Confessions* itself. Here again the intrication of ultimacy and its conventional vehicle turns out to be more intimate than one might expect.

Thus despite the powerful unity and simplicity of Augustine's experience, the harmony between Plotinian and biblical sensibility in his account of it harbors tensions that lie open to deconstructive interrogation.[8] The retrospective biblical recuperation of the Plotinian experience may be an act of hermeneutic violence, erasing the pluralism implicit in the difference between Plotinian ultimacy (Book VII) and Pauline ultimacy (Book VIII). Augustine is constantly weaving a unitary language of the spiritual realm from his two sources, the Platonist and biblical traditions, and the seam between them, with the occasional dropped stitches, marks the conventionality and constructed quality of his vision. The Augustinian system began to unravel when Luther pulled more heavily on the Pauline thread, releasing a dynamic of agape that could not be recuperated within the regime of Platonist interiority.

Intravi et vidi qualicumque oculo animae meae supra eundum oculum animae meae lucem incommutabilem, non hanc vulgarem et conspicuam omni

180

carni . . . sed aliud, aliud valde. "I entered and beheld with the eye of my soul, (such as it was,) above the same eye of my soul, above my mind, the Light Unchangeable. Not this ordinary light, which all flesh may look upon . . . but other, yea, far other."

The phenomenon that Augustine first names is a new intimacy with an inner depth in himself to which his access had been blocked. As Zen masters also testify, enlightenment is not merely a change in subjective vision; it is a return to the bedrock reality of one's being, from which one had been cut off by the fabric of habitual deluded thinking; hence the Japanese term for enlightenment, *kenshō*, "beholding (one's) nature." Immediately supervening on this is a new awareness of God as spirit, imaged as the Plotinian sun (the One) that rises above Intellect itself which contemplates it: "One should not enquire whence it comes, for there is no "whence": for it does not really come or go away anywhere, but appears or does not appear. So one must not chase after it, but wait quietly till it appears, preparing oneself to contemplate it, as the eye awaits the rising of the sun. What is the horizon which he will mount above when he appears? He will be above Intellect itself which contemplates him" (*Enn.* V 5, 8). The *intima mea* are not quite identical with the eye of the mind that perceives the divine light. The spiritual freedom that allows one to be fully present to oneself is the milieu within which the eye of the mind, the purified intellect, can open. In Augustine, the light and the mind that contemplates it differ as creator and created: *superior, quia ipsa fecit me, et ego inferior, quia factus sum ab ea*; "above to my soul, because It made me; and I below It, because I was made by It." Is this recognition of the light as creator a retrospective construction or was Augustine's experience conditioned by his biblical formation, recently renovated by the sermons of Ambrose? A retrospective refashioning of the experience would be facilitated by the fact that Plotinus, too, speaks of the Good as making all things (through the Nous and the Soul), so that the realization *ipsa fecit me* could have been part of Augustine's Plotinian vision without the fully developed biblical sense of a personal Creator.

The next phenomenon noted is the sense of unworthiness that overcomes Augustine when he is faced with the purity of the divine light:

Et cum te primum cognovi, tu assumpsisti me, ut viderem esse, quod viderem, et nondum me esse, qui viderem. Et reverberasti infirmitatem aspectus mei radians in me vehementer, et contremui amore et horrore: et inveni longe me esse a te in regione dissimilitudinis, tamquam audirem vocem tuam de excelso: 'Cibus sum grandium: cresce et manducabis me. "When I first knew you, you lifted me up, that I might see there was something I might see, and that I was not yet such as to see. And you beat back the weakness of my sight, irradiating upon me most strongly, and I trembled with love and awe: and I perceived myself to be far off from you, in the region of unlikeness, as if I heard your voice from on high: 'I am the food of adults; grow, and thou shalt feed upon me.' "

Joseph S. O'Leary

The Platonic language here corresponds to the sense of the numinous as *fascinosum* (inspiring *amor*) and *tremendum* (inspiring *horror*)—though, as the coiner of these terms points out, it is the *fascinosum* that prevails in Augustine.[9] The voice of God that is imagined to be speaking is a later gloss ("as if") on the gulf Augustine feels between his own want of being and the supreme reality of the spiritual realm. The gulf Augustine perceives will be interpreted in Pauline terms as a bondage to sin, to be broken at the end of Book VIII. But the Pauline and Platonic scenarios, with their respective traditional terminologies, do not coincide automatically. Throughout his oeuvre (notably in the *De Trinitate*) Augustine mutually adjusts these perspectives in a constantly reworked collage; but the classical topos of how the mind is dazzled and thrown back in mystical vision[10] has no immediate connection with the Christian topics of sin and faith. The same note of failure or incompleteness inheres in Augustine's post-conversion mystical moments also, and the explanation of it in terms of moral weakness is an extrinsic, ideological interpretation. In the anti-Pelagian writings the Pauline framework dominates and references to the mystical scenario recede, so that we have a more consistent but narrower Augustine. Both the Platonic language of vision and the Pauline language of grace were vehicles of encounters with ultimacy for Augustine, yet the tense pluralism between them, and between the corresponding experiences, is not erased in any leveling vision. Augustine needs to narrate his spiritual voyage, since no closed systematic presentation can do justice to the variety of encounters it embraced.

Augustine's encounter with the reality of God in this moment of intense vision yields a new vision of the reality of the world, a vision unfolded in calm reflection:

> *Et inspexi cetera infra te et vidi nec omnino esse nec omnino non esse: esse quidem, quoniam abs te sunt, non esse autem, quoniam id quod es non sunt* (VII 17); "And I beheld the other things below you, and I perceived, that they neither altogether are, nor altogether are not, for they are, since they are from you, but are not, because they are not what you are."

This vision is personalized by a quotation from the Psalms: *Mihi autem inhaerere deo bonum est (Ps.* 72:28); in my want of being I can truly be only by dwelling in the one who is. The biblical quotations serve throughout to Christianize the Plotinian experience. From the vantage-point thus established, he expounds his ontological vision of the convertibility of being and goodness, with the corollary that evil has no real existence—a vision which overcomes Manicheanism at its root (VII 18–22). Are these ontological considerations seamlessly derived from the religious experience, or is Augustine reading back the fruits of years of thought into a single dawning of fresh insight?

Does ontological speculation already begin to project a space of thought that is in tension with the space opened up by the vision, tending to screen it out? Is the vital immediacy of consciousness being replaced by a reflective objectification? Is speculative interest thwarting the unfolding of the phenomenological insight lying at the root of such convictions as the convertibility of being and goodness? If so, this process is carried further in the *De Trinitate*, where the experience of God as Spirit cohabits uneasily with the analysis of God as substance, and where analysis of triadic structures of an objectified "soul" is in tension with evocations of its pre-objective consciousness.[11]

Augustine tells how he sought to recapture the visionary moment by the practice of a Platonic ascent (as opposed to the complete gratuity of the initial enlightenment), passing by degrees (*gradatim*) from the beauty of bodies to that of the soul, and thence to the inner sense that even animals have, and to the reasoning faculty which judges the deliveries of that sense, until he reaches the level of intelligence, of *nous*, and above it the light whereby the intelligence judges. The ascent culminates in another ecstatic encounter with what truly is: *et pervenit ad id quod est in ictu trepidantis aspectus* (VII 23); "And thus with the flash of one trembling glance it arrived at That Which Is." Augustine again falls back, more quickly this time:

> *sed aciem figere non evalui et repercussa infirmitate redditus solitis non mecum ferebam nisi amantem memoriam et quasi olefacta desiderantem, quae comedere nondum possem.* "But I could not fix my gaze thereon; and my infirmity being struck back, I was thrown again on my wonted habits, carrying along with me only a loving memory thereof, and a longing for what I had, as it were, perceived the odour of, but was not yet able to feed on."

Here the labor of deliberate cogitation precedes the mystical moment rather than subsequently reaping its harvest of insight. This intrusion of intellectual reflection into the sphere of infused contemplation has led one author to suppose that there is nothing mystical about the Milan experiences at all. Even the first experience (VII 16) would represent "not a mystical intuition of God, but an implicitly reasoned ascent of the mind to the height of truth which is God . . . God is pictured as engaged in a brief I-Thou dialogue in which he tells Augustine that he is 'I am who am.' But this utterance is essentially an intellectual or quasi-theological locution, not a mystical deliverance."[12] This is a flat and literalistic paraphrase of Augustine's sublime words: *et clamasti de longinquo: immo vero ego sum qui sum. Et audivi, sicut auditur in corde.* "The analytical invocation of God's self-given name does not affectively move him or set his spirit afire; rather, it fills his mind with light . . . the satisfaction consequent upon a perception or experience characterized by expressions such as 'Aha!' or 'Eureka!' . . . He achieved intellectual fulfillment with an intense delight that Catholics born into the faith can abstractly conceive, but never concretely imagine."[13] "Arrival at the apex of his reasoning process is accompanied by an undeniable intellectual pleasure as well as a peripheral affective satisfaction; still, neither of these affective modes even approaches full-flowered mystical experience. Significantly, the decisive factor of passivity is missing."[14] The intellectual and the affective are dissociated here in a manner that cannot do justice to such passionate thinkers as Plotinus and Augustine, in whom intellect and passion work together in constant mutual illumination and stimulation. To see mysticism as a matter of "affectivity" and to suppose that because Augustine, following Plotinus, describes a mystical enlightenment of the mind, which also stuns the mind and exceeds its grasp, he must therefore be talking about something "merely intellectual" (though his language is charged with wonder and joy) is to bypass the phenomenon the text presents through reliance on cut-and-dried binary oppositions.[15]

Quinn finds genuine mystical passivity in the Ostia experience, and ascribes it to the grace of the sacraments Augustine received and the spiritual life he practised after his conversion. The idea that Augustine could have enjoyed mystical experience while in his unconverted state seems to Quinn to presuppose a special miracle, one God was unlikely to work. But there are many "mute inglorious Wordsworths" to vouch that mystical experience is not tied to the sacraments. Augustine does underline the greater perfection of the joy of Ostia, firmly rooted in the practice of agape, and of friendship, and the communion of saints. But the Milan experience, at least in VII 16, has the notes of passivity and grace as well, as the phrases *duce te* and *tu assumpsisti me* indicate. *Id ipsum, id quod est* is touched in a moment of pure ecstasy, *in ictu trepidantis aspectus*. *Ego sum qui sum* is no abstract proposition, as Quinn thinks, but *auditur in corde*—it is a homecoming to the maternal breast of being and to the paternal abode. The presence of God is with Augustine as a holy sweetness— *dulcedo mea sancta* (I 4), an inner light, food, strength, and the breast on which his thought reposes: *lumen cordis mei et panis oris intus animae meae et virtus maritans mentem meam et sinum cogitationis meae* (I 21).

The imagery of ascent can be translated into the more "passive" imagery of stripping-away, Plotinian *aphairesis*. Like the Zen suppression of thought and images (*munen musō*), it allows the mind to be receptive to phenomena. The ascent is inward, away from the tumult of sense involvement, and thus is in the direction of non-involvement in external activities, and of passivity before the higher light that enlightens the mind. Eckhart's reading of this passage, in a sermon on the feast of St. Augustine, responds sensitively to its witness to a *pati divina: quando scilicet lux divina per effectum suum aliquem specialem irradiat super potentias cognoscentes et super medium in cognitione, elevans intellectum ipsum ad id quod naturaliter non potest;* "when the divine light through one of its special effects irradiates upon the cognitive powers and the cognitive medium, elevating the intellect itself to that of which it is naturally incapable."[16] The language of elevation is perhaps misleading, and it irritates us now by a certain archaism. The One of Plotinus is not only "above"; it is also the reality nearest to hand. The negations of apophatic theology serve not to climb a ladder to a remote beyond, but to remove illusions that prevent God from speaking to us here and now. In Mâdhyamika and in Vedanta this is clearer; the dialectical negations serve not to take us beyond the world but to reveal emptiness or the Self in the here and now.[17]

Both Milan and Ostia are breakthroughs to ultimacy, but the Ostia experience is richer and more integrated. Between them lies the moral conversion made possible through the impact of the words of St. Paul (VIII 29), another breakthrough to ultimacy, which allowed Augustine to be serenely at one with himself and with his fellow-Christians. A crisis of Platonic eros is enacted in the "drop" Augustine feels after his first experience at Milan. The crisis is resolved when eros is inserted in the context of communal agape, *caritas*; at Ostia Monica and Augustine taste the delights of this more securely rooted contemplation. Augustine is now on a spiritual plateau, in daily enjoyment of the *internum aeternum* (IX 10). Though the language of the Ostia experience is still that of Platonic ascent, and in fact is close to the willed *tentative mystique* of Milan,[18] the affective tonality is very different. The subject of the experience is not an isolated philosophical seeker, but two friends united in serene praise of God in his creation.

> *Erigentes nos ardentiore affectu in id ipsum perambulavimus gradatim cuncta corporalia . . . Et adhuc ascendebamus interius cogitando et loquendo et mirando opera tua et venimus in mentes nostras et transcendimus eas, ut attingeremus regionem ubertatis indeficientis, ubi pascis Israhel in aeternum veritate pabulo . . . Et dum loquimur et inhiamus illi, attingimus eam modice toto ictu cordis; et suspiravimus et relinquimus ibi religatas primitias spiritus et remeavimus ad strepitum oris nostri* (IX 24). "Raising ourselves up with a more glowing affection towards the 'Self-same,' we passed by degrees through all things bodily. . . . We were soaring higher yet, by inward musing, and discourse, and admiring of your works; and we came to our own minds, and went beyond them, that we might arrive at that region of never-failing plenty, where you feed Israel for ever with the food of truth. . . . And while we were discoursing and panting after her [Wisdom], we slightly touched on her with the whole effort of our heart; and we sighed, and there we left bound the first fruits of the Spirit; and returned to vocal expressions of our mouth."

Here again Augustine's displays his inspired mastery of the conventional techniques of contemplation, of metaphysical analysis, of a rhetoric of eros mounting to meet the descending manna of agape (*ubi pascis Israhel*), and of the arts of fictional and dramatic presentation. Ostia might be seen as a synthesis or a dialectical result of the metaphysical vision of Milan and the moral liberation of the *tolle lege* scene, producing yet another form of experiencing ultimacy. Perhaps we might call it a Johannine ultimacy, given the key role of interpersonal love and the eloquence with which Augustine will discourse on this theme in his homilies on *I John*. The whole of Scripture is for Augustine a set of occasions for breaking through to the ultimate level of vision, and his hearers are urged to knock constantly until the light of intellectus dawns for them: *Surge, quaere, anhela desideria, et ad clausa pulsa . . .* (*Tractatus in Johannem* 18.7). The taste of ultimacy gives him great freedom in imaginative penetration of the biblical text, handled as a functional "skillful means" for evoking contemplative vision.

All of this work with conventions circles around the vividly experienced truth-event, the encounter with *id ipsum,* an intimacy with the divine in conjunction with a privileged moment of intimacy with a beloved human being or in communion with the quest of the praying pilgrim community. Fragile and elusive as the moments of *intellectus* are, their value as clues to the ultimately gracious nature of reality spurs us to work on the conventions of our religious discourse to make them more effective antennae for picking up such signals. Augustine's entire theological oeuvre is an effort to render the conventional transparent to the ultimate. He joyfully disposed the linguistic and intellectual resources of his culture into alignment with this contemplative ultimacy. The equivalent achievement for theology today would be to explore the horizon of ultimacy onto which the questions, the lack, the unease of modern civilization open out, and to revamp religious discourse so that it no longer obstructs access to this realm, but kindles experiences of ultimacy through a recognition of its own thorough conventionality.

Ultimacy under Fire: Psychoanalysts and Religious Experience

A religious experience such as Augustine describes bears witness to a dimension of reality that triumphs serenely over death and meaninglessness. The authority of this witness comes from the quality of ultimacy inherent in the experience itself, rather than from the metaphysical ideas and scriptural teachings linked with it. Of course, a scriptural word may be the occasion of the experience. Then it is that living word that has authority and ultimacy, not the mere text or secondary elucidations of it. The image of hearing a word may originate in the conviction that the experience is not merely subjective but is an encounter with the real. We saw how in the later account of his Milan experience, Augustine claimed that he heard the voice of God declare "I am who am." In Vedanta, too, the non-duality of atman and Brahman is not simply an insight, but a revelation, something heard (*śruti*), which, as in the case of the Prophets and the Quran, refers more to the mode of encounter with the divine than to the authority of canonical texts. Phenomenologically, the deliveries of religious experience impose themselves as unmasterable (Barth's *Unverfügbarkeit*), as "saturated phenomena" (J.-L. Marion), which we cannot go behind or seek to subordinate to any explanatory framework. The reality encountered is to be accepted entirely on its own terms, which are those of supreme being, awareness, bliss (the Vedantic *sat-chit-ananda*). Were one to grill it, to seek out its hidden background, to query its legitimacy, that would be a demonstration of phenomenological ill-breeding, or what Aristotle would call *apaideusia*. In the numinous moment, there is no room for doubt or questioning. The reality apprehended is more undeniable even than the reality of the everyday physical world: *non erat prorsus unde dubitarem, faciliusque dubitarem vivere me quam non esse veritatem . . .* (VII 16), echoed in Newman's reference to an "inward conversion of which I was conscious (and of which I still am more certain that that I have hands and feet.)"[19]

Nonetheless, the rights of the conventional will not be denied. Orthodoxy attempts to regulate and assess religious experience in terms of its conformity to doctrine. Mystics will have trouble honoring the constraints of doctrinal discourse, which may not fit well with their more vivid sense of the realities to which dogma points, since the entire realm of words and ideas belongs to conventional or world-ensconced truth whereas religious experience is a breakthrough to the *paramârtha* level. The wise mystic will patiently negotiate the realm of conventional reason. That Augustine could do so with such aplomb perhaps suggests that he was not primarily a mystical type at all; his contemplative serenity positively throve on the cut and thrust of doctrinal debate. Plotinus's cogitations are turned inward: he pursues his philosophical riddles as a spiritual exercise, in a spirit of play; the themes of Aristotle and the Stoics, even those of ethics, logic, and cosmology, are rehearsed, but in a perspective remote from their this-worldly concerns; they become the occasion of a perpetual rethinking that enacts the soul's effort to locate itself before the One.

Psychoanalysts practice a hermeneutics of suspicion that would trace everything back to the subject. While they respect experiences that show the subject engaging in the symbolic order in a realistic give-and-take, they tend to view religious experience as a saturnalian feast of the unconscious, in which all its repressed grandiose desires are given free rein. They assume it can be nothing more than an immanent psychic process, a blind jouissance, an oceanic feeling linked to pre-natal bliss. Many find in the *Confessions* nothing more than libido on the loose, ego inflation, masochistic self-annihilation before the super-ego. What a catastrophe it would be not only for religion, but for civilization, if these dismal diagnoses turned out to be the "truth" about Augustine.

Slavoj Žižek points out that in religious ecstasy, according to St. Ignatius Loyola:

> "the positive figure of God comes second, after the moment of 'objectless' ecstasy: first we have the experience of objectless ecstasy; subsequently this experience is attached to some historically determined representation— here we encounter an exemplary case of the Real as 'that which remains the same in all possible (symbolic) universes.'... precisely jouissance as that which always remains the same. Every ideology attaches itself to some kernel of jouissance which, however, retains the status of an ambiguous excess. The unique 'religious experience' is thus to be split into its two components, as in the well-known scene from Terry Gilliam's *Brazil* in which the food on a plate is split into its symbolic frame (a coloured photo of the course above the plate) and the formless slime of jouissance that we actually eat."[20]

Joseph S. O'Leary

To contest the phenomenological adequacy of this description, we must focus on the illuminative power of contemplative experience. The "inner witness of the Holy Spirit" lights up the biblical text and charges it with radiant meaning. Religious experience, as Augustine's account shows, is also a source of metaphysical insight, yielding a renewed vision of the world and of being. Even if one calls this body of scriptural and metaphysical insight an ideological construction, the relation between the insight and the ecstasy is more integrated than Žižek recognizes. To be sure, there is an excess of the joyful sense of ultimacy over the framework of understanding that it both confirms and shows up as "mere straw" (Thomas Aquinas), a vessel of clay. "We have this treasure in earthen vessels, to show that the transcendent power belongs to God and not to us" (2 *Cor.* 4:7). For Paul, the excess is a mark of the divine glory, not of an obscure psychic murk. The darkness of divine glory is further along the trajectory of dazzling insight that the religious experience conveys: "Dark with excessive bright thy skirts appear." If what is touched in mystical ecstasy exceeds the grasp of the mind—"what no eye has seen, nor ear heard, nor the heart of man conceived" (1 *Cor.* 2:9)—this is not because it is a slippery preconceptual slime, but because only the Holy Spirit can investigate it: "The Spirit searches everything, even the depths of God" (2:10). Contemplation is access to the dimension of Spirit, pneuma, marked by an intensification of the sense of reality, as 'seeing' gives way to 'touching.' (Here, though, I am again yoking together two disparate traditions, the biblical pneuma and the Neoplatonic touching, *thiggein*.)

If the core of religious experience is a blissful pneumatic illumination, this is in close conjunction with an illuminating word. Both aspects are transformative: the spiritual bliss is a liberation from chains of delusion, from psychic blockage; the word associated with it is a judgment of truth, cutting through the false or unreal positions in which one had been entangled and establishing a secure new perspective. Even if *jouissance* were always the same, the word in which it finds expression inevitably varies according to the context of the experience. The word cannot be a pure expression of ultimacy, as it invariably relies on the conventional data of the given context. One may also ask if even the core *jouissance* itself is shaped by its context, so that the effect of ultimacy could never be disentangled immaculately from the culture-bound contingencies of its emergence.

This dynamic of transformative illumination in religious experience is not undermined by the discovery of a connection with erotic drives. Those places in poetic or religious texts when we perceive the dawning of the sublime often bring a surge of erotic excitement or delight: consider the blissful release in the second variation of the third movement of Beethoven's Ninth Symphony (bars 99–114) or the vaulting quasi-fugato of the final movement (bars 432–525). To be "surprised by joy" is an erotic experience. But to reduce every summit of religious or aesthetic joy to instantiations of an invariable blind animal ecstasy is a doctrinaire curtailment of the phenomena and their significance. The idea that *jouissance* is always the same scarcely applies even to physical eroticism. The mood of sexual delight lights up intensely the varied beauty of the objects that elicit it. Analogously, the light and joy of the Spirit constantly reveal fresh aspects of the object of contemplation.

"In our era of modern science," says Žižek, "one can no longer accept the fable of the miracle of Resurrection as the form of the Truth-Event. Although the Truth-Event does designate the occurrence of something which, from within the horizon of the predominant order of Knowledge, appears impossible (think of the laughter with which the Greek philosophers greeted Paul's assertion of Christ's Resurrection on his visit to Athens), today, any location of the Truth-Event at the level of supernatural miracles necessarily entails regression into obscurantism, since the event of Science is irreducible and cannot be undone."[21] The primitive resurrection kerygma no doubt concerns a physical raising of Christ from the tomb, seen as the first fruits of the general resurrection of the dead. Demythologizers in the line of Schleiermacher and Bultmann have reinterpreted this ancient language as referring to a pneumatic eschatological event that no longer clashes directly with science. According to John Keenan, "The resurrected Jesus can be seen only in the conversion he came to preach about, not in some supernaturally perceptible coming back to show his new glorified body."[22] The miracle of resurrection is not the literal raising of a corpse but the conquest over exactly the dead-end beyond which Žižek believes it is impossible to go. "After Freud, one cannot directly have faith in a Truth-Event; every such Event ultimately remains a semblance obfuscating a preceding Void whose Freudian name is death drive." The resurrection obfuscates the Real manifested in Christ's death, "the lowest excremental remainder."[23] Yet in the Christian kerygma, this Real is not eluded: *Ego sum vermis et non homo* (Ps. 22:6). The abyss of the Triduum is the condition of the Paschal dawn.

Žižek himself speaks of revolutionary acts that "miraculously" break through the constraints of a given symbolic order. Correlative with resurrection is forgiveness, "the miracle of Grace which retroactively 'undoes' our past sins." Here it is not science that objects, but a scepticism based on the feeling that this is a tired old ideology. The phenomena of forgiveness and being forgiven provide, however, an empirical basis for belief in this miracle. The impact of Christ's revolutionary act of forgiveness can be described in Žižek's own terms: "An act proper 'miraculously' changes the very standard by which we measure and value our activity; that is, it is synonymous with what Nietzsche called 'transvaluation of values' . . . The act occurs when the choice of (what, within the situation, appears as) the Worst changes the very standards of what is good or bad."[24] Christ "becomes sin" to free us from sin, and his resurrection is perhaps the dialectical reversal brought about by this radical confrontation with sin and death. The joy of the resurrection is not sparked off

Joseph S. O'Leary

by the news of a fabulous miracle; rather, it is correlative with a vision of the full significance of Christ's teaching and his death, the vision that "God was in Christ reconciling the world to himself" (2 *Cor.* 5:19).

Beyond the finality of physical death lies the ultimacy of the death drive, the meaningless entropic noise at the heart of the universe. It is heard as a sublime interruption in a love-lyric of Catullus: *Nobis cum semel occidit brevis lux/Nox est perpetua una dormienda.* Freud and Lacan have increased the pervasiveness of this dark sublime. It, too, is unmasterable; there is no going beyond it. Yet Christ "abolished death and brought life and immortality to light through the gospel" (2 *Tim.* 1:10). The dark places of death are entirely comprehended by the light of the gospel word, so that their meaning changes. "The grace that is in Christ Jesus" (2 *Tim.* 2:1) is known on a nearer acquaintance with suffering and death. It is not by eluding the phenomena of sin and death, but by surrendering entirely to their claim, that one enters the domain of the forgiveness of sins and the resurrection from the dead.

Religious experience, then, is a miraculous breakthrough to a realm of freedom—be it nirvana, enlightenment, resurrection, the Vedantic Brahman, or the Plotinian One. Is there a specific form in which this "truth-event" is to be sought today? The leveling and alienating effect of the machine of global capitalism reduces all experiences to commodities. Religious vision is stymied by it much as artistic and political creativity are. When we study the breakthroughs to ultimacy recorded in the classic religious texts of the past and attempt to discern how they related to the historical and cultural contexts in which they emerged, we may find clues for an opening up of the contemporary context to a liberating ultimacy. A thorough recognition of the historical pluralism and the contingent, conventional status of all our languages of ultimacy will be a distinctive feature of a contemporary retrieval of mystical traditions, and we may draw from Buddhism the encouraging thought that to recognize the conventional *as* conventional is to be already aligned to the ultimate.

The Conventionality of Religious Experience

Religious experience should bring a sense of freedom and flexibility in dealing with the conventions of religious discourse. But when means and ends, the conventional and the ultimate, are confused, the result is a sclerosis of the religious tradition, some form of absolutism, fanaticism, or fundamentalism. To be sure, in the contemporary context a rigid fundamentalism may be more conducive to mystical breakthroughs than a liberal and pluralistic attitude. Yet perhaps if we go all the way with pluralism, recognizing the utterly contingent and conventional status of all religious constructions, we can traverse the religious fantasy (as Žižek might put it) and re-enact more skillfully the religious disposal of words, ideas, and actions in view of ultimacy. When people take up religious words and attitudes, they are aware that they are subscribing to an historical tradition. Today, that historical self-consciousness embraces not only one's own tradition but the wider community of faiths, bringing a critical sense of the non-absoluteness of one's mode of engaging with ultimate reality. The community that recites the Lord's Prayer is increasingly aware that they are enacting a specifically Christian convention, while neighboring communities enact conventions no less efficacious for them. Such awareness might undercut conviction at first, but subsequently it can renew one's relations to the forms one uses, as they are reappropriated in their fragile status as historically tried and tested means of opening to the divine. Can even the Eucharist be rethought in these terms? It is a form used by Jesus, drawing on all the riches of the Jewish heritage, and exhibiting the sense of his death. To re-enact that form is the richest way we have of realizing the Paschal sense of Christ's death, attuning ourselves to his pneumatic presence, and realizing communion with one another in him. The rite "works" for us as it did for Jesus. It is an eloquent and effective convention.

For Henri Poincaré, geometry is not an immediate datum of experience; neither is it a Kantian a priori structure, an inbuilt necessity of the mind. A geometry is freely chosen, as a conventional construct, constrained only by the necessity of avoiding contradictions. Einstein adds that physical geometry, or practical geometry, is constrained in addition by the empirical reality of solid bodies. When the purely theoretical conventions of mathematical geometry are put to practical use, we are forced to recognize a single specific geometry as that of our cosmos. This geometry turns out to be Riemannian rather than Euclidian, so that all the confirmations of Euclid and of Newton that centuries of experience provided now need to be recontextualized. But the move from theoretical to practical geometry is by no means a step out of conventions into transparent realities. Straight lines still remain idealized fictions that have no actual existence in nature.

If geometry is a convention, philosophical systems must be much more so. "In the endeavour to live up to traditional ideals of completeness and ultimate justification, a philosophical tradition or school tends to define and explain its basic notions in terms of the notions belonging to its own terminological core. Its arrangement of basic notions is in that sense circular, and it is by training and by allowing oneself to become convinced of its trustworthiness that one gets into that circle."[25] The world yields to the analytic methodology of a strong philosophical system, but the bulk of the system's progress lies in its internal self-confirmation and self-perfecting, sometimes to the point where it seems to exclude worldly reality from the crystal palace of its own purified reconstruction of the world (a critique addressed to Husserl by Adorno).

Analogously, Jonathan Z. Smith once compared religions to packs of cards. They are systems of conventional symbols and rules for playing with them. This conventionalist reading of religion has become very tempting as we take religious pluralism seriously, and realize that no one religion can set itself up as the ultimate norm whereby all the others are judged. Humans have forged religious systems from the materials available in their different cultures in complex historical trajectories. Faced with the contradictory variety of the results, we are forced to wonder if religious discourse has any substantial referent.

If we think of the chief referent of the biblical religions, God, it seems that God's "housing problem," long ago diagnosed by David Strauss, is more severe than ever. The notion of God has no steady place in our contemporary experience of worldhood. Even our grammar seems to exclude it, for the texture of signification no longer depends on a logocentric reference to stable substances. A Buddhist ontology of dependent co-arising, of a universal conditionality that functions without stable entitative causes, seems better suited to contemporary experience. As the most self-critical and thoroughly reflected of religions, Buddhism has a key role to play in resolving current questions about the status and function of religion and of theism. Buddhism is happy to see religions as conventional constructs, or as provisional skillful means to be used for the purposes of spiritual liberation.

Religious experience provides empirical confirmation to religious systems, just as the physical world confirms geometrical systems. But the confirmation does not take away the conventional status of the system. At best, it shows that the system has a useful function in favoring the occurrence of religious experience. Perhaps there is one correct "practical geometry" of the religious cosmos. Buddhism, the most methodical of spiritual paths, may have unveiled the lineaments of this realm. Or Buddhism may be one conventional map alongside others, and all the maps may have to be corrected as we close in on the true shape of religious reality. Or all the maps may be equally valid, and conventionalism thus may have a wider scope in spiritual than in physical space.

For Poincaré the question, "Is Euclidean geometry true?" had no meaning. Similarly, the questions "Is Buddhism true?" and "Is Christianity true?" could be construed as having no meaning. Both religions are skillful means for lighting up a spiritual space and traveling in it. Any other religion that works as effectively and as consistently would do just as well. We do not ask "Is Mozart true?" "Is Beethoven true?" as we travel in the space they open up. A conventionalist would say that within a certain geometrical set-up there are true and false propositions, while the question of the truth of the geometry as a whole cannot be asked, for there is no external, objective "space" with which one could compare it. Any non-contradictory geometry will fit our spatial experience, and the question, "which fits best?" reduces to the question of which is of most pragmatic value in a given context, or which best serves the evolution of the species. A religious conventionalist, analogically, could say that within a certain religious language-game there are true and false propositions, but the question of the truth of the religion as a whole cannot be asked, for there is no external, objective religious space with which one could compare it. A religion is a human method of tuning in to ultimate mystery. Its language generates propositions that have their own inbuilt, autonomous logic, just as those of geometry have. In Euclidean space, it is true that the angles of an equilateral triangle are equal, and false that they are not. The truth-effect is embedded in a context, inscribed within a web of writing that exceeds and encompasses it; and that writing itself eludes the question, "true or false?" as Derrida argues. In terms of the dyad of *samvrti-satya* and *paramartha-satya*, all propositional truth is conventional or world-ensconced truth, not ultimate truth. But the careful tending of the garden of conventional truth is a condition for the blossoming of ultimacy. Thus the dogmatic wrangles of the past had a point. Unfortunately, instead of being seen as labor on the conventional in service of the ultimate, they were seen as themselves ultimate, and thus they degenerated into a clash of absolutes.

In Christian religious space, it is true that God, Logos, and Spirit are equal, and false that they are not. But the dogmatic truths about the Trinity are embedded in a web of writing that ultimately eludes the question of truth or falsity. Mapping their experience in terms of God, Logos, and Spirit, the biblical writers were not aware of any tensions or contradictions of an ontological order. Only with the emergence of theology, fashioned after the Greek philosophical model by Philo and Justin, did questions about the ontological conditions and foundations of the biblical language begin to take a sharper character. The inspired utterances of the Johannine contemplative community offer little foothold for determining the ontological status of Christ; when John (1.1) writes that the Logos was *theos* (not *ho theos*), he is not stating that the Logos is lesser in divinity than the Father, but only apprehending the phenomenon of the Logos as one who comes from the intimacy of the divine realm. Conversely, when he has Thomas call the risen Jesus *ho theos* (20.28), he is not defining Jesus as truly God; it is a contemplative utterance, a recognition that the encounter with Jesus is an encounter with God.

The construction of trinitarian and christological orthodoxy is a skillful theological performance within an intellectual framework that is ill matched to the world of the texts on which it works, and not entirely suited to expounding the faith (though it was commonly taken to be the ideal, providentially supplied framework for clarifying Christian truth). Now that we have worked with the dogmatic framework for two millennia, we can see that for all its power it has a rigid and sterile cast and no longer provides a basis for creative development. Dogma developed according to its intrinsic metaphysical logic up to the fourteenth century, with the result that scholastic brilliance replaced authentic clarification of the biblical phenomena. From the Reformation on, creative theology has focused on tracing dogma back to its biblical roots. Systematic theologies in all Christian confessions today will normally adopt a biblical pattern of exposition, as in Melanchthon's *Loci* and Calvin's *Institutes*. This biblical refashioning of dogmatic thought has revitalized basic dogmatic claims, recontextualized others, and cast others into the shade. It has exposed as inadequate the classical frameworks of dogmatic thought, shaped by canons of rationality deriving from metaphysics.

Today, the intellectual space or regime of truth within which dogmatic truths enjoyed an immovable security has become obsolete. What is left of dogma survives only on the strength of biblical support and within a space of Christian thinking quite foreign to that of the Fathers, Councils, and scholastics. Little weight attaches to "dogmatic" claims unless they carry the mark of ultimacy—unless they could be candidates for a mystical level of contemplative apprehension. The Vedantic revelation, "that are thou" (*tat tvam asi*), and the Mahayana paradox, "samsara is nirvana," are claims of that sort. "He was delivered for our sins and rose for our justification" (*Rom* 4.25) and "The Word became flesh" (*Jn* 1.14) are such claims too, if apprehended in their original contemplative context without the intrusion of inappropriate ontology. The language of religion is primarily a language of mystical ultimacy, a language voiding itself before the numinous real, the divine. The more systematic down-to-earth explication of religious worldviews that most religions offer as well, the exoteric vision of *The City of God* for example will have little of the character of ultimacy, and the texts devoted to it will be much more imprisoned in their time and culture than those, like the *Confessions*, that boldly run up against the limits of language.

Ultimacy is not a thing, a noumenon, to which the merely phenomenal paths of the various religions would point. Ultimacy is rather adjectival, a quality attaching to a certain specific vision. Thus, the language expressive of it does not convey new substantive content, but a new depth of realization. Systems of religious thought centered on encounters with some ultimate reality, such as those of Plotinus, Augustine, or Sankara, retrieve previous tradition in a key of greater simplicity, radicality, and integration. Even if most of the traditions they rehearse are now outdated, their work on them is graced by a sense of the dual roles of the conventional and the ultimate. They handle the conventions with wisdom and respect, yet one senses that they all the time have a quiet awareness that the ultimate is around the corner, and that the conventions need not be worried about excessively. Augustine never becomes excited as he contemplates the fall of Rome and unrolls his panorama of history and eschatology; but when it comes to the topic of grace, a topic central to his encounter with God, his tone is urgent, impassioned. He becomes even fanatical, trapped in the horrendous theologoumena of predestination. Yet as in the case of Luther's reply to Erasmus, *On the Bondage of the Will*, the value of the texts lies in their exemplification of an indefectible sense of the reality of God and grace, a constant effort to let the ultimate be spoken in words that can only be the feeblest, most fragile of vessels. Though *The City of God* is weighed down by desultory lore, and though the writings on grace err through hammering too hard at the essentials, Augustine can stand as an exemplar of the interplay of ultimate and conventional, unfolding the doctrines from the central vantage-point of his contemplative vision, setting each element in its place, a relative and auxiliary one, as his mind ranges freely through the system in a spirit of play, knowing that all its constructions are mere provisional conventions at the service of the one thing needful, the *internum aeternum.*

What we call divine revelation is not an alien force that strikes from outside. It emerges within the conventions of a given historical world as a breakthrough to a new level of interiority or lucidity. Though it shatters the conventions prepared to receive it, as the real always shatters the merely notional, it does not offer a new empirical datum calling for categories not anticipated in the previous tradition. Although a revelation is stamped with the quality of ultimacy, that ultimacy always has a basis in the conventional; it is the ultimacy of this conventional world, the unconditioned that this particular set of conditions allows to emerge. Breakthroughs to ultimacy happen as a function of particular conventional set-ups. The irreducible and unmasterable core of the revelation event both fulfills and overthrows the context in which it emerges. It is not derived naturalistically from this preceding context, as a psychologist of religion is tempted to think: "Every religious phenomenon has its history and its derivation from natural antecedents."[26] But the manner in which its transcendence is manifest always exhibits a reference to the context. Even as the visionary struggles to express the "wholly other" character of what is manifested, the words that surge up to express it are those of the religious culture he or she had already acquired, words that now take wing, charged with new immediacy and fullness of sense.

In the Buddha's enlightenment, the conventional constructions of centuries of Indian religious exploration click into a new and luminous perspective. In the resurrection of Jesus, the conventional constructions of centuries of Jewish religious exploration find a new bearing. The resurrection is the happening of ultimacy amid the conventional. In the breakthrough to ultimacy, Gotama becomes Buddha, and Jesus becomes Christ: "descended from David according to the flesh, and designated Son of God in power according to the Spirit of holiness by his resurrection from the dead" (*Rom.* 1:3–4). Ultimacy is a radical transformation of the conventional world, and it can be known only in this way, starting from this conventional basis. The Pauline movement from flesh to spirit is the movement from conventional to ultimate.

Ultimacy, despite its "wholly other" quality, dwells in conventionality, and we remain open to it only in disposing the conventional world in line with its ultimate orientation. In Buddhist vision, ultimate reality is not some hidden thing-in-itself, but is fully accessible to enlightened awareness. The ultimate is not hidden behind the conventions. Etymologically, it is claimed, *samvrti-satya* is not merely "screening reality" but also "revealing reality"; to experience the conventions as conventions is already to be attuned to their emptiness, to ultimacy.

The mystical texts of the past give ample evidence of the flimsiness of even the most privileged religious language. To read them is to visit a museum of rusty old flying-machines. There is a whole collection built according to the Neo-Platonic model, and it includes Gregory of Nyssa, Augustine, Pseudo-Dionysius, Eckhart, and many other princes of Christian mysticism. That the machines flew need not be questioned, nor have the fundamental laws of aviation changed. But we no longer know how to build those contraptions. Despite the gap between the claims of ultimacy made by mystics and the manifestly culture-bound language they use, their fragile myths did function as vehicles of ultimacy for them—an ultimacy that could be expressed and experienced only in terms of those specific myths. Our present conceptions of spiritual space and of the technology for its conquest generate a very different body of conventions from those of classical mysticism, and these in turn will seem as farfetched to people in the future as the mystical maps of the past seem to us. Yet past texts, including the biblical ones, speak to us through the core phenomena of spiritual freedom to which they attest, despite the elaborate interpretative framework in which these phenomena are enshrined.

But are the core phenomena themselves a conventional formation, arising in dependence on a congeries of contingent historical conditions? In the case of the Protestant peasant who is related to have spent days lost in contemplation on reading *Romans* 8:1—"There is now no condemnation for those in Christ Jesus"—should we say that, rather than appropriating the meaning of Paul in a luminous communication, the reader constructed his own contemporary vision, kindled by Paul's words, and shaped by subsequent theological development, notably the creative retrieval of Paul in the Lutheran tradition?

A common core-experience cannot be distilled out of the various languages of ultimacy. Each is from the start a rich particular texture, and the ultimacy they secrete is the fine fruit of an entire religious culture. Like the experience of listening to a Beethoven quartet, "music heard so deeply / That it is not heard at all, but you are the music / While the music lasts" (T. S. Eliot), the interiorized appreciation of the images, truths, and presences constructed by a given religion is not an external confirmation of these, but their product. Yet as a musical ecstasy confirms the greatness of a musical opus, so does a religious ecstasy confirm the greatness of a religious vision. Something clicks, something chimes, and one cries: "That's it!"

A context-free description of ultimacy might be possible if it were essentially a psychological experience. Then one might discover the corresponding brain-waves. But ultimacy is a matter more of being than of consciousness. It is a quality of reality itself. To isolate that quality independently of the cultural vehicles that open access to it would entail finding a truer, more objective, more universal language of ultimacy than any concrete tradition has found. It is as if one were to seek a true, objective language of beauty that would surpass and replace the many languages of the great poets. One might trace general patterns of the emergence of ultimacy in religious traditions or of the emergence of beauty in poetry. But ultimacy and beauty are not things but "effects." The effect of beauty in poetry is on each occasion singular, unrepeatable. The effect of ultimacy in religion has a similar individual irreducibility. One can be initiated into a religious tradition and led to its vision of ultimacy, so that one "repeats" the experience of one's predecessors on this path. Similarly, one can come to appreciate a great poem and have the same experience of beauty as its previous readers had. There is a tradition of experience, as it is transmitted from mind to mind. But just as the poetry is not a dispensable vehicle of the experience of beauty it transmits, neither are the conventions of a religious tradition separable from the ultimacy they convey. They are not ways of cutting a pre-given experiential cake according to culturally conditioned conceptual or linguistic schemes. The schemes are intrinsic elements of the cake, which is always already rich in intelligible patterns.

Opposing talk of religious experience as culture-bound and historically contextualized, Anne Klein points to the direct perception of emptiness in Tibetan Mâdhyamika Buddhism. She claims that the immediate experience of ultimacy becomes independent of its conventional vehicles and, in consequence, attains a universality that common experience lacks. The conditioned makes the unconditioned possible, as the dissolution of conditions and the discovery of a realm of unconditioned freedom. It is thus that the ordinary mind can "experience a state that is unconditioned, omniscient, and pure," a "direct experience of the final or ultimate nature of things." "This knowledge and its object are unconditioned by particularities of history and thus accessible in the same form, albeit through different means, to all persons regardless of cultural or psychological particularity." The cultural particularity of religious paths fades into insignificance when the ultimate emerges. The conundrum of "how conceptual conditioning yields a non-conceptual experience of the unconditioned"[27] is solved by a gradualist approach in which conceptual analysis applied to the data of conventional awareness works in tandem with an abandonment of conceptuality for a non-conceptual, non-dualistic experience of emptiness. This abandonment is achieved through mental calming and concentration, which allay the tensions between conceptual thought and direct perception and reduce the impact of conditioned objects on the perceiving subject. Here a path of awareness opens up that is less and less subject to the conditioning that provides the basis for historicist and constructivist epistemologies. Insight into the constructed character of mental experience is not the highest insight for Buddhism, for such constructions are seen as interfering with cognition of the unconstructed, emptiness.

Against this, one might recall that in Mâdhyamika thought "emptiness" is always "emptiness of"; ultimate truth has as its basis some conventional truth; the unconditioned dawns on a conditioned mind, and emerges as the dissolution of just those conditions already in place. Buddhism may seem to preach a simple transcendence of constructions toward an experience of emptiness that is invariable, but in practice emptiness emerges on each occasion as a deconstruction of a given construction. Not the endless deconstruction of Derrida's *différance*, to be sure, but a deconstruction that finds something unconstructed, unconditioned at the heart of the constructed, conditioned. Ultimacy is always known as a conventionality deconstructed.

Thus, while in its inscrutable inner core the unconditioned may lie beyond all conventional contexts, in its actual emergence it appears in a variety of styles. Plotinus's One is not the same thing as Buddhist emptiness, though both are given as the ultimate nature of things. The One emerges as a simplicity transcending the noetic realm, as mapped in the theory of the Nous, whereas emptiness emerges in the quiescence of the distinctions of our conventional dealings with the dependently arisen world, as mapped in Buddhist theory. The unconditioned in each case takes its color and its mode of emergence from the conditioned set-up in terms of which it is sighted, even if it defines itself entirely by negation of the conventional conditions. A Pauline mysticism of grace, similarly, depends on a specific mapping of the human condition in terms of bondage to sin and death and condemnation by the Law; the unconditioned that emerges is the unconditioned of this particular conditioned. Even when mystics insist most radically on the unconditioned nature of their vision, they do so in a way that involves reference to specific cultural conditions: Plotinus has set up his entire conceptual machinery so as to allow the unconditioned to manifest itself in this way. In itself utterly simple, the unconditioned nonetheless comes into view in function of the conventions prepared for its apprehension. The various discourses about the unconditioned, whether it is envisaged as nirvana, Brahman, spirit, or the Good, converge in attributing to it such qualities as absolute simplicity. Yet the simplicity overcomes a different complexity in each system.

The Buddhist doctrine of the two-fold truth frees us, then, for a double reception of mystical witness: on the one had we recognize that the classic accounts remain beacons of ultimacy, and on the other we recognize the constitutionally broken character of these accounts, all linked to archaic historical contexts, when a certain makeshift human language served effectively as a provisional skillful means for tuning in to ultimacy. We rejoice in this brokenness and irreducible pluralism, since it clarifies the conditions of a contemporary quest for ultimacy, holding out the promise that the ultimate is not hiding in a recondite past but is ready to be found anew in our present rag-and-bone shop of samsaric conventions.

NOTES

1. Nâgârjuna, *Mûlamadhyamakakârikâ* 24:10, trans. J. Garfield, *The Fundamental Wisdom of the Middle Way: Nagarjuna's* Mulamadhyamakakarika (Oxford: Oxford University Press, 1995).

2. See G. Newland, *The Two Truths* (Ithaca: Snow Lion, 1992) and *Appearance and Reality: The Two Truths in Four Buddhist Systems* (Ithaca: Snow Lion, 1999).

3. See J. S. O'Leary, "Enjoying One Another in God: In Defence of Augustine's Eudaemonism," in *Archivio di Filosofia* (2001), 561–76.

4. Augustine, *Confessions*, VII, 16, ed. and trans. E. B. Pusey (New York: Modern Library, 1999), modified.

5. J.-P. Sartre, *La Transcendance de l'Ego* (Paris: Vrin, 1972), p. 26. The following citation is from p. 25.

6. Ibid., 66.

7. For Plotinus's own sense of grace, see R. Sorabji, *Time, Creation, and the Continuum* (Ithaca: Cornell University Press, 1983), p. 171.

8. See J. S. O'Leary, *Questioning Back: The Overcoming of Metaphysics in Christian Tradition* (Minneapolis: Winston-Seabury, 1985), chapter 4.

9. R. Otto, *Das Gefühl des Überweltlichen.* (Munich: Beck, 1933), p. 232.

10. See T. Finan, "A Mystic in Milan. *Reverberasti* Revisited," in F. X. Martin and J. A. Richmond, eds., *From Augustine to Eriugena* (Washington, D.C.: Catholic University of America Press, 1991), pp. 77–91.

11. See J. S. O'Leary, "Die-Esprit et Substance-Substance chez saint Augustin," *Recherches de science religieuse* 69(1981), pp. 357–90.

12. J. M. Quinn, "Mysticism in the *Confessiones;* Four Passages Reconsidered," in F. Van Fleteren et al., eds., *Augustine: Mystic and Mystagogue* (New York: Peter Lang, 1991), p. 258.

13. Ibid., 258–59.

14. Ibid., 265.

15. For the vibrant, indeed violent affectivity of Plotinian mysticism, taken up by Augustine, see Sorabji, *Time, Creation, and the Continuum*, pp. 159–60, 165, 169.

16. *Lateinische Werke* V 93–94; quoted in V. Lossky, *Théologie négative et connaissance de Die chez Maître Eckhart* (Paris: Vrin, 1998), pp. 180–81.

17. See J. S. O'Leary, "Where all the ladders start. Apophasis as Awareness," *Archivio di Filosofia* (forthcoming, 2003).

18. See P. Courcelle, *Recherches sur les Confessions de saint Augustin* (Paris: Études Augustiniennes, 1968).

19. J. H. Newman, *Apologia Pro Vita Sua* (Garden City, N.Y.: Doubleday, 1956), p. 127.

20. S. Žižek, *The Plague of Fantasies* (London: Verso, 1997), p. 50.

21. S. Žižek, *The Ticklish Subject: The Absent Centre of Political Ontology* (London: Verso, 1999), p. 142.

22. J. P. Keenan, *The Gospel of Mark: A Mahayana Reading* (Maryknoll, N.Y.: Orbis, 1995), p. 394.

23. S. Žižek, *The Ticklish Subject*, pp. 154, 228.

24. Ibid., 331, 307.

25. S. Stenlund, "Language and Metaphysics," *Theoria* 62 (1996): 196–97.

26. W. James, *The Varieties of Religious Experience* (New York: Mentor Books, 1958), p. 23.

27. A. Klein, "Mental Concentration and the Unconditioned: A Buddhist Case for Unmediated Experience," in R. E. Buswell and R. M. Gimello, eds., *Paths to Liberation* (Honolulu: University of Hawaii Press, 1992), pp. 269, 270, 271.

CONTRIBUTORS

JEFFREY BLOECHL is Edward Bennett Williams Fellow and Assistant Professor of Philosophy at the College of the Holy Cross in Worcester, Mass. He is the author of *Liturgy of the Neighbor: Emmanuel Levinas and the Religion of Responsibility* and a forthcoming book on philosophical anthropology between theology and phenomenology.

EMILIO BRITO is Professor of Fundamental Theology and Philosophy of Religion at the Catholic University of Louvain-la-Neuve. He has written numerous books in classical and modern philosophy of religion and Christian theology, including *Dieu et l'être d'après Thomas d'Aquin et Hegel, Heidegger et l'hymne du sacré*, and *Philosophie et théologie dans l'oeuvre de Schelling*.

JOHN D. CAPUTO is David A. Cook Professor of Philosophy at Villanova University, and a leading interpreter of contemporary European thought. His many books in the area include *Radical Hermeneutics, The Tears and Prayers of Jacques Derrida*, and *On Religion*.

RICHARD A. COHEN is Isaac Swift Distinguished Professor of Judaic Studies at the University of North Carolina-Charlotte. A prominent translator and interpreter of the thought of Emmanuel Levinas, Franz Rosenzweig, and other Jewish thinkers, he has published *Elevations: The Height of the Good in Rosenzweig and Levinas* and *Ethics, Exegesis, and Philosophy: Interpretation After Levinas*.

KEVIN HART is Professor of English at the University of Notre Dame. In addition to several works of criticism and collections of original poetry, he has published *The Trespass of the Sign* and has forthcoming books on the experience of God and on Maurice Blanchot.

JEAN-YVES LACOSTE has taught in Chicago, Tübingen, and Cambridge, where he is permanent fellow of Clare Hall. He has written *Expérience at Absolu* and *Le monde et l'absence d'oeuvre*, and edited the monumental *Dictionnaire critique de la théologie*.

Contributors

JOHN C. MARALDO is Professor of Philosophy at the University of North Florida, and a leading interpreter of the Kyoto School of Buddhist thought. In addition to many articles and two forthcoming books in that area, he has also published *Der hermeneutische Zirkel. Untersuchungen zu Schleiermacher, Dilthey, und Heidegger,* and an edition (with James Hart) of Heidegger's writings on theology, entitled *The Piety of Thinking.*

JOSEPH S. O'LEARY teaches at Sophia University in Tokyo. His work ranges from Patristic theology to contemporary European philosophy and Buddhist thought. He has edited, with Richard Kearney, *Heidegger et la question de Dieu,* and written *Questioning Back: Overcoming Metaphysics in Christian Theology; Religious Pluralism and Christian Truth;* and a forthcoming book on conventionality in religious experience.

ADRIAAN PEPERZAK is Arthur Schmitt Professor of Philosophy at Loyola University of Chicago. His many books in European philosophy and Christian theology include *System and History in Philosophy, Platonic Transformations: With and After Hegel, Heidegger, and Levinas,* and *Before Ethics.*

BEN VEDDER is Professor of Philosophy at the Catholic University of Nijmegen, and was previously chair of the theology department at the Catholic University of Tilburg. His books include *Wandelen met Woorden, een weg van de filosofische hermeneutiek naar hermeneutische filosofie* and is completing a book on the relation of Heidegger's philosophy to religion and theology.

IGNACE VERHACK is Professor of Philosophy at the Higher Institute of Philosophy in Leuven, where he teaches in the areas of philosophy of religion, contemporary European philosophy, and metaphysics. In addition to essays on Wittgenstein, Heidegger, and Levinas, he has published *De mens en zijn onrust,* and is writing a book on immanence and transcendence in contemporary philosophy.

INDEX

Absolute, 3, 5, 6, 15, 50–67, 91, 105, 174, 179; absolute dependence, 15, 16; "absolute near side" (Nishitani), 179; Nothing, 37–49; as absolutely self-contradictory self-identity, 37–38; as moving absolute, 105; non-substantial absolute, 179

Adorno, Theodor, 191

Affect, Affection, 72–92, 98, 104; affective answer, 103; affective response, 84–85; 89, 98–99; affective tonality, 78; affective understanding and sensible understanding, 85; affectivity and mysticism of Augustine, 184; auto-affection, 78; original Affection, 101; making world or earth appear, 86. *See also* Feeling; Heidegger, *Befindlichkeit*

Aise (comfort), 91

Aisthèsis, 72, 91, 98

Alquié, Ferdinand, 72

Ambitio saeculi, 28

Ambrose, Saint, 178, 181

Analogia entis, 55

Anselm of Canterbury, 129, 155

Anthropomorphism, 17, 57

Anxiety, 22, 42–43, 72, 73, 76, 83, 87

Aphairesis, 184

Aphanology, 54

Apophansis, 12, 35, 41, 54, 101, 102, 175. *See also* Theology, negative; *via negativa*

Aporia, 11, 161–162

Appearance, Appearing, 68–93; co-appearing, 78, 79; "malappearing," 70; non-appearing, 69–70; over-appearing (*surapparaître, Überfluss*), 88–89, 90

Arianism, 128

Aristotle, 24, 29, 105, 186, 187

Art, 8, 22, 69–72; as disclosure, 72; and perception, 71–72; and phenomenological reduction, 72; as presence that imposes itself, 83–84; and truth, 74–77, 81–83, 90; work of, as appearing, 68–93; work of, as

phenomenological object par excellence, 90; work of, as phenomenon-for-affect, 89; work of, irreducible to aesthetic object, 75

Articuli fidei, 155

Askesis, 103

Attention, 78; as power of appearing, 78

Augustine, 2, 6, 8, 12, 26, 27–29, 125, 155, 156, 167–168, 175, 176, 177–188, 194, 196; anti-Pelagian writings of, 182; on *beata vita*, 27–28; *City of God*, 194; *Confessions*, 177–186, 187, 194; on *concupiscentia carnis* and *concupiscentia oculorum*, 28; *De Trinitate*, 182, 183; as Greek thinker (Heidegger), 29; Heidegger's interpretation of *Confessions*, X, 27–29; as influenced by/in relation to Neo-Platonism, 177–190; readings of *libri Platonicorum*, 180; and *veritas redarguens*, 2

Balthasar, Hans Urs von, 161, 168, 179

Barth, Karl, ix, 161, 186; *Unverfügbarkeit*, 186

Being, viii, 4–5, 6, 7, 10, 24, 25, 31–49, 50–67, 68–93, 106–118, 112, 116; anonymous, 61; and appearing, 68–93; being-as-ground, 115; being-before-God, 91; being-in-the-world, 7, 8, 78; being-on-the-way, 113; being-toward-God, 7; goodness of, 114–115; and having, 36; and/as Nothing, 6, 31–49; middle of, as no-thing and as religious, 114–116; and Sacred, 51–67; transcendence of, 51–57, 112–116

Benamozegh, Rabbi Elijah, 135–152; on "Hebraic cosmopolitanism," 147; *Israel and Humanity*, 141, 149

Benedict, Saint, 157

Bergson, Henri, 151

Bernard of Clairvaux, 179

Blanchot, Maurice, 120, 124; *Writing of the Disaster*, 120

Blondel, Maurice, 63–64; *Action*, 63

Index

Index

Psychoanalysis, 186–190
Pure experience (James), 42

Quinn, J. M., 184

Rahner, Karl, 156, 159, 161, 162–163, 167
Rappaport, Joyce, x
Religious sentiment, 3. *See also* Affection;
  Feeling, of absolute dependence
Richard of St. Victor, 164
Rilke, Rainer Maria, 80
Ritschl, Albert, 157
Roman Catholicism, 63, 118, 142, 156, 167,
  183
Rorty, Richard, 123
Rosenzweig, Franz, 63

Sacer, 53
Sacred (*das Heilige*), 51–67
Same, ix, 37, 58; as *das Selbe* and as distinct
  from *das Gleiche* (the similar), 58
Sankara, 196
Sartre, Jean-Paul, 179
Scheler, Max, 60–62
Schelling, F.W.J., 59, 62
Schleiermacher, Friedrich, 3, 6, 14, 15–18,
  24, 25, 50, 61, 91, 157, 159, 164, 189; on
  absolute dependence, 15, 16;
  Glaubenslehre, 61, 157; *Reden über die Reli-
  gion*, 17; on religious sentiment or religious
  feeling, 3, 16
Schopenhauer, Arthur, 3
Schweitzer, Albert, 160, 162
Sign(s), 10, 18, 119, 121–129; Husserl's theory
  of, 121–122; Derrida's interpretation of
  Husserl's theory of, 122–125; Marion's
  interpretation of Husserl's theory of, 125–
  129
Sinai, 63, 138, 139
Smith, J. Z., 191
Sokal, Alan, 124, 133
soku, 39–41; as distinct from *ist zugleich* and
  sive, 39
Speech, 9–10, 23, 96–97, 105, 119, 121–125,
  132–133, 175; Derrida's conception of,
  122–125; Husserl's conception of, 121–
  122; and promise (Derrida), 120, 131; and
  response, 96–97; "without knowing," 133
Spinoza, Baruch, 14, 15, 16, 25, 138, 145
Strauss, D. F., 192
Subject, viii, ix, 6, 12, 16, 17, 35, 42, 74, 88,
  93, 96, 114, 179; "abyssal," 93

Subjectivism, 50, 57, 62; of Heidegger, 57
Summum bonum, 28, 62
Symmachus, 151

Tanabe Hajime, 48
Tautology, 52, 54, 55; and Heidegger's conceptions of Being, language, and the
  Sacred, 52
Temporality, 5, 25–26, 51, 56, 74, 104. *See
  also* Eschatology
Tertullian, 156
Theiology, ix
Theion, 33
Theism, 4, 107
Theology, vii, ix, 6, 8, 11, 12, 13, 14, 26, 33–
  35, 40, 45, 46, 56, 58, 63, 67, 91, 94, 95, 96,
  103, 110, 126–129, 132, 153–173, 176–
  198; of "absence," 128; biblical, 163; Catholic, 157; as charismatic kerygma, 94; dogmatic, 154; liberal, 161–162; metaphysical,
  67; mystical, 126–129; negative, 14, 45 (*see
  also* Apophansis; *via negativa*); philosophical, 26, 56, 58; pseudo-theology, 63; of religions, 167; sacramental, 160; spiritual, 103
Theophilus, 156
Thomas Aquinas, 59, 77, 89, 112, 154, 170,
  188, 193; on beauty as "splendor of the
  truth," 77, 89; on grace and nature, 112;
  rejection of Joachim's theology of history by,
  170
Titian, 74
Totality, ix, 25, 38, 86
Trace, 51, 52, 110, 112, 113, 116, 130, 161,
  167–168; of absolute singularity of Jesus
  Christ, 168; of divinity, 51; of fullness of
  being, 113; of gift, 110; of God, 161; of salvation, 52; of Trinity, 168. *See also* Vestigium trinitatis
Trakl, Georg, 80
Trinity, 11, 40, 153–173; economic and
  immanent, 159, 162–163, 167; exceeding
  dogma, 155; preceding history, 164
Two-truths theory (*da-satya*), 174–175

Ultima ratio, 109, 117
Universal, universality, 11, 24, 135–152; holy
  as universal, 135; Judaism as universal religion, 136 and 135–152 passim
Upâya (skillful means), 176, 185

Value, 97
Vandenbossche, Stijn, x

208